MARKETING OF TRIBAL PRODUCTS

MARKETING OF TRIBAL PRODUCTS

By

Dr. Rabi N. Misra

and

Dr. Narayana Panda

DISCOVERY PUBLISHING HOUSE
NEW DELHI-110002

First Published-2004

ISBN 81-7141-794-9

Published by

DISCOVERY PUBLISHING HOUSE
4831/24, Ansari Road, Prahlad Street,
Darya Ganj, New Delhi-110002 (India)
Phone: 23279245 • Fax: 91-11-23253475
E-mail:dphtemp@indiatimes.com

Printed at:
Tarun Offset Printers, Delhi-53

Preface

Orissa is an under-developed state in spite of its vast natural and other resources. Due to lack of infrastructural facilities, inadequate marketing facilities and due to other problems, the vast natural resources of the state have not been exploited effectively. The hilly areas of the state are mostly inhabited by scheduled tribes and scheduled caste people. The tribals live upon agriculture and collection of forest products like hill-broom, siali-leaves, mat-grass, genduli, gum, medicinal herbs and roots. Orissa has the second largest tribal population in the country next to Madhya Pradesh.

The tribals was exploited by the Sahukars, moneylenders and others. They purchase the forest products directly from the tribals at throw away prices and sell these products in the regular markets at high prices. For this purpose Agency Marketing co-operative Society Ltd. of Tikabali was established on 1947 and purchased the forest products from the tribals through their procurement centres. It purchases forest products from the tribal people at a fixed and reasonable prices and thus saves them from the exploitation of the private traders.

R.N. Misra

N. Panda

Acknowledgements

We are very much thankful to the librarians of Utkal University, Berhampur University and Sambalpur University. Again we also express our thanks to the librarians of Vaikunth Mehta National Institute of Co-operative Management, Pune, Gokhle Institute of Economics and Politics, Pune and National Library, Kolkata, (W.B) for their help and co-operation in providing information for the purpose of the study.

We are also very much thankful to all informants for providing information as per questionnaire.

We are also thankful to all friends and relatives who were helped us in writing this book.

Last but not least, we are also very much thankful to Sri Tilak Wasan, Proprietor, Discovery Publishing House, New Delhi, who had rapidly accepted our proposal in spite of their heavy pressure in publishing the book.

R.N. Misra

N. Panda

Contents

1

Introduction

Co-operation has played a vital role since the existence of human civilisation. It has focused the light for the growth and development of various co-operative societies in the country. Co-operation is generally considered as a weapon for fighting with the evils of capitalism in the society. The co-operative movement was introduced in India to uplift the standard of living of the rural poor. To save the farmers who are born in debt, live in debt and die in debt from the clutches of the moneylenders, co-operative movement has come into existence to shift their burden and to bring them to a manageable stage.

The introduction of Co-operative Credit Societies Act in 1904 marked the beginning of co-operative movement in India. After 1950, the co-operative movement marched ahead on various directions to uplift the economic standard of the poorer class. Considering the importance of co-operation, the Government of Orissa has taken various steps for its development during different plan periods.

A market consists of all the potential customers sharing a particular need or want who might be willing and able to engage in exchange to satisfy that need or want.[1] It is rightly observed that marketing is born and grows as society moves from a home handicraft economy of self-sufficiency into a socio-economic system which involves division of labour, specialisation, factory industrialisation, mass production, and urbanisation of population. Marketing has developed in an evolutionary rather than a revolutionary fashion. The village artisans need to exchange their products for food, raw materials and for other necessaries. So exchange of goods for goods known as barter system was developed. In order to remove the difficulties of barter system, a common medium of exchange was sought for. After using copper, bronze, gold etc. money was used as a medium of exchange. Due to development of large-scale enterprises, demand of market has increased. After the introduction of globalisation, the importance of market has reached its optimum. In a perfect market, the buyer is aware of the product and seller also knows the details about the buyer. There are mainly two types of markets *viz.*, primary market or daily market and secondary market or weekly market (commonly known as hat in Orissa). In rural areas, weekly markets are playing an important role to bring buyers and sellers together to a particular place *i.e* market place or hat.

The tribals of Kandhamal district were exploited by the non-tribals. They sell forest and agricultural products to local traders at abnormally lower price. But the operation of co-operative societies has been considered as a *sine qua non* in the tribal life and economy. In the tribal areas, the co-operatives serve four important objectives:[2]

(*i*) to protect the tribals from the exploitation of the middlemen
(*ii*) to provide credit facilities to the tribal members
(*iii*) to procure daily requirements of the members in the tribal community
(*iv*) to make necessary arrangements for the marketing of surplus agricultural produce and minor forest produce of the members

In order to save the tribals and the weaker sections of the society from the exploitation of the private traders and moneylenders, the Agency Marketing Co-operative Society (AMCS) was established on 19-11-1947 at Tikabali, 37 kms. from Phulbani Town, which is the district headquarters and important market place in Kandhamal. Although it is a primary co-operative society, its area of operation generally covers the entire districts of Kandhamal and Boudh, Mumbai and also other metropolitan cities of the country. The AMCS purchases minor forest produce and surplus agricultural produce from the tribals of the districts of Kandhamal and Boudh by establishing various procurement centres in different rural areas at a previously fixed reasonable price and save them from the exploitation of the private traders. The Society also provides loans to the tribals and the time of their necessity and adjust the loan amount at the time of purchasing minor forest produce and surplus agricultural produce from them. Thus the Society tries its best to improve the standard of living of the tribal people in Kandhamal district.

Due to the change in the policy of Forest and Environment Department, Government of Orissa executed vide letter No. 5503/E & E dated 31-3-2000 (Appendix—II), selected agents are allowed for collection of minor forest produce under the policy of Joint Forest Management. For the remaining items of Non Timber Forest Produce (NTFP) other than minor forest produces, the dealers are permitted to register their names at Divisional Forest Offices. In all these cases, the registered dealers are required to pay royalty to the local Forest Range Officer at the rate fixed for the quantity of produce allotted. For all NTFP items including NFP, the committee appointed by Government in SC and ST Development Department will fix the minimum procurement price for each collection season or part thereof.

The implementation of this policy of the government adversely affected the functioning of the AMCS, Tikabali. At present the private traders are able to appoint their agents at the Panchayat level and collect the products from the tribals. Though a price has been fixed by the government the money minded traders are able to manipulate the tribals in quantity and size. Ultimately neither the AMCS, Tikabali nor the tribals are benefited by this new government policy.

Relevance of the Study

District Kandhamal of Orissa occupies a privileged place for the tribals. The tribal people generally depend on minor forest produce. To save the tribals from the clutches of the private traders, the Agency Marketing Co-operative Society (AMCS Ltd.), Tikabali has played an important role for the marketing of minor forest produce and surplus agricultural produce.

Marketing of tribal products is highly essential. The tribals are poor and their standard of living lies below the poverty line. For the minor forest produce collected by them, the tribals should be paid a reasonable price. If they are not able to sell their products or sell their products at below the reasonable price, it will hamper the day-to-day life of the tribals. So how far the AMCS is helpful to the tribals of the district regarding marketing of forest and agricultural products in comparison with the local traders need to be studied taking 1,000 samples.

Under the circumstances mentioned above, it is highly essential to study the behavioural attitude of the tribals regarding selling MFPs and SAPs as it is very much relevant in the present context.

Review of Literature

In the field of co-operative marketing, particularly in AMCS, Tikabali, very few scholars have made studies at different times. Mishra Rabindra Nath in his thesis entitled "*Co-operative Marketing in the Perspective of Economic Development of Orissa*" submitted in the year 1982 at Berhampur University, has studied nine marketing societies for the purpose of his Ph.D study. Mr. Mishra tried his best to explore the working conditions of marketing societies of Orissa. For this purpose, he has taken only secondary data. Mr. Mishra has given some suggestions on the development of RMCS of the state of Orissa. He has not studied the problems faced by the sellers and problems faced by the co-operative staff for the procurement of the products.

Mr. Srikant, L.M. in his book *The Scheduled Tribes of India* emphasized the development of the co-operatives in tribal areas to fight against poverty. Mr. Srikant has made an observation that ignorance is one of the causes of exploitation and suggested that the LAMPS should come forward to provide better facilities to the tribals.

Tiwari, R.G. in his book *Role of Co-operatives in the Development of Hill Areas and Hill State* has pointed out that the people who are residing at hilly areas are neglected in the development process of the country. The problems of these people are still in dark. The forest products which are available plentily are not being utilised or marketed. So he suggested that the co-operatives of the tribal areas should come forward for the procurement of the forest products from these people.

Sahu, N.C. in his book *Economics of Forest Resources* suggested that the forest resources played a significant role in the development of the region. He, therefore, suggested that a good network system should be operated by the co-operative societies for the marketing of the forest resources of the tribals.

Mr. Behera, K.K. in his article "*A Revamping LAMPS for Better Marketing Services*" published in the Orissa Journal of Commerce volume 21 in 1997 has taken 20 LAMPS as sample and observed their performances in purchasing the SAP and MFP from the tribals at daily markets and weekly markets. For this purpose, he has taken 5 years and chosen Koraput as sample district.

Tripathy, S.N. published an article "*Role of LAMPS for the Development of Tribals in Orissa*" in his edited book *Co-operatives—*

Its Growth and New Dimensions has taken 5 years for the purpose of his study and he has observed how the LAMPS in Orissa marketed SAP and MFP during his period.

Nadkarni, V.R. in his article "*Challenges Before Co-operative,*" Vol. 31, March 1994 has given importance on the marketing of the products by the co-operatives. He has suggested that a co-operative society should come forward for the marketing of the surplus products of its members to save them from the clutches of middlemen, moneylenders and the like.

Bhadu, B. in his article "*Marketing Co-operatives in the Liberalization Scenario,*" published in the *Co-operator* in June, 1997 has explained that during the last three decades, the marketing co-operative societies have played a tremendous role. But, in this liberalization period, he forecast that the marketing co-operative sector will face different problems and challenges regarding the marketing of products through co-operatives in the decades to come.

Nalwaye, K.L. in his article "*Trends in Marketing Co-operatives*" published in the *Co-operator,* May 1994, has narrated that the marketing in the present scenario need great attention of all. The co-operative societies, starting from the PACS, have to play an important role in the marketing of surplus products of the rural poor to uplift their standard of living.

Mr. Palo, R.N. in his thesis entitled "*Tribal Development Fostered through Agency Marketing Co-operative Society, (AMCS Ltd.) Tikabali*" has narrated the role of AMCS, Tikabali for the economic development of the rural people of that area. His thesis work is purely based on the secondary data. He has studied the role of different agencies for the rural development in different plan periods. Finally he has taken the procurement of different products along with its quantities by the AMCS, Tikabali.

The studies mentioned above have taken only secondary data for their purpose. But they have not studied the tribals at individual level. The problem faced by the innocent have not been narrated in these above-mentioned studies.

The present study aims to focus on the role played by the AMCS, Tikabali from its inception in marketing the tribal products. Further it also explains how far it could save the tribals from the clutches of middlemen for exploitation. For this purpose, primary data form the sample selected tribals are collected and analysed. An attempt has also been made to highlight the various points on the aspect of marketing of tribal products in detail.

Objective and Scope of the Study

The problem of marketing of forest and agricultural products of the tribal people of Orissa in general and that of Kandhamal district in particular has become a constant source of anxiety. The innocent tribal people are exploited by the sahukars and the like. So they are forced to sell their products to the local traders at lower price. In this context, the AMCS Ltd. of Tikabali plays an important role in the marketing of the forest and agricultural products of the district at reasonable price as fixed by the Government.

The present study, being a fact-finding research, aims at finding out the magnitude of the problem regarding the marketing of products at AMCS Ltd., Tikabali. The problems faced by the tribal people are also taken into consideration.

Since it is empirical in nature, the study is confined to AMCS Ltd., Tikabali. Further the scope of the study is made limited only to the marketing of forest and agricultural products of the tribal people of the district.

Period of the Study

The study has covered a period of ten years form 1991-1992 to 2000-2001. This period is selected to study the effects of the globalisation on tribal people who mainly depend on the forest products and to study the effects of the change in the policy by the government of Orissa regarding selling of the forest products freely by the tribal people.

Hypotheses

The study aims at testing a set of hypotheses with the help of findings after evaluation. Following hypotheses are formulated keeping in view the overall analysis of the data. After analysis, the following issues shall be examined which may either be confirmed or rejected:

1. The personnel of AMCS, Tikabali influence the sample respondents to sell their produce at different recognised centres of the society;

2. Mostly females and illiterate respondents come forward to sell their produce at different procurement centres;
3. Sample respondents mostly approach the procurement centres everyday to sell their produce;
4. Mostly elderly women of the sample district come forward to the marketing centres to sell their produce;
5. The personnel of AMCS, Tikabali provide necessary training facilitates to the sample women respondents to get finished produce form them;
6. The sample respondents save their time, transport expenses etc. as the local traders come to their door-step after implementation of New Government Policy, 2000;
7. The traders appointed by the Panchayats (after new government policy) influence the tribals and others to sell their produce at their collection centres instead of selling at AMCS, Tikabali;

Methodology Applied

Methodology applied for the study is illustrated below in detail.

Collection of Data

The data for the study are collected from two sources. They are: primary source and secondary source. Primary data have been collected with the following objectives:

(*a*) To study the socio-economic conditions of the tribal people of Kandhamal district;

(*b*) To study the purchasing style of the AMCS, Tikabali regarding minor forest produce of the area;

(*c*) To study the purchasing style of recognised local traders regarding the minor forest produce from local tribal persons;

(*d*) To study the behavioural attitude of the tribal persons in selling of forest products;

(*e*) To find out the probable reasons in connection with the improvement of the marketing system of minor forest produce by the tribals.

For the purpose, a suitable questionnaire is designed (Appendix—I). The questionnaire was shaped with the objective of collecting quantitative as well as qualitative informations.

The scheduled of questionnaire has been divided into six parts. Part I is designed to collect general information of the tribals of Kandhamal. Part II is designed to collect information about land holding of the tribal and borrowing from AMCS to sell the minor forest produce and surplus agricultural produce in advance. Part III deals with the repayment style of loan by the triabls. Part IV has been formulated to find out the marketing of tribal products by the tribal people at daily and weekly markets. Part V is designed to study the opinion of the tribal people about the marketing society of Tikabali. Part VI deals with the opinion of tribal people regarding selling their products through Panchayat level agents. All the primary data are collected through administration of the questionnaire by direct interview method.

Sampling Design

For sampling design, keeping in view the objective and scope of the study, it was decided to choose tribals on the basis of representative sampling instead of taking the whole universe. As per the census 2001, the district Kandhamal has 6,47,912 population out of which the population of tribal persons are 3,33,584. So one thousand sample tribals have been taken in proportion to the population of the sample district Kandhamal for the study. The sample tribals are taken into consideration to study the behavioural attitude towards the marketing of minor forest produce to AMCS, Tikabali and to the private traders of the district selected by Panchayats according to the new Government policy of 2000.

Method of Analysis

The analysis of the study has been divided into there parts. The first part of the analysis (Chapter II) is designed on the socio-economic condition of the tribal people of District Kandhamal of Orissa.

The second part of the study has been designed to highlight the growth and development of co-operative marketing in general and AMCS Tikabali, in particular (Chapter IV and V)

In the third part (Chapter VI), the collected data have been analysed to find out the style of marketing of AMCS Tikalbali and private traders with respect to marketing of minor forest products of the district Kandhamal.

Tools of Analysis

For the analysis of collected data, a number of statistical tools like percentages and average, have been used. A number of graphs and charts have been furnished to make the study illustrative and clear. For making the data comprehensive, it was felt necessary to present the collected data in the form of tables. Therefore, a large number of tables are also used in the course of study.

Limitations of the Study

Due to limitation of time and resources, only tribals of Kandhamal district have been selected for this study. Further the period of study was confined to only 10 years from 1991-92 to 2000-2001. To study the behavioural attitude of tribals regarding selling minor forest produce and surplus agricultural produce, one thousand samples have been selected at random from Kandhamal district. The larger sample and longer period of coverage could not be taken up. Limitation of random sampling technique also exists.

The primary data are collected as per the information given by the sample tribals of the study district. The information supplied by them (as per questionnaire) at the time of survey cannot be taken as hundred per cent accurate.

Similarly, hundred per cent accuracy cannot be attached to the secondary data used in the study. As they are of secondary nature, all the limitations of the secondary data are also found in this study. Further, for the purpose of analysis various statistical devices and accounting ratio have been used and they have their own limitations.

Chapter Design

The main object of the study is to find out how the tribals of Kandhamal district sell the minor forest produce and surplus agricultural produce to the AMCS, Tikabali. For the elucidation, the scope of the study has been divided into two parts—First part consists of two chapters and second part three chapters, the other two chapters being introduction and conclusion.

The details of the study has been divided into the following chapters:

Chapter 1 : Introduction and Methodology

The Chapter—1 deals with the objectives and relevance of the study with a brief introduction of the problem. It also deals with the formulation of hypotheses and methodology used in the study.

Chapter 2 : Socio-Economic Profile of District Kandhamal

The Chapter—2 deals with the socio-economic condition of the tribal people in the district Kandhamal.

Chapter 3 : Growth of Co-operative Movement in India and Orissa

Chapter—3 of the study tries to highlight the growth and development of co-operative movement before independence and during Five Year Plan periods in the country as well as the state of Orissa with the help of a number of tables.

Chapter 4 : Approach and Strategies for the Development of Co-operative Marketing

The development of marketing co-operative societies in India during different plan periods are discussed in this chapter with the help of various tables.

Chapter 5 : History and Growth of AMCS, Tikabali

This chapter deals with the history of Agency Marketing Co-operative Society of Tikabali of Kandhamal district.

Chapter 6 : Marketing of Minor Forest Produce and Surplus Agricultural Produce: An analysis

This chapter is devoted entirely for the analysis of marketing of minor forest produce and surplus agricultural produce of the tribals. The steps taken by the AMCS to purchase the MFPs from the tribals are taken into consideration.

Chapter 7 : Findings and Suggestions

Being the concluding chapter of the study, this chapter deals with the findings of the study, testing of hypotheses (as formulated in the first chapter) and a few suggestions are offered.

REFERENCES

1. Kotler, Phillip, *Marketing Management—Analysis, Planning, Implementation and Control*, Prentice Hall of India, (P) Ltd., New Delhi, 1988, p-11.
2. Vidyarthi, L.P. and Rai, B.K., "*The Tribal Culture of India*, New Delhi, Concept Publishing Company, 1985, p. 440.

2

Socio-economic Profile of District Kandhamal

Historical Background

The early history of Boudh and Khondmals is still in obscurity. There is no accurate account of the origin of the ruling dynasties of this region. Yet a glimpse into the history indicates that in different periods, the territory of Boudh and Khondmals was ruled by the Bhanjas, the Somavamsis, the Cholas and the Gangas.

The territory of Boudh and Khondmals was occupied by the Marathas in 1800 A.D. during the reign of Bhonsla Raja of Nagpur. At the fag end of 1803 when the Britishers occupied Cuttack after defeating Marathas the latter took shelter in the domain of the Raja of Boudh. But the King of Boudh took a hasty step to give solicitation to the Britishers and extended his helping hand to them by which Boudh was occupied in 1804. The Bhonsla Raja of Nagpur claimed Boudh in the year 1810. Subsequently in 1818, he got jurisdiction over that state.[1] In 1852 Boudh was finally surrendered to British Government by Madhoji Bhonsla. Till the year 1819, the king of Boudh had jurisdiction over Athamalik. Then in that year, the British Government made a separate Kabuliyat with the Samanta of Athamalik. In 1852, after the death of Chandra Sekhar Dev, the king of Boudh, Anthamalik became independent. The king of Boudh had suzerainty over Kandhamal from early times.[2]

Although the king of Boudh had jurisdiction over Khondmals, he had no real control over the tract. The Kandhs, the main inhabitants of the tract, did not recognise the authority of the king. So in 1845, Khondmals was separated from Boudh. For the

Suppression of Meriah sacrifice (Human sacrifice) in the hill tracts, an Act was passed in 1845. An Agent was appointed by the Governor-General to take over the charge of Boudh, Daspalla and some other hill tracts. He was given adequate powers to suppress human sacrifice. In 1853, a revolution was started under the leadership of Chakra Bisoyi for the enthronement of the deposed king of Ghumsur. The leader of the rebellion took shelter with the Kandhs in the Southern hill tracts of Boudh. In order to control the rebellion, the Boudh state was replaced under the direct charge of the Superintendent of the Tributary Mahals of Orissa. The rebellion was suppressed by Mr. Samuells, the Superintendent of Boudh. As a result, Chakra Bisoyi and his followers were driven out of the country. After taking over Khondmals, Mr Samuells established a police Thana and also appointed one Dinabandhu Pattnaik as an Agent/Tahasildar to work under the direct control of the Superintendent of Tributary Mahals.[3] Due to this effective administration was possible and human sacrifice was controlled. On 15th February, 1855, he issued a proclamation for annexing Khondmals with British territory.[4] Thus Khondmals was surrendered by the tributary chief of Boudh.

In 1891, after the amalgamation with the headquarters at Angul, Khondmals were made a sub-division of Angul district. Bisipada which is 6 kms. south from Phulbani was the headquarters of Khondmals sub-division. As Angul was situated at a distance of 128 kms. from Khondmals, it created problems in the effective administration of this region. In 1904, the subdivisional headquarters was shifted to Phulbani from Bisipada by Mr. A.J. Ollenbach, the then sub-divisional officer of Khondmals.[5] This district with Angul and Khondmals sub-divisions continued up to 1936.[6]

On 1st April, 1936, Orissa became a separate province and then the Khondmals sub-division was incorporated with the district of Ganjam. Prior to the British administration, the Khondmals was much less known to the outer world. During British rule, the area was a part of Bengal-Bihar-Orissa state, then a part of Bihar-Orissa State and finally an integral part of Orissa state after its separation.[7] The formation of the district of Boudh-Khondmals with headquarters at Phulbani was made with two sub-divisions viz., Boudh and Khondmals on 1st January, 1948. The Boudh state was an ex-state ruled by the Kings of Boudh. The Kings were receiving sanand from British Government up to 1913. After the death of

Jogendra Dev, the King of Boudh in 1913, Narayan Dev was enthroned as the king and during his period of reign, the state of Boudh was merged with Orissa on 1st January, 1948.[8] Subsequently the taluks of G. Udaygiri, Baliguda of Ganjam district and 51 villages of Dahia Police Outpost of Balangir district were added to this district in the year 1949.[9]

It may be mentioned here that there was no line of demarcation between Boudh and Khondmals in the map prepared by the Surveyor General of India till the year, 1903. The name 'Khondmals' was not mentioned in the district map. But later the Southern hill tracts of Boudh was designated as Khondmals by the Government.[10]

Unlike most of the districts of Orissa, this district does not derive its name from the name of its headquarters town which is popularly known as Phulbani. Several changes are noticed in the name of the district. It is even known as Boudh Phulbani district. The Government Publications bear that combined names of its two sub-divisions, Boudh and Khondmals. Its nomenclature remained in tact even after the reorgnisation of the district in the year 1949.[11]

Baliguda sub-division was formerly a part of the special Assistant Agents Division which included R. Udaygiri taluk of Ganjam. The area was known as 'Agency' which is derived from the term 'Agent' in whose special charge these tracts were placed as per the provisions of the Ganjam and Vizagpatnam Act, 1839.[12] The Collector, Ganjam was appointed as the Agent for the area as it was integrated with the district of Ganjam.[13] As the normal district administration pattern was introduced, this sub-division was detached from the district of Ganjam and added to the district of Boudh-Khondmals with effect from 1st April, 1949.[14] In 1959, the sub-divisional headquarters which was functioning at Phulbani shifted to Baliguda.[15] The district 'Boudh-Khondmals' was divided into two districts viz. Boudh and Kandhamal in the year 1992. At present Kandhamal district comprises of two sub-divisions viz. Phulbani and Baliguda. It has four Tehsils such as Phulbani, Baliguda, G. Udaygiri and Daringbadi. The district is further divided into 12 blocks, with 144 Gram Panchayats for administrative convenience. Out of the 12 blocks, 9 blocks are Tribal Development (TD) blocks and the other three are Community Development (CD) blocks (Table 2.1).

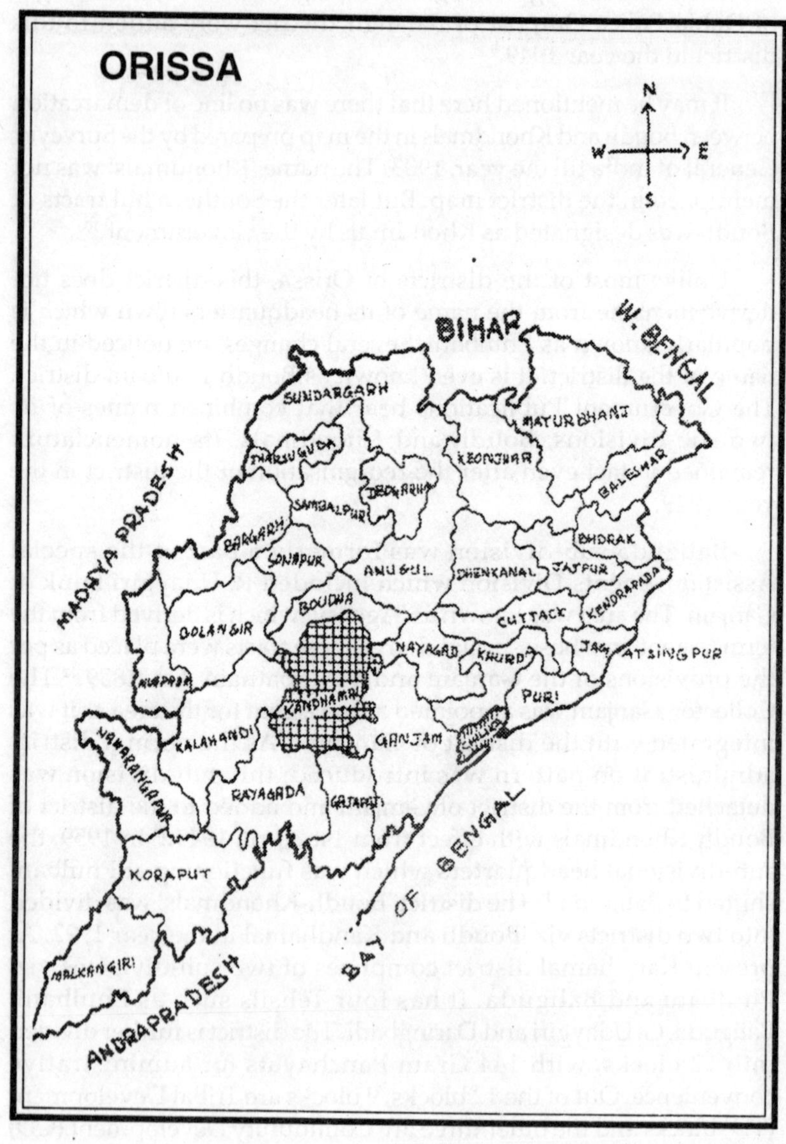
ORISSA
N
W
E
S
BIHAR
W. BENGAL
SUNDARGARH
MAYURBHANJ
JHARSUGUDA
KEONJHAR
DEOGARH
BALESHAR
SAMBALPUR
BHDRAK
BARGARH
SONPUR
ANUGUL
DHENKANAL
JAJPUR
KENDRAPADA
BOUDHA
CUTTACK
BOLANGIR
NAYAGAD
KHURDA
JAGATSINGPUR
NUAPADA
PURI
KANDHAMAL
CHILKA
NAWARANGAPUR
KALAHANDI
GANJAM
RAYAGADA
GAJAPATI
KORAPUT
MALKANGIRI
MADHYA PRADESH
ANDRAPRADESH
BAY OF BENGAL

Location and Boundary

Kandhamal district is one of the thirty districts of the state of Orissa. It is centrally located in the state. It lies between 19.36° S and 20.53° N latitude and 83.33° W and 84.48° E longitude.[16] The total geographical area of the district is 7,650 sq. kms.[17] It is about 4.9 per cent of geographical area of the state. Kandhamal district is surrounded by six districts of the state. The district of Boudh is in the North, Rayagada and Gajapati districts are in the south, Ganjam and Nayagarh in the East and in the West is Kalahandi (Map—1).

Table—2.1 Administrative Divisions of Kandhamal District

Sl. No.	*Administrative divisions*	*Name of the tehsils*	*Name of the blocks*	*No. of G.Ps. in each block*	*No. of villages*
1.	Phulbani	Phulbani	1. Phulbani	11	205
			2. Khajuripada	13	237
			3. Phiringia	19	390
2.	Baliguda	1. Baliguda	1. Baliguda	12	239
		2. G. Udaygiri	2. Daringbadi	23	259
		3. Daringbadi	3. Chakapad	08	138
			4. G. Udaygiri	08	76
			5. Raikia	10	138
			6. Nuagaon	11	173
			7. Tikabali	11	133
			8. Kotagarh	10	142
			9.Tumudibandh	08	206
	2	4	12	144	2,336

Source: District Statistical Handbook, 1995 and records of the Block.

Topography, Climate and Soil

Topographically the district has one specific geographical region . The hill-cum-forest tracts of Baliguda and Phulbani sub-division consists of all the twelve blocks of the district (Map-2)

Maximum and minimum temperature of the district is 40.6°C and 1.3° respectively.[18] During the year, summer is felt from March to June. May is the hottest month of the year in the district. From the

MAP OF
KANDHAMAL DISTRICT
BOUDH DISTRICT
KHAJURIPADA
PHULBANI
PHIRINGIA
NAYAGARH DIST.
KALAHANDI DIST.
BALIGUDA
K. NUAGAON
TIKABALLI
CHAKAPAD
G.UDAYA GIRI
TUMUDIBANDH
KOTAGAD
DARINGBADI
RAIKIA
GANJAM DIST.
RAYAGADA DIST.
GAJAPATI DIST.
N
INDEX
DISTRICT BOUNDARY
SUB-DIVISION
BLOCK BOUNDARY
ROADS
RIVERS
HILLS
DISTRICT HQR
SUB-DIVISION
BLOCK HQR
TAHSIL
P.S
N.A.C

middle of November to the end of February, the atmosphere is very cold. Usually December and January are considered coldest months in the district.

Rainfall

Generally monsoon starts in 1st week of June and continues till September. The average rainfall of the district is 159.76 cms which is beneficial for Khariff and early Rabi crops. But unusual heavy rainfall in the beginning of the monsoon and dry spell of drought towards the end very often result in crop failure. The district gets rainfall for the average of 45 days during a year. The month-wise actual rainfall of Kandhamal district from 1993 to 1995 is explained in table 2.2.

Table—2.2 Month-wise Actual Rainfall in the District of Kandhamal (in mm)

Month	Year		
	1993	*1994*	*1995*
1. January	—	1.1	85.00
2. February	—	45.20	14.50
3. March	0.8	4.90	15.90
4. April	55.50	63.10	38.60
5. May	93.80	60.60	429.40
6. June	195.80	264.70	99.10
7. July	323.00	558.60	366.20
8. August	280.90	644.20	250.10
9. September	234.50	378.60	207.50
10. October	87.50	63.90	145.20
11. November	—	3.40	165.40
12. December	—	—	—
Total	1271.00	2088.30	1816.90

Source : District Statistical Handbook, Kandhamal, 1995, p. 13.

During the year 1993, the actual rainfall is 326 mm less than the actual average rainfall of 1597 mm. But during 1994 and 1995, there was a record difference of 501 mm and 219.9 mm. rainfall from normal to actual in the district.

Soil

The soil of the district is moderately fertile and varies considerably in composition. Six types of soil have been identified in the district.[19] The red laterite soil and the red sandy soil is suitable for cultivation of paddy, turmeric, pulses, ginger, mustard, jowar and minor millets, paddy, cotton, sugarcane and Rabi crops are also grown in black soil in the district. The other types of soil such as red, yellow, scalital, and forest brown soil are also suitable for the cultivation of turmeric, pulses, mustard and jowar.

Mineral Resources

Geologically the district of Kandhamal is composed of laterite, sandstone and archaean rocks. The soil varies considerably in composition due to the variation in character of the original rock. Laterite is found on the top of the hills in the district which is porous, gray and is the product of the variety of rocks.

The mineral resources of the district are mainly composed of manganese, mica and rock-crystal. Some deposits of lime stone, graphite, quartz, felspar and coal are also found in the district. The quality of the minerals is of low grade and so those have not been exploited commercially. Though the district is gifted with several mineral resources, no mineral of economic importance is found in the district.[20]

Forest Resources

Kandhamal district is rich in forest resources which covers 4457.78 sq. kms. area. Nearly 58.27 per cent of the total geographical area is covered by the forests in the district. The forest area of the district is divided into two major divisions, viz. Phulbani and Baliguda. Phulbani forest division covers 1684.87 sq. kms. forest area which comprise 4 (four) forest ranges with 7(seven) revenue blocks such as Phulbani, Phiringia, Khjuripara, G. Udaygiri, Raikia, Tikabali and Chakapad. As regards Baliguda forest division, it covers 2772.91 sq. kms. area under forests. It consists of five forest ranges which included 5 (five) revenue blocks such as Baliguda. Nuagaon, Daringibadi, Tumudibandh and Kotagarh. Phulbani forest division occupies 50.86 per cent of its geographical area. In Baliguda forest division 75.85 per cent geographical area is covered under forests (Table—2.3).

Table—2.3 Division-wise coverage of forest area as on 1.4.1996 (Area in Sq. Kms.)

Sl. No.	*Name of the forest division*	*Geographical area*	*Forest area*	*Percentage of forest area to geographical area*
1.	Baliguda	3655.7	2772.91	75.85
2.	Phulbani	3312.6	1684.87	50.86

Source : District Statistical Handbook, 1995 Kandhamal, p. 27.

The forests of the districts of Kandhamal are divided into two types such as Northern tropical semi-evergreen forests and Northern tropical moist decidous forests.[21] The Northern tropical semi-evergreen forest is found in Baliguda sub-division. The important economic species of this division are Sal (Shorea Robusta), Asan (Terminalia Tomentosa), Bija (Ptero Carpus Mzrsupium), Kurum, (Adina Cardifolia), Dharua (Anogessus Latifolia), Sisoo (Dalbergia Latifolia) and Gambhar (Gemeline Arboria) Bamboo, Sabai grass and medicinal plants are also plentily grown in this forest. The northern tropical moist deciduous forest is found in Phulbani and Baliguda forest divisions. Sal, Bija, Sisoo, Bamboos etc are grown in these forests. Besides these, some minor forest produce (MFP) such as siali leaves, brooms, tamarind, sal resin, Genduli gum, mats arrowoods etc. are grown in these forests. The tribals in the direct collect these products which help them for earning their livelihood.

The division-wise classification of forest area by legal status in Kandhamal district is shown in the Table—2.4.

Out of total forest area of 4457.78 sq. kms., the reserved forest area accounts for more than 45 per cent. The area covered under unclassified forest is about 0.04 per cent which is very much less than that of undemarcated forests.

In Kandhamal district, different programmes were executed in order to increase the size, quality and area of the forest. During the year 1988, social forestry project was introduced in the whole of the district. Village wood lot afforestation, barren hill plantation, forest farming for rural poor, agro based forest, rehabilitation of

Table—2.4 Division-wise classification of forest area by legal status in Kandhamal district as on 1.4.1996

Sl. No.	Types of forest	Area in sq. kms.
1.	Reserve forest	2010.06
2.	Demarcated protected forest	1755.91
3.	Un-demarcated protected forest	689.82
4.	Unclassified forest	1.99
	Total	4457.78

Source : District Statistical Handbook, 1995, Kandhamal, p. 27.

degraded forests, farm forestry programmes were implemented in the waste lands, depleted forest lands and hill slopes of the district.[22]

During the mid of the twentieth century, in different parts of the forests of the district, large number of wild animals were found. So far the lovers of wild life and hunters, the Kandhamal forest was considered as the paradise.[23] Now-a-days because of the rampant destruction of the forests, the number of wild animals has reduced to a large extent. Wild elephants, tigers, leopards, wild pigs, wolf, bear, deer, fox, sambar, wild buffalo are found in the dense forests of the district. Birds like peacock, jungle fowl etc. are also found in these forests. Sometimes wild animals destroy the crops and damage the forests by uprooting young saplings and stripping of the bark of valuable trees.[24]

Demographic Features

According to 1991 census, the total population of Kandhamal district was 546-281 thousands. Out of this, 273.234 were females.[25] In this district, the rural population and urban population was 510.6 thousands and 35.6 thousand respectively. Out of the total population of the district, 100 thousand belonged to scheduled castes and 281 thousand belongs to scheduled tribe communities. The percentage of the district population to the state population was 1.73. The number of females per 1000 males was 999. The total population of the district according to 2001 census is 6,47,912. Out of this, 3,22,674 are males and 3,25,238 are females. The decennial growth rate of population from 1991 to 2001 was 18.60. (Appendix-III)

Density of Population

The district is thinly populated as compared to other districts of Orissa (Appendix—IV). According to 2001 census, the population per sq. km. is 81 persons.[26] It is much less than the state average of 206 persons.[27] Due to lack of adequate natural resources in the district, projects and industries have not been established for which the people from outside are not interested to come to the district for settlement. The reason for low density is also due to unhealthy climate of the district in which people suffer from indigestion or from malaria. In the district of Kandhamal, there are 179 uninhabited villages. In village like Dangamila, Lundruketa, Budhakhan, Salpada and Hatiraj of Baliguda block, less than 10 persons live. The density of population in Baliguda Tahasil of the district is highest having 136 persons per sq. km. and in Kandhamal Tahasil, it is lowest having 93 persons per sq. km.

Sex Ratio

The impact of the social welfare measures on the society depends on the sex ratio of population. If in a closed population, the females outnumber males, reproduction will be high that very much increases the total population. According to 1981 census, the females outnumbered males. The sex ratio was 1037 females per thousand males. But in 1991 census, the number of males exceeded the number of females. It shows a ratio of 999 females per thousand males as compared to 971 in the state. According to 2001 census number of females per 1000 males in the district Kandhamal is 1008. However, the females outnumber of males in the tribal community. As per 1991 census, the sex ratio in this case is 1027 per thousand males. In case of scheduled caste community, the sex ratio of 997 females per thousand males.

The number of males and females in different blocks of the Kandhamal district is shown in table 2.5.

It is seen from table 2.5 that in five blocks such as Baliguda, Khajuripada, Kotagarh, Phulbani and Tumudibandh, the sex ratio is in favour of males. In all other blocks, the sex ratio goes in favour of females. The sex-wise ratio of tribals of the district (as per block-wise) is explained in table 2.6.

Table 2.6 shows that the sex ratio of the tribals goes in favour of females in all the blocks of the district. But in Phulbani N.A.C. area, the sex ratio is found in favour of males.

Table—2.5 Sex ratio in blocks (1991 census) of Kandhamal district

Name of the block	*Total population*	*Male*	*Female*	*Sex ratio per thousand*
1. Baliguda	52,409	26,536	26,873	975
2. Chakapad	36,168	18,012	18,156	1,008
3. Daringibadi	73,688	36,010	37,678	1,046
4. G. Udaygiri	35,770	17,693	18,077	1,022
5. Khajuripada	42,562	21,363	21,199	992
6. Kotagarh	32,313	16,222	16,091	992
7. Nuagaon	40,259	20,081	20,178	1,005
8. Phiringia	59,680	29,665	30,015	1,012
9. Phulbani	57,963	30,185	27,778	920
10. Raikia	42,194	20,863	21,331	1,022
11. Tikabali	42,915	21,414	21,501	1,004
12. Tumudibandha	30,360	15,190	15,170	999

Source : District Statistical Handbook—1993, Kandhamal, p. 8.

Working Population

The total number of main workers, marginal workers and non-workers by sex is explained in table 2.7.

From table 2.7, it is found that 2,12,946 were main workers and 2,85,405 were non-workers. Non-workers were highest in the district.

Occupational Pattern

The occupational distribution of population is an index of economic development. With the development of an area, there occurs occupational shift in the population from the primary to the secondary and tertiary activities.

The occupational pattern of the district is predominantly agricultural in character. The classification as per occupation per worker is illustrated in table 2.8.

Table—2.6 Sex ratio of tribals in blocks (1991 census) of Kandhamal district

Name of the block	*Male*	*Female*	*Total*	*Sex ratio per thousand*
1. Baliguda	11,870	11,907	23,777	1,003
2. Chakapad	8,531	8,551	17,082	1,002
3. Daringibadi	20,572	22,000	42,572	1,069
4. G. Udaygiri	8,566	8,880	17,446	1,037
5. Khajuripada	10,912	10,931	21,843	1,002
6. Kotagarh	9,128	9,173	18,301	1,005
7. Nuagaon	10,181	10,407	20,588	1,022
8. Phiringia	17,190	17,820	35,010	1,037
9. Phulbani	8,538	8,601	17,139	1,007
10. Raikia	10,981	11,617	22,598	1,058
11. Tikabali	11,512	11,814	23,326	1,026
12. Tumudibandha	8,500	18,742	17,242	1,028
URBAN				
1. G. Udaygiri (NAC)	883	984	1,867	1,114
2. Phulbani (NAC)	1,444	1,151	2,595	797

Source : District Statistical Handbook, 1993, Kandhamal, p. 8.

In the occupational structure, no change is marked. Agriculture still continues to be the chief support of economy of the district.

Human Settlement

In Kandhamal district, there are 2,336 inhabited and 179 un-inhabited villages. Table 2.9 gives a picture of the residential houses and census villages in different blocks in the district.

Table 2.9 illustrates the composition of population with reference to village and household break-up in different blocks of the district. It is seen from the table that population less than forty thousands live in five blocks such as Chakapad, G. Udaygiri, Kotagarh, Phulbani and Tumudibandh. These blocks accommodate lowest number of households than those of other blocks. The number of people living in these five blocks is also less as compared to other blocks.

Table—2.7 Number of main workers, marginal workers and non-workers (sex-wise) of Kandhamal district

Sl. No.	Type	Male	Female	Total
1.	Main workers	1,47,593	65,353	2,12,946
2.	Marginal workers	5,130	42,800	47,930
3.	Non-workers	1,20,511	1,64,894	2,85,405

Source : District Statistical Handbook, 1993, Kandhamal, p. 10.

Table—2.8 Classification of workers in Kandhamal district (1991 census)

	Name of the occupation	Number of people engaged	Percentage
1.	Cultivator	1,02,929	48.34
2.	Agricultural	73,727	34.62
3.	Livestock, Forestry Fishing, Hunting & Plantation Orchards and allied activities.	3,285	1.54
4.	Mining & Quarrying	63	0.03
5.	Manufacturing, processing servicing & Repairs:		
	(*a*) In household industries	4,731	2.22
	(*b*) Other industries	1,918	0.90
6.	Constructions	1,036	0.49
7.	Trade & commerce	7,094	3.33
8.	Transport, Storage & Communications.	1,324	0.62
9.	Other services	16,839	7.91
	Total	2,12,946	100.00

Source : District Statistical Handbook, 1993, Kandhamal, p. 10.

There are only two Notified Area Council (NAC) towns in the district viz., Phulbani and G. Udaygiri. Table 2.10 indicates the

Table—2.9 Population as per block-wise of the Kandhamal district (1991 census)

Name of the blocks/towns	*Population*	*Number of residential houses*	*Number of households*	*Number of villages inhabited*	*Number of villages uninhabited*	*Total*
1	2	3	4	5	6	7
1. Baliguda	52,409	11,258	11,386	239	19	258
2. Chakapad	36,168	8,050	8,087	138	18	156
3. Darngibadi	73,688	15,694	15,786	259	15	274
4. G. Udaygiri	27,262	6,377	6,407	76	6	82
5. Khajuripada	42,562	9,352	9,416	237	11	248
6. Kotagarh	32,313	7,465	7,484	142	5	147
7. Nuagaon	40,259	9,108	9,152	173	39	212
8. Phirngia	59,680	13,148	13,223	390	20	410
9. Phulbani	30,809	6,694	6,727	205	13	218
10. Raikia	42,194	9,253	9,300	138	11	149
11. Tikabali	42,915	9,919	10,020	133	12	145
12. Tumudi-bandha	30,360	6,823	6,852	206	10	216
URBAN						
1. G. Udaygiri (NAC)	8,508	1,790	1,799	–	–	–
2. Phulbani (NAC)	27,154	5,759	5,820	–	–	–
Total	5,46,281	1,20,690	1,21,459	2,336	179	2,515

Source : District Statistical Handbook, 1995, Kandhamal, p. 8.

growth of population in these two towns. Phulbani has acquired the urban status in 1971. In 1981 G. Udaygiri was given the urban status. Phulbani is the district headquarters town. Out of the total population of the district, about 6.5 per cent people live in Urban areas.

Education

During the year 1994-95, there were 1,329 primary schools, 209 middle English Schools, 73 High Schools and 12 colleges in the district. Out of this, 6 High Schools, 5 Ashram Schools and Kanyashrams and 89 Sevashrams have been established by the

Harijan and Tribal Welfare Department of the State Government for providing better education facilities to the students belonging to S.C. and S.T. communities in the district.

Table—2.10 Growth of population in the towns of Kandhamal district since 1971 census

Name of the towns	*1971*	*1981*	*1991*
Phulbani	10,677	17,682	27,154
G. Udaydiri	..	6,841	8,508

Source : District Statistical Handbook, Phulbani, 1990-91, pp. 5-6 and District Statistical Handbook, Phulbani, 1995, p. 9.

In Kandhamal district, about 37.23 per cent of the total population are literate. The literacy percentage of the district is less in comparison with the state and national average. The literacy rate among the tribals is lowest i.e. 27.49 per cent of the total tribal population in the district. Among them the percentage of literacy of the males and females are 43.93 and 11.56 per cent respectively. Thus it is clear from the census records of 1991 that about 88 per cent females among the tribals were Literate.

Agriculture

Agriculture is the predominant activity in the district under study. It is seen from the occupational pattern that more than 80 per cent of the people are working as cultivators and agricultural labourers. The land utilisation pattern of the district and the blocks are shown in Appendix. The forest area of the district is 1,42,497 hectares. Raikia block in Baliguda sub-division has more cultivable area and Kotagarh block has the least cultivable are (Appendix—V).

The area operated by the class of operational holding reveals that (Table—2.11) about 94 per cent of total individual holding is below 4 hectares. It shows that land holding exceeding 10 hectares is less than one per cent of the total operational holding of the district.

Cropping Pattern

The cropping pattern mostly depends on the climatic conditions of the district. Drought occurs when the moisture in the soil is not adequate for a sustained crop growth. The hilly areas in the 12 blocks of the district are suitable for paddy, mustard, nizer, turmeric, ragi, maize, millets and ginger.[28]

Paddy and maize are the principal crops of the district. Turmeric is the main commercial crop. The other minor crops of the district are mustard, groundnut, green gram, black gram , horse gram, til, ragi, and potato. The people of the district especially the Kandhas grow a single crop in the year due to lack of irrigation failities.[29] Shifting cultivation is widely followed by the tribals of the district in the hilltops. The cultivation of turmeric is hereditary of the tribes of the district.

The total cultivable area can be divided into high lands, medium lands and low lands. The high land constitutes more in the hilly areas than the plains. It comes to 74 per cent of the total cultivable areas in the district. The medium land and low land are 17 per cent and 9 per cent respectively.

Area under Different Crops

Table 2.12 reflects the area under production of different crops in the district during 1993-94, 1994-95 and 1995-96.

It shows that area under cultivation of rice increased from 52,648 hectares in 1993-94 to 60,545 hectares in 1994-95 and decreased to 57,695 hectares in 1995-96.

Table 2.12 reveals that the area under cultivation of maize increased from 4,399 hectares in 1993-94 to 4,435 hectares in 1994-95 and decreased to 3,926 hectares in 1995-96. Ragi constitutes the second important crop in the district. There has been an increase in the area under ragi from 122 thousand hectares in 1993-94 to 166 thousand hectares and 132 thousand hectares in 1994-95 and 1995-96 respectively. Similarly the area of production under green gram increased from 188 thousand hectares in 1993-94 to 254 thousand hectares and 213 thousand hectares in 1994-95 and 1995-96 respectively. Area under cultivation of black grams and horse grams also increased from 1993-94 to 1995-96. There is a fall and rise in the area under total oilseeds in between the years from 1993-94 to 1995-96. It was (486 + 359 + 4860) i.e. 5,705 thousand hectares in 1993-94 and (520 + 353 + 4,284) i.e. 5,157 thousand hectares in 1995-96.

Table—2.11 Class-wise number and area of operational holdings of the district Kandhamal for the year 1990-91

Sl. No.	Class in hectares	All social groups: Number			Areas		
		Rural	Urban	Total	Rural	Urban	Total
1.	Below 0.02	635	4	639	10	–	10
2.	0.02-05	32,790	452	33,242	9,006	103	9,109
3.	0.5-1.0	31,212	140	31,352	23,004	102	23,106
	Marginal	64,637	596	65,233	32,020	205	32,225
4.	1.0-2.0	31,293	136	31,429	44,343	181	44,524
	Small	31,293	136	31,429	44,343	181	44,524
5.	2.0-3.0	14,659	47	14,706	34,852	116	34,968
6.	3.0-4.0	4,665	24	4,689	15,933	78	16,011
	Semi-Medium	19,324	71	19,395	50,785	194	50,979
7.	4.0-5.0	3,015	7	3,022	13,118	35	13,153
8.	5.0-7.5	2,071	28	2,099	12,301	147	12,448
9.	7.5-10.0	877	2	879	7,308	11	7,319
	Medium	5,963	37	6,000	32,727	193	32,920
10.	10.0-20.0	442	3	445	5,695	41	5,736
11.	20.0 and above	76	–	76	2,179	-	2,179
	Large	518	3	521	7,874	41	7,915
	Total	1,21,735	843	1,22,578	1,67,749	814	1,68,563

Table—2.12 Area under different crops in the district from 1993-94 to 1995-96. (Area in 000' hectares)

Sl. No.	Different crops	1993-94	1994-95	1995-96
1.	Rice	52,648	60,545	57,695
2.	Wheat	–	3	–
3.	Maize	4,399	4,435	3,921
4.	Ragi	122	166	132
5.	Greengram	188	254	213
6.	Blackgram	206	229	211
7.	Horsegram	1,796	1,863	2.089
8.	Til	486	477	520
9.	Groundnut	359	381	353
10.	Mustard	4,860	5,053	4,284
11.	Potato	420	519	539
12.	Sugarcane	4	10	21

Source : District Statistical Handbook, 1995, Kandhamal, p. 19.

Table—2.13 Production of different crops in the district of Kandhamal from 1993-94 to 1995-96

Sl. No.	Different crops	1993-94	1994-95	1995-96
1.	Rice	61,542.2	84,400	70,787.4
2.	Maize	41,41.6	23,256	38,08.1
3.	Ragi	59.1	72.2	59.3
4.	Pulses	682.3	570.0	756.0
5.	Oilseeds	1,188.3	1,301.4	1,216.6
6.	Potato	2,654.6	3,575.1	3,003.8
7.	Sugarcane	210.7	470.0	830.8

Source : District Statistical Handbook, 1995, Kandhamal, pp. 18-19.

Production of Different Crops

Table 2.13 deals with the production figures of different crops of the district during 1993-94, 1994-95 and 1995-96. It shows that the production of rice in the district increased from 61,542 tonnes in 1993-94 to 70,787 tonnes in 1995-96. But the production of maize had decreased from 4,141 tonnes in the 1993-94 to 3,808 tonnes in

1995-96. Although the production of ragi increased to 72 tonnes in 1994-95 from 59 tonnes in 1993-94, it again reduced to 59 tonnes in 1995-96. The total production of pulses was 682 tonnes, 570 tonnes and 756 tonnes in 1993-94, 1994-95 and 1995-96 respectively. As regards the production of oilseeds, it increased to 1,301 tonnes in 1994-95 from 1,188 tonnes in 1993-94; but the production decreased to 1,216 tonnes in 1995-96. Similarly the production of potato and sugarcane increased to 3,003.8 tonnes and 830.8 tonnes in 1995-96 from 2,654.6 tonnes and 210.7 tonnes in 1993-94 respectively.

Land Utilisation

The total geographical area of the district is 7,650 sq. kms. The potentiality for agriculture and the position of agricultural land is shown in table 2.14.

Table—2.14 ***Block-wise land utilisation pattern of the district Kandhamal (area in 000' hect.), 1994-95***

Sl. No.	*Name of blocks*	*Land put to non-agricultural uses*	*Barren & uncultivable land*	*Current follows*	*Other follows*	*Net area shown*
1.	Tumudibandha	1,307	2,654	1,897	1,654	5,730
2.	Kotagarh	708	5,236	831	935	2,966
3.	Daringibadi	2,283	15,003	5,166	2,103	11,449
4.	Raikia	923	9,580	1,516	2,167	6,754
5.	G. Udaygiri	404	1,698	832	823	2,929
6.	Chakapad	1,225	4,703	1,503	649	8,680
7.	Tikabali	1,201	1,690	1,715	583	5,933
8.	Nuagaon	2,111	10,086	2,101	2,113	5,226
9.	Baliguda	2,136	6,545	2,095	1,443	8,551
10.	Phiringia	2,459	23,256	3,240	1,397	13,459
11.	Phulbani	1,129	8,457	1,684	1,009	5,362
12.	Khajuripada	1,774	12,585	2,087	1,638	6,636
	Total	16,660	1,01,493	24,617	16,514	83,675

Source : District Statistical Handbook, 1995, Kandhamal, p. 16.

Landholding pattern of a population can be taken as an index of economic development. It is an indicator of the socio-economic position of the rural areas. Land-wise holding of the people of Kandhamal district is explained in table 2.15.

Table 2.15 shows that more than 45 per cent of farmers are having less than one hectare of land for cultivation.

Shifting Cultivation

Most of the tribes in India depend upon agriculture. They follow two methods of cultivation such as traditional shifting method and settled or plough cultivation. Shifting cultivation has been known by different names such as Jhum in north-eastern states, Bewar or Dahya in Madhya Pradesh, Podu in Andhra Pradesh and Koman or Bringal in North Orissa.[30]

Table—2.15 Class-wise number of operational holding of the district Kandhamal (1990-91)

Class in Hectares		*Number*		
		Rural	*Urban*	*Total*
1.	Below 1-0 (Marginal)	26,278	153	26,431
2.	1.0-2.0 (small)	16,317	84	16,401
3.	2.0-4.0 (semi-medium)	9,971	35	10,006
4.	4.0-10.0 (medium)	3,078	8	3,086
5.	10.0-20.0 (large)	172	-	187
6.	20.0 above (large)	15		
	Total	55,831	280	56,111

Source : District Statistical Handbook, 1995, Kandhamal, p. 22.

Under the method of shifting cultivation, a patch of hilly forest region is selected every year. Then after cutting the trees and bushes, fire is set to burn them. By following this procedure, a field covered with ash is prepared for cultivation. During summer season, showers of rainfall help the tribals to dig the cleaned areas of the hilltops by hand hoes. Then seeds of dry crops such as Johar, Mandya and Olisi are scattered at the top of the cleared space and are washed down the hill slopes by the monsoon rains. Due to the fertilising effect of the wood ash, the yield, rate of crops was

Table—2.16 Irrigation potential created in different districts of Orissa up to 1997-98 ('000 hectares)

Sl. No.	Name of the district	Major & medium		Minor (flow)		Minor (Lift)	
		Kharif	Rabi	Kharif	Rabi	Kharif	Rabi
1.	Angul	9	3	19	3	9	6
2.	Balasore	20	7	8	2	36	22
3.	Bargarh	92	57	19	3	8	5
4.	Bhadrak	75	12	1	–	16	10
5.	Balangir	8	1	13	3	7	4
6.	Boudh	20	2	10	1	5	3
7.	Cuttack	89	53	16	3	20	12
8.	Deogarh	8	6	4	–	2	1
9.	Dhenkanal	15	8	19	4	10	6
10.	Gajapati	–	–	21	2	5	3
11.	Ganjam	114	8	96	7	22	13
12.	Jagatsingpur	27	17	–	–	8	5
13.	Jaipur	62	33	5	1	26	15
14.	Jharsugada	–	–	4	1	3	1
15.	Kalahandi	62	2	20	5	10	6
16.	Kandhamal	2	1	8	3	3	2
17.	Kendrapada	63	41	–	–	29	17
18.	Keonjhar	27	6	23	5	15	9
19.	Khurda	44	26	16	2	6	4
20.	Koraput	39	21	6	2	9	5
21.	Malkangiri	64	18	1	–	1	1
22.	Mayurbhanj	37	14	36	3	15	9
23.	Nabarangpur	4	2	5	1	6	4
24.	Nayagarh	10	3	16	4	5	3
25.	Nuapada	13	5	5	2	4	2
26.	Puri	105	67	–	–	10	6
27.	Rayagada	8	2	20	5	13	8
28.	Sambalpur	27	23	16	2	6	4
29.	Sonepur	54	22	6	1	6	3
30.	Sundargarh	13	7	22	4	10	6
	Orissa (T)	1111	467	435	69	325	195

Source : District at a glance 2000, Directorate of Economics & Statistics, Orissa.

very good in most of the patches of the forest regions. The tribals in the district of Kandhamal are very much inclined to the shifting cultivation.

In order to dissuade the people of the hilly regions from the Podu cultivation, different programmes are executed by the Government for campaigning the evil effects of this system of cultivation. Soil Conservation Department of the Government has recently taken many steps in this regard and thus people become conscious of the adverse effects of shifting cultivation. Construction of water harvesting structures, Jhola land development, contour bunding, economic plantation such as Cashew plantation, coffee plantation, land shaping and land development have been taken up in this region.[31]

Irrigation

In Kandhamal district, there are only two medium irrigation projects Viz Salki and Pilla Salki. It has not major irrigation project. medium irrigation projects, lift irrigation points, minor irrigation project, dug wells, water irrigation structures etc. are the sources of irrigation in the district, which are shown in table 2.16.

It is seen from table 2.16 that irrigation potential created in the district upto 1997-98 is very much less in comparison with other districts of Orissa. Out of the total 2602 thousand hectares irrigation potential created in the state, only 19 thousand hectares irrigation potential was created in the district.

Fertiliser

Fertiliser plays an important role in the agricultural production. The consumption of chemical fertiliser of different districts of Orissa is explained in table 2.17.

Consumption of fertiliser is sporadic in the district. Table 2.17 shows consumption of fertiliser in different districts of the state in 1994-95. From the table it seen that nitrogenous, phosphatic and potassic fertilisers of 0.48 tonnes, 0.14 tonnes and 0.13 tonnes respectively were used in the district. Out of the total 290.8 thousand tonnes fertilisers used in the state, 0.75 tonnes was used in the district. It is noticed that the position of the district *vis-à-vis* other districts of the state is the least.

Table—2.17 ***Consumption of fertiliser in different districts of Orissa in 1997-98 (in '000 mts.)***

Sl. No.	*Name of the district*	*Nitrogenous*	*Phosphatic*	*Potassic*	*Total (N+P+K)*
1.	Angul	4.41	1.31	0.70	6.42
2.	Balasore	15.14	5.25	4.04	24.43
3.	Bargarh	21.12	8.33	6.32	35.77
4.	Bhadrak	11.84	4.89	2.79	19.52
5.	Balangir	5.25	1.86	1.29	8.40
6.	Boudh	1.30	0.43	0.30	2.03
7.	Cuttack	8.34	1.59	2.26	12.19
8.	Deogarh	1.72	0.51	0.20	2.43
9.	Dhenkanal	2.72	0.92	0.60	4.24
10.	Gajapati	3.16	0.21	0.16	3.53
11.	Ganjam	23.43	2.45	1.96	27.84
12.	Jagatsingpur	6.45	0.94	1.07	8.46
13.	Jaipur	8.23	2.26	2.10	12.59
14.	Jharsugada	3.56	1.31	0.41	5.28
15.	Kalahandi	6.65	2.55	0.93	9.13
16.	Kandhamal	0.48	0.14	0.13	0.75
17.	Kendrapada	5.61	1.58	1.26	8.45
18.	Keonjhar	5.08	1.97	0.74	7.79
19.	Khurda	5.83	0.54	1.01	7.38
20.	Koraput	3.06	0.84	0.74	4.64
21.	Malkangiri	1.71	0.80	0.36	2.87
22.	Mayurbhanj	7.08	2.80	1.69	11.57
23.	Nabarangpur	6.00	1.00	0.87	7.87
24.	Nayagarh	4.62	0.31	0.23	5.16
25.	Nuapada	1.80	0.47	0.21	2.48
26.	Puri	8.25	1.67	2.15	12.07
27.	Rayagada	3.66	0.71	0.63	5.00
28.	Sambalpur	11.66	4.72	2.91	12.29
29.	Sonepur	4.20	1.20	0.50	5.90
30.	Sundargarh	4.44	1.97	0.91	7.32
	Orissa	195.80	55.53	39.47	290.80

Source : District at a glance—72000, Orissa Directorate of Economics and Statistics, Orissa, Bhubaneswar.

Livestock

Livestock development in the past was almost negligible. Although the I.T.D.A has taken some steps for upgrading the animals, it has not yet become popular. The cattle in this district are of inferior breed and milk yield from local cows is very low for want of proper cattle feed and fodder. In 1995-96, total cattle were 3,08,767 and of which 2,435 were cross breed and 3,06,332 were indigenous.[32] During this period, the total number of buffaloes, sheep, goats, pigs and fowl were 76,230, 7,336, 193,685, 56,293 and 536,957 respectively.[33]

Industry

Kandhamal district is the most backward in the state in the field of industrial establishment. Large and medium scale industries have not been established in the district. Whatever industrial units exist are either in small scale or in the household sector.

Table—2.18 ***Number of industries, total employees and net value added by manufacturers under annual survey of industries in Kandhamal district***

Sl. No.	*Items*	*1993-94*	*1994-95*	*1995-96*
1.	No. of Reporting units	4	4	3
2.	No. of workers	384	317	286
3.	Persons other than workers	30	29	29
4.	Total no. of employees	414	343	315
5.	Fixed capital ('000 Rs.)	4,741	1,639	508
6.	Working capital ('000 Rs.)	– 319	– 1,153	324
7.	Productive capital ('000 Rs.)	4,422	486	832
8.	Value of output ('000 Rs.)	24,421	32,464	31,960
9.	Value of input ('000 Rs.)	7,612	7,023	2,109
10.	Depreciation ('000 Rs.)	702	271	50
11.	Net value added by manufacturer ('000 Rs.)	16,107	25,170	29,801

Source : District Statistical Handbook, 1997, Kandhamal, Directorate of Economics and Statistics, Orissa.

Table 2.18 shows the number of industries, total employees and net value added by manufacturers under survey of industries in Kandhamal district. It is seen from the table that during 1995-96, there were only three industrial units operating in the district. But in 1993-94 and 1994-95, there were four industrial units. Thus one industrial unit in the district was closed during the year 1995-96.

The table reveals that total productive capital invested in the industrial units of the district was only Rs. 8.32 lakhs. But during 1993-94, the industrial units of the district invested Rs. 44.2 lakh in manufacturing operations. Thus it is seen that there is a decreasing trend in the subsequent year regard the productive capital invested in the industrial units of the district. The total number of employees working in the industries similarly reduced from 414 during 1993-94 to 315 during 1995-96. But the net value added by manufacture was increased from Rs. 1.61 crores to Rs. 2.98 crores.

Transport and Communication

The transport and communication of the district is explained in table 2.19.

Table—2.19 Length of different categories of road in Kandhamal district (in Km)

Sl. No.	*Category of road*	*1994-95*	*1995-96*	*1996-97*
1.	National highways	—	—	—
2.	State highways	340	340	340
3.	Major district roads	143	143	143
4.	Other district roads	63	63	63
5.	Forest roads	323	323	323
6.	Gram panchayat roads	5,651	5,651	5,651
7.	Classified village roads	253	279	279
8.	P.S. roads	532	532	532
9.	Village roads	587	371	371
10.	Urban roads	88	196	212
	Total	7,980	7,898	7,914

Source : District Statistical Handbook, 1997, Kandhamal, p. 48.

Table 2.19 indicates the present position of roads and communication facilities available in the district. No national highway goes through the district. The total length of roads in the district is 7,914 kms. of which 340 kms are state highways, 143 kms are major district roads, 63 kms are other district roads, 323 kms are forest roads, 5,651 kms are G.P. roads, 279 kms are classified village roads, 532 kms are P.S. roads, 372 kms. are village roads and 212 kms are Urban roads. Kandhamal district is a backward district in Orissa which has no railway line.

The number of post offices of the district (block-wise) is explained in table 2.20.

Table—2.20 Post Offices in different blocks and urban area of Kandhamal district as on 31.03.1997

Sl. No.	*Name of the Block/NAC*	*Head post offices*	*Sub-post offices*	*Branch post offices*	*Total*
1.	Baliguda	—	3	37	40
2.	Chakapad	—	3	15	18
3.	Darngibadi	—	2	32	34
4.	G. Udaygiri	—	3	18	21
5.	Khajuripada	—	2	19	21
6.	Kotagarh	—	1	12	13
7.	Nuagaon	—	2	15	17
8.	Phiringia	—	1	26	27
9.	Phulbani	—	2	17	19
10.	Raikia	—	2	16	18
11.	Tikabali	—	2	19	21
12.	Tumudibandh	—	1	11	12
	Urban 1				
1.	G. Udaygiri (NAC)	—	1	—	1
2.	Phulbani (NAC)	1	6	—	7
	District Total	1	31	237	269

Source : District Statistical Handbook, 1997, Kandhamal, p. 49.

Table 2.20 reveals that there are 269 post offices in the district of which only 1 is head post office, 31 are sub-post offices and 237 are branch post offices. Thus the district has no well developed communication system.

Health

The people of Kandhamal district suffer mostly from common diseases like malaria, anaemia and dysentery. For the treatment of the people of the district, one district headquarters hospital, one sub-divisional hospital, five other hospitals, 7 community health centres, 34 primary health centres, 8 mobile health units have been established by the year 1998-99. There are also 13 Ayurvedic and 16 Homoeopathic hospitals and dispensaries in the district. To take care of the health of the people, 406 beds have been provided in the hospitals of the district. There is one blood bank at the district headquarters.[34] In the year 1997, the total number of patients treated in the hospital was 1,29,565.[35]

Family Welfare

Family welfare programme, earlier known as family planning programme started functioning in the district form the year 1964.[36] At present, there are 12 rural family welfare centres located in each of the 12 block headquarters. Besides these, 2 mobile family welfare units are also functioning in Kandhamal district.

Drinking Water

The provision of safe drinking water supply is necessary for healthy living. This explained in table 2.21.

Table 2.21 indicates that in the district, 4 villages have no source of drinking water. On 31st March 1997, the number of working tube wells, sanitary wells, piped water projects were 4882, 345 and 9 respectively and they covered 2,085 villages, 246 villages and 15 villages respectively. In summer season, some of the sanitary wells become dry and people mostly depend upon the tube wells for drinking water.

Electrification

Out of 2,336 inhabited revenue villages, only 1,087 villages have so far been electrified. So 1,249 villages i.e. 53.47per cent of the total number villages in the district have not yet been electrified.[37] This is a pointer to the fact that most of the villages have not been developed.

Table—2.21 ***Availability of drinking water facilities in different blocks of Kandhamal district. As on 31.3.1997***

Sl. No.	Name of blocks	No. of villages having no source of drinking water	Tube wells		Sanitary wells		Piped water	
			No. of working tube wells	No. of villages covered	No. of working sanitary wells	No. of villages covered	No. of piped water projects	No. of villages covered
1.	Baliguda	1	449	202	50	36	1	1
2.	Chakapada	—	376	123	45	14	—	—
3.	Daringibadi	2	540	220	39	37	1	1
4.	G. Udaygiri	1	263	70	9	5	—	—
5.	Khajuripada	—	444	226	21	12	1	2
6.	Kotagarh	—	275	123	24	19	1	1
7.	Nuagaon	—	387	153	25	20	1	1
8.	Phringia	—	697	354	50	36	1	2
9.	Phulbani	—	400	201	11	4	—	—
10.	Raikia	—	364	116	25	22	1	2
11.	Tikabali	—	360	118	14	14	1	4
12.	Tumudibandh	—	327	179	32	27	1	1
	District Total:	4	4,882	2,085	345	246	9	15

Source : District Statistical Handbook, 1997, Kandhamal, p. 71.

Public Distribution System

The public distribution system of the district is explained in table 2.22.

It seen from table 2.22 that there are 247 retail shops functioning in different blocks of the district. During the year 1996-97, total allotment of essential commodities such as rice, wheat, sugar and kerosene under public distribution system in different blocks of the district was 28,474 Mts., 920 Mts., 2,218 Mts., 4,406 K. Lits. respectively.

Table—2.22 Number of retail shops, allotment of essential commodities under public distribution system in different blocks and urban areas of Kandhamal district (1996-97)

Sl. No.	Name of block/ULB	No. of retail shops	Allotment of essential commodities Rice (in MT)	Wheat (in MT)	Sugar (in MT)	Kerosene (in K. Lit.)
1.	Baliguda	36	2894.7	77.5	267.4	487
2.	Chakapada	14	1926.6	42.5	115.3	252
3.	Daringibadi	35	357.1	57.5	223.9	536
4.	G. Udaygiri	12	1623.0	42.5	94.9	192
5.	Khajuripada	20	2223.4	42.5	133.0	391
6.	Kotagarh	12	1580.2	39.5	84.9	180
7.	Nuagaon	16	2064.9	42.5	125.5	282
8.	Phringia	28	3187.6	47.5	194.6	355
9.	Phulbani	14	1725.5	45.5	98.8	236
10.	Raikia	17	2279.6	42.5	135.9	376
11.	Tikabali	17	2293.7	47.5	133.2	367
12.	Tumudibandh	10	1595.0	42.5	92.5	180
			ULB			
1.	G. Udaygiri (NAC)	7	315.5	102.0	135.2	120
2.	Phulbani (NAC)	9	1190.2	248.0	376.7	452
	Total	247	28,474.0	920.0	2211.8	4406

Source : Civil Supply Office, Kandhamal

Socio-Economic Condition of Tribals

According to 1991 census, the tribal population constitutes 51.51 per cent of the total population in Kandhamal district. 27 types of tribes are found in the district, out of which 7 types of tribes are numerically important. They are Gond or Gondo, Khond or Kandha or Sita Kandha, Mirdhas, Munda, Pentia, Saora or Savar or Saura Shabar or Lodha.[38] They constitute 99.2% of tribal population of the district.[39] Of the 12 blocks in the district of Kandhamal, tribal population is highest in Daringibadi block and lowest of Phulbani block. Table 2.23 reflects the concentration of tribal population in different blocks of the district.

Numerically the Khonds are the largest group in the district. They are heavily concentrated in the 12 blocks of the district. They are divided into the three branches viz. Kutra Khonds, Dangric Khonds and Desia Khonds. The Kutia Khonds reside mainly in Kotagarh, Tumudibandh and Belghar area of Baliguda sub-division. In the highland regions of the district, the Dongaria Khonds or Malua Khonds are found. The Desia or Oriya Khonds generally live in the plains areas of the district with the non-tribals. Their number according to 1991 census was 2.8 lakhs of which 1.39 lakhs were males and 1.42 lakhs were females. Next to Khonds, Gonds or Gondas are the second most important scheduled tribes of the district under study.

The word Khond is derived from the Telugu word Konda, which means a hill or from Oriya word 'Kanda', an arrow. They are variably named by different authors such as Khonds, Konds, Kandhs, Kondhas, Naguli Khondas or Sita Khonds.

Table—2.23 Block-wise tribal population in Kandhamal district. 1991 census (in Nos)

Sl. No.	*Name of the blocks*	*Total population*	*S.T. population*	*Percentage of tribal population*
1.	Baliguda	52,409	23,777	45.37
2.	Chakapada	36,168	17,082	47.23
3.	Daringibadi	73,688	42,572	57.77
4.	G. Udaygiri	27,262	17,446	63.99
5.	Khajuripada	42,562	21,843	51.32
6.	Kotagarh	32,313	18,301	56.64
7.	Nuagaon	40,259	20,588	51.14
8.	Phringia	59,680	35,010	58.66
9.	Phulbani	30,809	17,139	55.63
10.	Raikia	42,194	22,598	53.56
11.	Tikabali	42,915	23,326	54.35
12.	Tumudibandh	30,360	17,242	56.79
		NAC		
G. Udaygiri		8,508	1,867	21.94
Phulbani		27,154	2,595	9.56

Source : District Statistical Handbook, 1997, Kandhamal, p. 19.

Major Macpherson describes the Khonds as they are "filled by physical constitution to undergo the severest exertions and to ensure every form of privation. Their forms are characterised by strength, and symmetry. The muscles of the limbs and body are clean and bodily developed. The skin is clean and glossy, the heel is in a line with the back of the leg, the foot is comparatively larger and the instep most highly arched although the Khonds have extra-ordinarily speed on foot. The forehead is full and expanded. The cheek bones are rather high and prominent. The lips are full but not thick, the mouth is rather large. The whole physiognomy is generally indicative of intelligence and determination blended with good humour.[40] The men are active and average in height. The women are short, robust and sturdy. They are very simple, frank and naive in nature. Their behaviour is pleasant and hospitable. They are courageous before the wild animals but timid before an unarmed stranger. They are characterised as "bold and fitfully laborious, mountain peasantry of simple but not undignified manners, upright in their conduct, sincere in the superstition, proud of their position as landlords and tenacious of their rights".[41]

Food Habits, Dress, Ornaments, House, Language and Utensils of Tribals

The staple food of the tribals consists of rice and dry grains boiled into a sort of porridge. The drink peja (gruel of rice) and also use it as sick diet. When they go outside of their village, they don't use fingers for taking rice. A scoop made up of leaf is used for the purpose of eating. They are very much fond of meat. They don't take milk because in their community it is considered as a food of the meek and orphan. In their opinion 'meat' and 'wine' are necessary for man to become strong and stout. The Kondhas don't take the meat of crow, eagle, vulture, owl, frog and snake. Fish and crabs are taken by the Kondhs. The women of the Kondh community are not allowed to take eggs and meat of the pigs. Mushrooms are taken as staple food by the tribal people during the rainy season.

According to the language of Kondhs, wine is called 'Kalu'. Two types of liquor such a 'Salap handia' (made kalu) and 'Mahua liquor' (Erpi kalu) are taken by them. As a matter of customary habit, they smoke and chew tobacco leaves.[42] Tobacco is considered as an essential commodity for consumption in the tribal community because most of them are smokers. Different crops such as ragi, tamarind, kandula and maize are cultivated by the tribals. Those commodities produced by the Kondhs are not adequate for their consumption throughout the year. After the consumption of these things for a period of 4 to 6 months in a year, they have to live on tamarind seed powder, mango stones, edible roots and tubers during the rest of the year.[43]

The Kondhs wear a simple dress. The men wear a long and narrow cloth (dhoti) which passes round the waist and between the legs. The ends of this cloth are brightly coloured and hang down behind like a tail.[44] The Kondh men are used to keep a long hair which they forterned in front by a knot. In this they usually stick cigar, locally known as Kahali, which is made up of tobacco rolled in sal leaf. The Knodh women wear two small clothes one around the waist and the other for upper portion of the body. Women wear only one loin cloth in Kutia Konth community. In case of small tribal women, the ends of the cloth are usually tied in a knot over the left shoulder instead of being tucked in at the waist.

The Kondh women have intense love for ornaments and wear gold and silver necklaces, ear-rings and hair ornaments. The most peculiar fashion among them is the ornamentalistion of the ear. The girls bore the entire rim of the ear and insert small thin sticks in them. But after marriage, the sticks are being replaced by silver rings. Before the marriage ceremony of girls they tattoo their faces profusely. The women in the tribal community use silver coins as necklaces. They also wear aluminium anklets in legs and rings in toes. But now a days this peculiar fascination is fast disappearing due to the spread of education.

The Kondhs live in hill slopes. Their houses are generally small and constructed either of puddled earth or of jungle wood poles struck vertically on the ground and then covered with a thin caking of mud. Their houses are well terraced with wild grass or date palm leaves. Their houses are generally neat and clean for which the women folk take the pride of it. But due to lack of windows, problem of ventilation arises. The Kondhs keep domestic animals and fowls inside the house which make an unhealthy atmosphere.

The Kondhs used to speak different dialects which had no written characters. In 1848, J.P. Frye, an officer of the Madras

Government, a leading linguist, took great interest in the Khonds and wrote an elementary book on the Khond vocabulary, grammar and alphabets and another book entitled *"A Series of Progressive Reading Lessons"* in the Khond language. These two books bestowed an entity to the Khond language as a separate one, which looked more akin to Oriya, for it had accepted Oriya character as those of its own.[45]

The Khonds speak "Kui" language. This is their mother tongue, which belongs to intermediate group of Dravidian languages.[46] But most of the Khonds of the district speak Oriya.[47]

For the purpose of carrying water and cooking food, earthen pots as utensils are used in Kondh community. They use bamboo baskets to keep crops, eatable items etc. A plate prepared out of leaves is used by them for taking meals. Brass and aluminium utensils are used in well-to-do Kondh families.

Social and Religious Life of Tribals

A Kondh family is generally having a small family consisting of husband, wife and unmarried children. After marriage, the daughter goes away to her husband's house and stays there. When the son gets married, he is also allowed to have his separate household. The average size of a Kondh family generally consists of four to five members. Both the husband and wife shoulder equal responsibilities in the matters of economic, religious and social significance. Both of them work inside and outside the house.

In their day-to-day life, all capable members of a family including the wife and children co-operate with the head of the family in collecting forest products and working in farms. The Kondh women are industrious and more responsible than male members. In most of the days during a year, the male members spend their time in drinking and the women folk go to work in the field or to collect the fruits, leaves etc. from the forest for their daily bread.[48]

The Kondhs live in villages where ten to twenty houses stand in rows. Each village is headed by a "Malika" or a "Maju" or a "Padara" (Headman). A group of villages formed a "Mutha" (sub-division).[49] The mutha is headed by mutha mallik or mutha sardar. After the abolition of statutory panchayat, the office of the mutha head became administratively defunct. But it has not yet lost its prestige and value. Under the muthas, the village has a well knit organisation having a secular head called "Bisimajhi" and a religious functionary called "Jani". The Bisimajhi is very effective in discharging some quasi-administrative functions without any official sanction behind it. Then Jani is the priest of the village and "Disari" is the native doctor who administers traditional medicine prepared from local herbs and also prescribes ritual offering.[50]

From E.A. Samuell's statement it is proved that the Kondhs were good and efficient administrators. While praising the Kondh system of local self-Government, E.A. Samuell, a British official, stated that "there is probably no established community in the world which might with so much of justice appropriate the motto of liberty and equality. In their deliberate assemblies, all voices are equal and each cultivator is the sole proprietor of the soil he tills. In every Kondh village, there were separate colonies for the Panos and Dambas.[51]

Polygamy is not seriously objected in Kondh society. A second wife can be easily taken by a Kondh person. Generally a Kondh boy marries at the age of 18 or 20 and a girl at the age of 16 to 18. There is a common house in every village of the tribal community in which all the unmarried girls of the village accompanied with an old woman sleep. It is called "Dinda Ghar" (Spinsters' dormitory). The young boys from the neighbouring village visit the dormitory at night with flute and Khanjani to perform folk dance. After dance is over, at night they used to sleep in the same house. During this period, the boys and girls choose their life partners. Sometimes in local weekly markets and fairs, their marriage negotiations take place.[52] Marriage between the members of the same clan is punishable with death. Matrimonial alliances are regulated by avoiding common ancestors.[53] In Kondh family women have an independent status.[54] But an opposite view has been expressed by Somanath Rath.

Stating the place of Kondh women during the British era, he stated that "women remained deprived of many rights and privileges. They were in no way equal to their male counterparts in socio-economic-regligious and in any other field. They were required to keep their husbands ever content and happy by playing the games of love, romance and sex with the husband.[55]

An elderly woman known as midwife attends on the expectant mother at the time of child birth. When the child takes its birth, the umbilical cord is cut by an arrow by the mother of the infant. With the help of castor oil and turmeric paste, the infant's body is smeared for one month. After giving birth to a baby, the mother goes to her brother's house and returns with a fowl and some liquor as a presentation to her husband.

When a person dies, his dead body is wrapped in a new cloth. The dead body is taken to the burial ground. It is followed by the relatives and women upto the burial ground. After the burial, the relatives observe "Pidra Puja" (worship to dead soul) and give a fowl to village priest "Jani" for sacrifice. On this occasion, country liquor is served to all of them.

Religion of Tribals

The Kondhs have an organised religion which believed in as many as 84 deities. The most supreme among the deities is the God of light or the sun called "Boora Penu". The names of the Kondh Gods are:

(1) *Tada Penu:* (Mati Debata or God of Earth) He is believed to promote the allround well-being of a person;
(2) *Saru Penu:* (Parabat Debata or God of Mountains). He helps men and animals to move freely in the jungle;
(3) *Jaker Penu:* She is believed to be the sister of Tada Penu;
(4) *Turki Penu:* He is believed to live in the garbages;
(5) *Dharma Penu:* He is believed to be the witness of the work done by men;
(6) *Ruja or Yuga Penu:* He is believed to help in raising agricultural production;
(7) *Maulaka:* He is believed to be the cause of creating diseases, illness and to bring in danger.

The Kondhs are God fearing and rigid in their religious beliefs. There is a common belief in their community that if they don't satisfy the God and Goddess, mishaps in their family in the form of disease, death, loss of cattle, property, crop etc. may occur. So before consuming anything they offer their produce to the God or Goddess. They also follow Hindu customs and rites. They worship big trees, stones and forest because of their belief in the manifestation of God in these forms. In the past, they were practising human sacrifice called "Meriah sacrifice" which was stopped by the Government.

It is said that "the Khonds have never forgiven Meriah sacrifice and that deep down in the Kondh heart is an essential lawlessness and disregard for human life. Some of the Kondh priests are now having dream and say that if they want their forest back, they must restart human sacrifice.[56]

Now-a-days the Konds are used to kill buffaloes, goats, pigs and fowls in social and religious functions. They too follow Hindu customs and rites. They observe Car festival, Siva Puja, Ganesh puja, etc.[57]

In the Kondh community, the people like to enjoy during social functions and festivals. They live in an open atmosphere and observe different festivals in different seasons. The Kondh girls participate in folk-dance. They perform "Kedu" by killing buffalo so that their land would produce more crops. Dalkhai dance, Krahanda dance, hunting dance are observed in different seasons. The Kondhs have given up such traditions due to the spread of education.[58]

Music and Dance

The Kondhs usually pass their leisure time by drinking, dancing and singing. They like to song love songs, marriage songs and harvest songs. They use locally made musical instruments like Nagara, Singha, Dhol, Gini etc. during dancing. Dhangudi dance is performed in Kondh society. Except Kutia Kondhs, other Kondhs do not dance with the girls of the same village. Such dances form a prelude to love-making and marriage. Their songs are composed in Kui language. The theme of the song is mainly based on love, beauty of nature and devotion to their Gods and Goddesses. On the Thursday of the month of Margasira, the Dalkhai dance is performed by the Kondhs. On this occasion, they worship the Goddess of forest and crop.

Standard of Living of Tribals

The standard of living of Kondhs of Kandhamal district is very low as compared to that of the non-tribals. The average per capita annual income of the tribes in Kandhamal district is Rs. 660. The main items of expenditure are food and drinks which constitute 88 per cent of the total expenditure.

Due to low income and disproportionate expenditure on different festivals the majority of the tribals of the district are indebted. It is estimated that 62.5 per cent of the tribals are indebted in Baliguda Sub-division and 72 per cent in Kondhmal Sub-division.[59] The extent of indebtedness is aggravated due to the ruthless exploitation by the unscrupulous traders and non-tribals.

The uneconomic landholding, low productivity , soil erosion, illiteracy, indebtedness and lack of infrastructure facilities taken together are responsible for the stagnation of the tribal economy and appalling poverty of the people.

* The socio-economic survey conducted by ITDA, Phulbani project in 2000-2001 reveals that 16 per cent of the household derive their income from agriculture. The rest 84 per cent are below the poverty line. They have to undergo semi-starvation and starvation conditions subsisting on many non-food materials like mango, jack-fruit, mango carnels, mahua flowers, tamarind seeds and many other roots, fruits and vegetables. The survey also reveals that 51per cent of the surveyed households face such starvation for varying number of days between 1 to 45 days in a year and 22per cent of the households pass such conditions between 46 to 120 days in a year.

REFERENCES

1. "Orissa District Gazetteers, Boudh and Khondmals", Department of Revenue, Government of Orissa, 1983, p. 34.
2. "Orissa District Gazetteers, Boudh and Khondmals", *op.cit*, p. 40.
3. Bailey, F.G., "Cost and Economic Frontier (A village in Highland Orissa)", Chapter I, p. 30.
4. "Gazetteers of India, Boudh, Khondmals", 1983, *op.cit*, pp. 42-43.
5. Dr. Das, Binayak, "Development Strategy of the *Tribal People* of Phulbani, Orissa", 1988, p. 32.
6. Report of the District Reorganisation Committee, Orissa, Vol. I, 1975, p-15.
7. "District Statistical Handbook of Phulbani District", 1969-70 pp. 3-4.
8. Gazetteer of India, Boudh Khondmals, 1983, p. 83.
9. "Census of India, Orissa Boudh-Khondmals", 1961, p. 6.
10. Gazetteer of India, Boudh Khondmals, 1983, p. 42.
11. *Ibid.*, p. 2.
12. Macpherson's Report on Khonds of the districts of Ganjam and Koraput, Section II, p-6.

13. Statistical Handbook, Boudh Khondmals, 1969-70, p. 34.
14. 'Census of India', Ganjam District, 1969, p. 23.
15. Statistical Handbook, Boudh Khondmals 1969-70, p. 4
16. District Statistical Handbook, Phulbani, 1964, P-III.
17. District Statistical Handbook, Kandhamal, 1995, P-1.
18. *Ibid.*, p. 14.
19. Dr. Das Binayak, "Development Strategy of Tribal People in Phulbani, Orissa", 1988, p. 40.
20. "District Credit Plan", Boudh, Kandhamal, 1983-85, p. 1.
21. Gazetteer of India, Boudh Khondmals, Govt. of Orissa, p. 14.
22. "Information on Social Forestry Project", Phulbani Division, Phulbani, 1988.
23. "District Gazetteers/Boud-Kandhamal", pp. 1-5.
24. *Ibid.*, 1983, p. 20.
25. State's Economy in figures 1996, Orissa, p. 2.
26. Paper-II of series 22 of Census of India, 2001, p. 61.
27. *Ibid*.
28. District Credit Plan, Phulbani, 1983-85, p. 2.
29. District Credit Plan, 1974-75, p. 25.
30. Padhy, K.S. & Satapathy, Purna Chandra, Tribal India Today., p. 48 (Ashish Publishing House, 1988).
31. An Evaluation Study of I.T.D.A. Baliguda, 1985-86, p. 33.
32. An Evaluation Study of ITDA Baliguda, 1995-96, p. 35.
33. District Statistical Handbook, 1997, Kandhamal, p. 43.
34. District at a glance 2000, Orissa.
35. District Statistical Handbook, 1997, Kandhamal, p. 57.
36. Dr. Das, Binayak "Development Strategy for the Tribal People in Phulbani, Orissa", p. 53.
37. Districts at a galance, 2000, Orissa.
38. Census India, 1961, Orissa, District Census Handbook, Boudh-Kandhamal pp. 15-16.
39. *Ibid.*, p. 16.
40. Dr. Das, Binayak, "Development Strategy for the Tribal People of Phulbani, Orissa" (Memio) 1988, p. 72.
41. Taylor, H.D. (Collector and Agent to the Governor) Memoir on the Ganjam Maliahs in the Presidency", Ganjam, p. 2.
42. "Orissa District Gazetteers", Boudh Khondmals, Govt. of Orissa, 1983, p. 73.

43. *Ibid*., p. 73.
44. *Ibid*., p. 70.
45. Behera, Dandapani, "The Bhanjas and the Khonds of Orissa (Calcutta Punthi Pustak, 1987, p. 140)
46. T. Sangama, "Adivasi" Vol. III, July, 1966, p. 3.
47. "Orissa District Gazetteer", Boudh Khondmals, Govt. of Orissa, 1983, p. 73.
48. Statistical Handbook, Phulbani, 1971, p. 3.
49. Behera, Dandapani, The Bhanjas and the Kondhs of Orissa, Calcutta, Punthi Pustak, 1987, p. 140.
50. Benchmark Survey Report of Balliguda Project, 1973, p. 26.
51. E.A. Samuell's Report to Secretary, Govt. of Bengal, 14th Feb., 1855 Vol. 1853-1856, B.R.A.
52. Statistical Handbook, Phulbani, 1973, p. 3.
53. Orissa District Gazetteer, Boudh Kondhmals, Govt. of Orissa, 1983, p. 71.
54. Tribal Development, Govt. of Orissa, Jan. 1977, T & R.W Deptt. Bhubaneswar, p. 22.
55. Rath Somanath, "Upendra Bhanja, Sidelights on History and Culture of Orissa (Edited by M.N. Das), New Delhi, S. Chand & Co. 1977, p. 698.
56. Dr. Elwin Varrier, supplement to "A Brief Survey of the Aboriginal Tribes of the Districts of Ganjam and Koraput, pp. 4-5.
57. Orissa District Gazetteer, Boudh Kandhmals, Govt. of Orissa, 1983, p. 73.
58. *Ibid*., p. 69.
59. Development Strategy for the Tribal People, Phulbani, Orissa (Memio) Dr. Das, Binayak, 1988, p. 83.

3

Growth of Co-operative Movement in India

Introduction

Co-operation means working together. Co-operative has played a vital role since the existence of human civilisation. Co-operation has given light to the man which enables him to live together, work together and help each other in times of stress and strain. The principles of co-operation has given light to the human race. Modern civilisation cannot achieve its target and economic progress without the help of co-operation.

The basic concept of co-operation is the inspiration of self-reliance of individuals to be realised through mutual aid and group action. Even though the main objective of a co-operative is the meeting of economic needs of the members, the method of meeting them is as much important to a co-operative as the objective itself. The goal of co-operation is to develop man so that he may rise to a full personal life and collectively to full social life.

Co-operative societies are mainly formed for the people of low economic strata, low means, agricultural workers, self-employed people, and the like. It is the co-operative societies through which the people (members) get collective benefits and achieve their goal of economic prosperity.

Co-operation is inextricably linked with India's historical traditions and cultural mosaic. The Indian is basically social and works best with his family and his community. Gandhiji used this characteristic to great advantage in fashioning the tools to drive out those for whom the sun would never set on their empire. Thus, coopertion was basically a process and an educational process and this places India's co-operative objectives squarely in the great co-operative objectives squarely in the great co-operative tradition.

For Jawaharlal Nehru co-operation was not merely a useful organisational device of economic production and intermediation for the economically disadvantaged. It was at the very core of his economic philosophy of a desired social pattern. He saw in co-operatives a "higher form of social organisation", and visualised a co-operative commonwealth in which the smallest of individuals could have the means of access to modern technology and larger resources of money and management, yet not lose their individuality in the process. In his vision of India, co-operatives and community development were to be the twin animators of rural regeneration. Self help, self-reliance and self-regulation was the spirit of both.

Co-operative idea invokes the spirit of man and accepts 'universality' in man—the same 'atman' residing in each of us. Co-operation believes that all men are created by God and inequality is the creation of a particular form of social organisation. A co-operative form of organisation based on mutuality endeavours to harness the finer qualities of man for a better man and better society.

"Co-operative form of organisation emerged as a reaction to the depredations of capitalistic system, where competition actually results in cut-throat competition allowing each other for maximisation of their profit, resulting in extreme inequality in the sharing of the cake. Man ceases to be man and treated as a machine and there is mass unemployment and misery in this situation.

Growth of Co-operative Movement in India

The co-operative movement which received legal sanctity in the year 1904 and will be soon completing its century, could play a dynamic role in achieving our objectives. Vaikunthabhai Mehta was the doyen of the co-operative movement in the country. During the past 95 years, co-operative movement has entered several sectors like credit, banking, processing, housing, warehousing, irrigation, transport and even industries. Due to the growth of credit co-operatives, it was possible to weaken the stronghold of moneylenders on thousands of poor families and free them from their bondage.

The growth of dairy co-operative and sugar co-operative made India as a major nation in the world in milk and sugar production.

The co-operative movement in the country is at crossroads and has been passing through a critical phase like our economy. In such circumstances, acceptance of self-reliance and swadeshi and non-dependence on foreign funds, is the only alternative. Growth with social justice along with due care of environment for sustainable development must be the new direction of the co-operative movement. The co-operative movement in India made significant strides only after independence when it was thought of as a potential means of eradicating poverty from the face of India. Before that it had been conceived of mainly as an agency to cater to the credit needs of the farmers. It was only under the benign patronage of persons like Pandit Jawaharal Nehru that it was given an important place in the economic programmes aimed at overall development of the country. The movement, therefore, gradually diversified itself and spread its tentacles far and wide. The rapid strides that it took make it today one of the largest movements in the world.

Movement from 1904 to 1912

The introduction of the Co-operative Credit Societies Act in 1904 marked the beginning of the co-operative movement in India. The Co-operative Credit Societies Act was passed on 25th March, 1904. In the above period, the Government was the prime mover of the movement. This Act was started with the motive of establishing credit societies both in rural and urban areas to provide cheap credit facilities to the persons of limited means. In 1909, the Government subscribed 22 per cent of the working capital as alone to the members of the societies.

Mr. Lallu Bhai Samal Das and Mr. G.K. Gokhale of Bombay took interest for the movement. Mr. Samal Das has organised the first Central Co-operative Bank in Bombay in 1911. Another Co-operator, Mr. Chiromule has organised a society of 20 sweepers at Sitara. The members were all indebted to Pathans, who charged extra-ordinary rate of interest. The society freed the members of that debt and spread the reputation of the movement.[1]

Table 3.1 indicates the growth of co-operative credit societies in India during the period (1906-07 to 1910-11)

Table—3.1 Progress of co-operative movement in India from 1906-07 to 1910-11

Year	No. of societies	No. of members (in thousands)	Working capital (Rs. in lakhs)
1906-07	843	90.84	23.72
1907-08	1,357	149.16	44.14
1908-09	1,963	180.34	82.32
1909-10	3,428	224.40	124.68
1910-11	5,321	305.06	203.05

Source : Mathur, B.S. 'Co-operation in India', Sahitya Bhawan, Agra, 1990, p. 55.

From the figures in the above table, it is seen that there was significant progress of the credit societies during the initial stages. There was hardly any state where the new doctrine did not strike root. The Maclagan Committee stated that "the movement did not take long to outgrow the dreams of its members."[2] The Act of 1904 could not meet the growing needs of the movement due to the following reasons:

(1) Legal protection was not given to the societies formed for the purposes other than credit;

(2) For the financing of primary societies, provision for the formation of a central agency such as the central banks was not made;

(3) There was arbitrary classification of societies as rural and urban and it was found unsuitable.

Movement from 1912 to 1918

In 1912, Co-operative Societies Act was passed to remove the defects of the 1904 Act. After passing this Act, the co-operative movement entered into the second stage of its progress.

Table 3.2 indicates the growth of co-operative credit societies in India during the period from 1912-1918.

It may be seen from the figures in the table that there was steady increase in the number of societies, their membership and the amount of working capital during the above period. Thus, the growth of the co-operative movement received a fresh impetus due to the new Act of 1912.

Table—3.2 ***Progress of the co-operative movement from 1911-12 to 1917-18***

Year	*Societies*	*Membership (in lakhs)*	*Working Capital (Rs. in lakhs)*
1911-12	8,177	4.7	335.7
1917-18	25,192	10.9	760.09

Source : Mathur, B.S., *op. cit*., p. 68.

The number of agricultural societies and non-cultural societies was 23,714 and 1,451 with membership of 8.5 lakhs and 2.4 lakhs respectively by the end of 1917-18.

In 1904, a committee under the chairmanship of Sir E.D. Maclagan was appointed by the Government of India to study whether the co-operative movement was progressing on sound lines or not. The committee, in its report, warned on the hurried expansion of the movement and recommended that utmost care was to be exercised in the formation of a society.

Movement from 1919 to 1929

After the conclusion of World War-I, the Reforms Act of 1919 was introduced and co-operation became a provincial subject and was placed under the charge of a Minister. During this third stage of co-operative movement, the initiativeness of the development ministers, post-war boom and rising prices provided fillip to the co-operative movement. For the rapid progress of the co-operative societies, in 1925 a new Act was passed. Bombay, Madras, Bihar, Orissa and Bengal also passed new Acts during the later years.

Table—3.3 ***Progress of co-operative movement from 1919 to 1929***

Year	*No. of Societies (in thousands)*	*Membership (in lakhs)*	*Working capital (Rs. in crores)*
1920	28.4	11.3	15
1929	94.0	37.0	75

Source : Bedi, R.D., 'Theory, History and Practice of Co-operation', Loyal Book Depot, Meerut, 1977, p. 194.

From the figures in the above table 3.3 it is seen that number of members of agricultural credit societies increased more than three-times, while their working capital moved up five-fold. In non-credit sector, the progress was even more. The number of non-credit societies increased from 1,971 in 1918-19 to 9,761 in 1928-29 while the membership moved from 2.62 lakhs to 9.92 lakhs recording about a four-fold increase in both the cases. During this period, the increase in working capital of these societies from Rs. 2.17 crores to Rs. 13.63 crores recorded a six-fold increase. But the number of rural families brought within the co-operative fold was very small which was about 2.8 per cent. During this period, various committees namely Royal Commission on Agriculture, the Central and Provincial Banking Enquiry Committee, the Oakden Committee, the King Committee and the Townsend Committee were formed to give report of the co-operative movement in the country.

Movement from 1929-30 to 1938-39

During this period, the great depression of the thirties resulted in substantial fall in prices of agricultural commodities. As it affected repaying capacity of the agriculturists, overdues mounted up. In some provinces such as the central provinces and Berar, Bihar, Orissa and Bengal, the movement nearly collapsed.[3] In many provinces different committees were appointed to assess the real situation and make suggestion for the development of the movement. During this period rectification and rehabilitation was the objective of the co-operative department. The number of agricultural credit societies decreased from 93,512 in 1930-31 to 92,226 in 1933-34. Close supervision, strict scrutiny of operations, all-out efforts made to recover overdues resulted in the sign of recovery from 1935-36. After the establishment of Reserve Bank of India in 1935, various problems regarding agricultural credit were studied and organisation of multi-purpose co-operative societies was emphasized. Co-operative Movement from 1939 to 1947 is reflected in table 3.4.

The inflationary trend during the second world war increased the repaying capacity of the former. So the overdues decreased from Rs. 14.05 crores in 1938-39 to Rs. 8.52 crores in 1945-46.

The progress of the movement could be judged from the fact that in 1945-46, there was one society for every 3.8 villages and about 10.6 per cent of the population had been covered by the movement as against one society for every 5.4 villages and 6.2 per cent population in 1938-39.[4]

The second world war period broadened the functional rank of the co-operative movement and it brought about a shift in the lop-sided emphasis from the credit aspect to the productive and distributive function or to its multi-purpose potentialities—"a long-felt need for imparting that richness and balance which is necessary for the proper development of the movement.[5]

Table—3.4 Progress of co-operative movement from 1938-39 to 1945-46

Year	*No. of societies (in thousands)*	*Membership (in lakhs)*	*Working capital (in crores)*
1938-39	122	53.7	106.47
1939-40	137	60.8	107.10
1940-41	143	64.0	109.32
1941-42	145	67.4	112.42
1942-43	146	69.1	121.14
1943-44	156	76.9	132.21
1944-45	160	83.6	146.63
1945-46	172	91.6	164.00

Source : Review of the Co-operative Movement in India, 1939-46, p. 3

The co-operative planning committee appointed by the Government of India during this period under chairmanship of Shri R.G. Saraiya fixed an overall target of bringing 50 per cent of the village and 30 per cent of the rural population in the ambit of the co-operative movement within a period of ten years.

In 1947 before the independence, in our country there were 1.39 lakhs societies with membership of 91 lakhs having a working capital amounting to Rs. 156 crores. The laissez faire policy of the Government, general illiteracy of the masses, want of trained staff, lack of supervision and co-ordination were the important reasons for the limited progress of the co-operative movement before independence.

Co-operative Movement after Independence

The co-operative movement in India which is more than 90 years old made significant strides only after independence when it was thought of as a potential means of eradicating poverty from the face of India. Before that it was considered as an agency to cater to the credit needs of the farmers. It was only under the benign patronage of persons like Pandit Jawahar Lal Nehru that it was given an important place in the economic programme aimed at overall development of the country in different five-year plans. The movement, therefore, gradually diversified itself and spread its tentacles far and wide. The rapid strides that it took make it to-day one of the largest movements in the world.

Co-operative Movement through Five-year Plans

The progress of co-operative movement through different plans are discussed below:

The First Five Year Plan

The First Five Year Plan which was launched in 1950-51 described the co-operative movement as an indispensable instrument of planned action in the country is discussed in table 3.5.

Table—3.5 Progress of co-operative movement during the first plan period (1950-51 to 1955-56)

	1950-51	*1955-56*
1. No. of primary agricultural credit societies	1,15,462	1,59,939
2. Membership (in lakhs)	51.54	77.91
3. Average working capital (Rs)	3,547	4,946
4. Percentage of rural population served	10.30	15.60

Source : Mathur, B.S. 'Corporation in India', Sahitya Bhawan, Agra, 1990, p. 66.

The figures in the above table show that by the end of June 1956, about 15.6 per cent rural population has come within co-operative sector. The Planning Commission laid emphasis on the co-ordination between village panchayats and co-operative societies for the achievement of co-operative socialism during the first Five Year Plan. In 1951, the All India Rural Credit Survey was conducted by the Reserve Bank of India and its report was published in 1954. One of the findings of the survey was that the co-operatives supplied only 3.1 per cent of the total credit requirements of the farmers. It was also revealed in the survey that a larger part of the co-operative credit went to the bigger agriculturists. For strengthening and revitalising co-operative movement, the survey committee recommended an 'Integrated scheme of Rural Credit' based on the principles of state partnership, constitution of long-term operations fund by the R.B.I., emphasis on crop loan, establishment of large-sized societies, linking of credit with marketing, training of personnel and effective and supervision and audit.

Second Five Year Plan

During the second Five Year Plan, co-operative movement was not confined to credit societies alone, but it was widely extended to marketing, warehousing and buffer stocks etc. On the basis of recommendations of Rural Credit Survey Committee, plans for the co-operative was formulated during this plan period as explained in table 3.6.

Table—3.6 Progress of the co-operative movement during the second plan period (1955-56 to 1960-61)

		1955-56	*1960-61*
1.	Number of Societies (in lakhs)	2.40	3.32
2.	Membership of Primary Societies (in lakhs)	176.00	342.00
3.	Average working capital per society (Rs)	4,946.00	12,913.00
5.	Percentage of villages covered	—	75.00

Source : Mathur, B.S., *op. cit.* p. 84.

From the above table it is indicated that during the second plan, the number of societies increased from 2.40 lakhs in 1955-56 to 3.32 lakhs in 1960-61 and the number of members increased from 176 lakhs in 1955-56 to 3.42 lakhs in 1960-61.

In 1958, the National Development Council resolutions brought a radical change in the policy and programmes of the co-operative movement. During the second plan, a number of communities and working groups, namely, the Committee on Co-operative Credit, the Working groups on Panchayats and Co-operatives, the Study Team on Co-operative Training, the Committee on Consumers' Co-operation made very valuable recommendations for the development of co-operative movement.

Third Five Year Plan

During the third Five Year Plan, Rs. 80 crores was provided for the development of the co-operatives. For strengthening the co-operative movement, many working groups and committees on Industrial Co-operatives, Housing Cooperatives, Transport Co-operatives, Fishery Cooperatives, Dairy and Animal Husbandry Co-operatives were constituted by the Government.

In 1963, a committee under the chairmanship of Shri V.L. Mehta was appointed which made valuable suggestions for sound administration, audit, supervision and training of staff. In 1964, an expert committee under the chairmanship of Prof. M.L. Dantwala was appointed to review the present pattern of marketing co-operative societies. The committee made valuable suggestions such as introduction of two-tier structure, mixed membership and location of primary marketing societies at mandi centres for increasing the efficiency of marketing societies.

In 1964, a committee on co-operation, constituted under the chairmanship of Shri R.N. Mirsha, submitted its report in August, 1965 recommended criteria to determine the genuineness of co-operative societies and suggested certain restrictions regarding admission to the membership of co-operative societies.

As against 100 per cent coverage aimed at in the Third Plan, 5,02,816 villages out of the total of 5,63,629 villages in the country in June, 1966 had been covered by primary agricultural societies. The percentage of the villages covered by the active societies worked out to be 82. At the end of year 1965-66, the number of societies was 1,91,904. In June, 1966, the total number of members of the credit societies was 26.1 million. During the Third Plan, co-operative processing and consumer co-operatives made considerable progress.

Before the implementation of Fourth Five Year Plan, co-operative movement made a headway under Annual Plans. In 1966-67, Rs. 33.5 crores, in 1967-68, Rs. 36.3 crores, in 1968-69 Rs. 34 crores were spent for the development of co-operative societies in the country.

Fourth Five Year Plan

During the Fourth Five Year Plan, the target was to bring all the villages and there-fourths of the population under co-operation. Growth with stability was expected to the key-note of the co-operative movement during this plan period. Reorganisation of primary credit structure, rehabilitation of weak central banks, reduction of overdues deposit mobilisation, orientation of policies of credit co-operative and land development banks in favour of small cultivators, considerable emphasis on co-operative marketing structure, organisation of new processing units and consolidation and strengthening of existing consumer co-operatives were the main objectives of this Plan period.

In 1969, All India Rural Credit Review Committee under the chairmanship of Shri B. Venkatappiah was appointed by the Reserve Bank of India to review the supply of rural credit during this plan period. The reorganisation of rural credit in the Reserve Bank, involving the establishment of an Agricultural Credit Board, the setting up of a Small Farmers Development Agency in each of a number of selected districts throughout the country, the creation of Rural Electrification Corporation which among other things is to benefit under developed areas with an agricultural potential, the formulation of a more active and much bigger role for the Agricultural Refinance Corporation, and the adoption of various measures for ensuring the timely and adequate flow of credit for agriculture through co-operation and commercial banks—these are among the highlights of the recommendations of the Review Committee.

The establishment of a Consultancy and Promotional Cell within the National Co-operative Consumers Federation for providing expert guidance to consumer co-operatives was another significant development during this plan period. With regard to cooperative marketing of agricultural produce, fourth plan targets were exceeded. In case of co-operative credit and co-operative storage, the progress was according to the plan targets. But in other fields, there were shortfalls against the plan targets.

Fifth Five Year Plan

During the Fifth Plan, special emphasis was given on the requirements of farmers, workers and consumers. The Draft Fifth Five Year Plan (1974-79) stated:

"Co-operation is eminently suited to bring about desired socio-economic challenges in the context of the existing conditions in the country. There is no other instrument as potentially powerful and full of social purpose as the co-operative movement."[6]

During the Fifth Five Year Plan, the specific objectives for the development of co-operatives were (*a*) to strengthen the network of agricultural co-operatives (credit, supply, marketing and processing); (*b*) To build up a viable consumer co-operative movement; (c) To take steps for removing regional imbalances in the level of co-operative development particularly in the field of agricultural credit; (*d*) restructuring and reorienting the co-operatives for the benefit of small and marginal farmers and other under-privileged section of the people.

For the benefit of small and marginal farmers, organisation of Farmers Service Society as envisaged by National Commission on Agriculture was emphasised during Fifth Plan. Structural reformation on a district by district basis of a large number of weak primary agricultural credit societies, district central co-operative banks and consumer co-operative stores was contemplated.

In the Fifth Plan, a substantial increase in the flow of institutional credit to small farmers, marginal farmers, tenants and share croppers was an important objective of credit policy. Some steps such as consolidation and strengthening of existing agricultural marketing co-operatives, intensification of co-operative training and education programmes, establishment of management cadres, reduction of inter-state imbalances in the co-operative were taken during the fifth plan. The total public sector outlay for co-operative development during Fifth Plan was Rs. 423 crores as against an estimated expenditure of Rs. 258 crores in the Fourth Plan.

Sixth Five Year Plan

During the Sixth Five Year Plan, special attention was given to the following tasks:

(1) An action programme to be prepared to strengthen the primary village societies with a view to enable them to act effectively as multipurpose units catering to diverse needs of their members;

(2) To reorganise the existing policies and procedures of the

co-operatives in order to ameliorate the economic conditions of the rural poor;

(3) Reorganisation and consolidation of the role of co-operative and expansion of agricultural sector;

(4) To develop professional cadres for different managerial positions.

The promotion of voluntary scheme and social action programme, promotion and strengthening of Mahila/Yuvak Mandals, pilot projects of Public Co-operation implemented by the State Governments, research studies in the field of rural development were the important programmes undertaken during the sixth plan period.

During the sixth plan, the total public sector outlay on various schemes of co-operative was Rs. 914.23 crores. The short-term loans, medium term loans and long-term loans amounted to Rs. 2,500 crores, Rs. 250 crores and Rs. 500 crores respectively by the end of the sixth plan. The amount of marketing of agricultural products increase to Rs. 2,700 crores by the end of 1984-85. At the end of 1984-85, the capacity of the constructed co-operative godowns was 8 million tonnes. At the end of this plan, the number of co-operative sugar factories and co-operative spinning mills were 185 and 90 respectively. During the sixth plan, another major development was the establishment of National Bank for Agriculture and Rural Development (NABARD) in July, 1982.

Seventh Five Year Plan

During the Seventh Five Year Plan, the total expenditure for co-operation was Rs. 1,400.58 crores, out of which expenditure of the centre was Rs. 500 crores, for states Rs. 870.18 crores and for Union Territories the outlay was of Rs. 30-40 crores.

The Planning Commission after making a review of the progress made by the co-operatives noted that although quantitative progress was made during different plan periods, the co-operative movement had not picked up in the North Eastern Region. So during the Seventh Plan, comprehensive development of primary agricultural credit societies, realignment of the policies and procedures of co-operatives, special co-operative programmes for implementation in the North Eastern Region, strengthening of consumer co-operative movement in urban and rural areas, promotion of professional management and strengthening of effective training facilities were emphasized.

During the seventh plan, greater stress was also laid on the following:

(*a*) to ensure adequate flow of credit to the weaker sections;

(*b*) to supervise proper utilisation of the loans;

(*c*) to improve recovery climate and reduce overdues;

(*d*) to implement a pilot scheme of mobile credit delivery system;

(*e*) to intensify co-operative training and education programmes.

Eight Five Year Plan

During the Eighth Five Year Plan, Government of India took some steps for the implementation of an integrated development approach by means of extension and organisation of co-operatives in tribal areas. In order to help the tribals to get reasonable price in marketing of minor forest produce, the Tribal Development Co-operative Corporation (TDCC) was organised for collecting and marketing of minor forest produce.

The co-operative societies were re-oriented and restructured to achieve the above objectives. The large sized Agricultural Multi-purpose Societies (LAMPS) were also organised in order to fulfil the necessaries of the tribal people relating to the marketing of MFP and supply of essential commodities at a responsible price. During this plan period, identification of different occupational groups among the tribals, proper training in co-operative education and entrepreneurial skill and leadership among them was created for greater participation in the field of co-operative movement.

Ninth Five Year Plan

During the Ninth Five Year Plan (1997-2002), the focus was laid on "growth with social justice and equity". It gave priority to agriculture and rural development in order to generate adequate productive employment and eradication of poverty. In the Approach Document for the Ninth Plan, the overall growth rate for Gross Domestic Product (GDP) at constant prices had been fixed at 7 per cnet per annum and that for the agriculture sector at 4.5 per cent per annum. The Union Agriculture Ministry exhorted various segments of the co-operative movement to help in attainment of the target for agriculture sector stipulated for the ninth plan. For this, the co-operative sector had to supplement the efforts of the non-cooperative organisations to achieve the stipulated growth rate. In order to facilitate this role in the co-operative sector, the co-operatives have to adopt themselves to the postulates of the growing competitive economy. The co-opertives have to strengthen their productive apparatus in terms of supply of agriculture inputs like quality seed, fertilisers, pesticides, agricultural implements etc. The co-operatives already have an edge over other sectors in so far as their organisational structure is concerned. The federal organisational structure, despite its weakness, provides a very wide network to link up primary producer/consumer to the tertiary level of economy.

The approach document to the ninth plan has stated that co-operatives ought to the efficient, competitive and commercially viable through the development of professional efficiency, diversification of activities and sufficient volume of business. In the context of a market oriented economy, the situation demands induction of efficient personnel at various levels of co-operative administration and management. In this context, there was the need for wholesale reformulation and modification in policies relating to human resource development in co-operatives during the ninth plan period. The co-operative sector should take advantage of the New Rural Infrastructural Development Fund and submit suitable bankable projects relating to co-operative economic activities. This is likely to help in financing the capital expenditure of the ongoing projects of the co-operative sector and would ultimately help in improving the capital formation in this sector.

During the ninth plan, the co-operatives disbursed 59 per cent of the total flow of institutional credit in the agricultural sector at all-India level. The co-operatives also substantially increased their role in the distribution of fertilisers, improved seeds, farm implements at reasonable prices and at appropriate time to the farming community. The grand success of co-operative during experiment achieved at Anand in Gujarat should be an eye-opener for other components of agricultural growth and rural development for adoption and implementation during the ninth plan period. The need for extension of dairy co-operative philosophy to other sub-sectors like poultry, fishery, fruits and vegetable co-operatives was very much felt during this plan period.

As the level of post-harvest facilities and services is grossly inadequate in the country, there are losses ranging between 25 per cent to 30 per cent in the case of fruits production. In value terms, the post-harvest wastage and losses per year have been estimated at over Rs. 3,000 crores. During the ninth plan period, the co-operative institutions made concerted efforts to step up their contribution towards improving post-harvest services such as handling, storage, transportation, processing and marketing of horticultural and vegetable products. The attainment of higher contribution of co-operatives to the attainment of higher growth rate could be facilitated during the ninth plan period if the co-operatives would have made efforts to have closer interaction with other institutions like panchayats, research institutions, extension agencies and Krishi Vigyan Kendras.

Co-operative Movement in Orissa

Before Plan Period

The co-operative movement in Orissa dates back to 1904, when Co-operative Credit Societies Act was passed. The origin of the movement in the co-operative sector in the state can be traced back sufficiently before the Act. There were a few co-operative socieities operating in different districts of Orissa long before the Co-operative Societies Act, 1904 was enacted. The economy of Orissa is based mostly on agriculture. According to 1991 census, out of the total population of 3.17 crores, 86.6 per cent people in Orissa live in rural areas. As per the agricultural census of 1991, about 46.94 per cent people in Orissa directly depend on agriculture to earn their livelihood and among them the small marginal farmers constitute about 76 per cent of the farming community.[7] The size of their holding varies from 0 to 5 acres. About 20 per cent of the cultivable land is possessed by them. Further 38.4 per cent of the total population constitute the S.T. and S.C. population in the state.[8] Most of the farming communities in Orissa belong to the backward and financially weaker sections. The farmers suffer a lot of uncertainty of rainfall, lack of infrastructural facilities and lack of improved sources credit.

In order to overcome the difficulties, mainly on short-term credit facilities in agricultural sector, co-operative movement in Orissa was started. It followed the all India pattern. Raiffeisen model of co-operative was favoured in Orissa (Appendix VI). Orissa was the pioneer in the field of co-operative movement in India. A society was formed at Nimapada in Puri district with the help of Government loan of Rs. 500. The co-operative societies were also formed by Mr. P.C. Lyon, Director of Settlement of Agriculture at Balugon, Taraboi and Bolagarh in Khurda sub division with the Government loan of Rs. 1,250. About 21 co-operative societies were operating as credit institutions at Charchika, Subarnapur and Baraput in Cuttack district as early as 1905 with a grant of Rs. 1,000 drawn from the Board of Revenue of the Bengal Presidency.[9] During the British rule, late Rai Bhadur Bidyadhar Panda and late Balmukunda Kanungo, the then Deputy Collector of Banki took the leadership to spread the message of co-operation among the people in Orissa as the torch bearer of the movement.[10] In accordance with the recommendations of the Famine Commission of 1901, some other co-operative societies were also organised during and after the Act of 1904. Due to this, the objectives like thrift, self and fellow feelings developed among the farmers against the exploitation of local money lenders and sahukars.

As adequate scope was not provided in the Act of 1904 for the growth of co-operative in other areas, the Co-operative Societies Act, 1912 was promulgated to bring about important changes and diversification into non-agricultural fields. In 1912, Central Banks at Banki and Khurda were established to provide finance to the affiliated societies and also to safeguard the interest of the people. There were 82 credit societies functioning during this period.

Orissa was divided into two parts. The North Orissa part was under Bihar-Bengal-Orissa State.[11] Similarly the South portion was in the Madras Presidency until the formation of separate Orissa State on 1st April, 1936.[12] The Berhampur Urban Co-operative Bank formed in 1906 was the 1st co-operative society in South Orissa.[13] There was no much expansion of the co-operative movement in this region till 1915. Nineteen co-operative societies were operating in this region being financed by the Madras Central Bank.[14] In the year 1916, for the purpose of financial facilities, all the co-operative societies were affiliated to Madras Central Urban Bank. In order to provide finance to the co-operative societies of Ghumsur, Khallikote and Athagarh estates, another Central Co-operative Bank was established at Aska in the year 1918. A Central Co-operative Bank was also established at Paralakhemundi in the year 1920. But, on account of financial weakness, it was merged with Berhampur

Central Co-operative Bank in the year 1924.[15] Three Central Co-operative Banks and 185 primary Co-operative Societies with 9264 members and Rs. 6.83 lakhs working capital were operating in the South Orissa. The growth of co-operative societies decreased in Northern Orissa due to separation of Bihar and Orissa from Bengal. Two CCB and 82 societies with 3182 members and Rs. 2.78 lakhs of working capital were functioning in North Orissa.[16] For financial assistance to the Central Co-operative Banks, the Bihar and Orissa Provincial Co-operative Bank was established in April 1949. Some steps were taken through non-official, rural gentlemen for the extension of the co-operative movement to rural areas in order to influence the rural mass. In 1918, the first guarantee union was started for spreading education, sanitation, agriculture and creating an interest for the co-operatives among the people.[17] The Bihar Orissa Co-operative Federation was established in the latter part of 1918 for the purpose of encouraging efficient system of supervision, audit and control of all Co-operative Banks to promote and develop agricultural, industrial and other special forms of co-operatives.[18] The famine relief assisted in the achievement of sound progress of co-operative movement.

In Orissa, the growth in the co-operative movement was slow during the World War-II. After the enactment of the Co-operative Reforms Act in 1919, the provincial Governments were empowered to look after the development of co-operatives. The provincial Governments were also vested with powers to retain or modify the existing Act of 1912.

The Government of India appointed a committee in the year 1922 to give advice on the financial aspects of the co-operative movement in Bihar-Orissa State. In 1923, another committee was appointed by the Government to give advice on the procedures of audit and schemes of financial assitance. Both the committees submitted their reports and the Government accepted and executed them. Due to mounting overdues, many societies suffered financial difficulties during this period. In order to overcome the financial difficulties rapidly, a review was made. The co-operative societies faced serious threat to their existence because of the great depression of 1930. The effects of great depression was seriously felt in Orissa. During this period, many co-operative societies were closed. In some provinces like Bihar, Orissa, Bengal, the movement was collapsed.[19]

There were 9,404 primary societies with 2.66 lakhs members and capital of Rs. 2.8 crores during this period (Table 3.8).

After Orissa became a separate state on 1st April, 1936, Ganjam and Koraput districts of Madras province were included in it. Then co-operative societies were organised, developed and managed in Northern Orissa and Southern Orissa separately by the state government till 1939. In North Orissa, Mr. N. Bakshi I.C.S. and in South Orissa, Mr. S.M. Majumdar remained in charge of management of the societies. Then co-operative societies in North and South Orissa were amalgamated and the Registrar of Co-operative Societies with headquarters at Cuttack remained in charge of all societies in the state.[20] During this period, there was a strong consensus for a third circle officer covering entire Sambalpur and Balangir district.[21] Although the registration of Orissa provincial Co-operative Bank was effected in the year 1936, it could not operate till 1948 because of dispute between the banks of Bihar and Orissa in connection with the distribution of their assets.

In 1938, K.D. Mudaliar, the Dewan Bahadur, was appointed by the Government of Orissa to review the progress of the movement in the co-operative sector. Mr. Mudaliar was also assigned the responsibilities to study the financial position, production, distribution and sale of co-operatives. The sub-committees were appointed in different districts to help Mudaliar Committee in investigation (Table 3.7). The committee visited all the 15 central co-operative societies. The members of the committee also met many members and received 243 statements in support of village credit co-operative societies. A conference was also convened by the committee to make an elaborate study of the co-operative movement in Orissa (Table 3.7).

For the purpose of direct finance to the primary societies, the committee suggested that provincial Co-operative Banks should be formed. In order to increase the confidence of the depositors, the financial assistance was also sought from the state Government on the basis of the recommendations of Mudaliar Committee. The constitution of the Central Co-operative Bank was also altered to bring a comprehensive programme of rehabilitation and to freeze off a portion of overdues outstanding against Co-operative Societies.[22]

Table—3.7 Mudaliar district sub-committee, 1938

Sl. No.	*Name of the Districts*		*Name of the members*
1.	Cuttack	(*a*)	Sri Bhagirathi Mahapatra
		(*b*)	Sri Gouri Prasad Mahapatra
		(*c*)	Sri Harihara Mahapatra
		(*d*)	Rai Bahadur B.C. Pattnaik
2.	Balasore	(a)	Sri Jaganath Das
		(*b*)	Sri Maulavi Md. Hanif
3.	Sambalpur	(*a*)	Sri Ramani Ranjan Bose
		(*b*)	Sri Biswa Nath Panigrahi
		(*c*)	Sri Prahalad Railath
4.	Puri	(*a*)	Sri Jagannath Mishra
		(*b*)	Sri Banamali Das
5.	Ganjam	(*a*)	Sri Khetramani Panda
		(*b*)	Sri Balakrishna Patra
		(*c*)	Sri N. Ramakrishna Rao

Source : Extract of the report on the condition of the 'Co-operative movement in Orissa, Diwan Bahadur, K.D. Mudaliar, AVL, Officer-in-charge, Co-operative Enquiry Committee, Orissa, Dt. 31.3.1938.

The Provincial Co-operative Land Mortgage Bank with headquarters at Berhampur was established in the year 1938-39 for advancing long-term loan to the farmers. The Central Co-operative Banks acted as the agents of the Land Mortgage Bank. The members were not interested to form new co-operatives due to the auction of their private assets during the British regime. During this period, there were 2715 co-operative societies with a membership of 1.06 lakhs and Rs. 1.32 crores as working capital (Table 3.8).

In Orissa, the co-operative movement received enormous impulse due to the second world war. During this period, the poor farmers received much benefit due to much increase in the price of the agricultural commodities. The co-operative movement gained a remarkable progress due to generation of ray of new hope in the mind of the farmers. It led to the reorganisation of many old credit societies. During this period, non-credit movement also progressed and the Government took much interest to distribute the essential products both in rural and

Table—3.8 Progress of co-operatives movement in orissa from 1904-1950

Sl. No.	*Year*	*No. of societies*	*No. of members (in thousands)*	*Working capital (in lakhs)*
1.	1904-1905*	6	NA	0.03
2.	1905-1906	9	NA	NA
3.	1906-1907	16	NA	NA
4.	1907-1908	18	NA	NA
5.	1908-1909	18	NA	NA
6.	1909-1910	18	NA	NA
7.	1910-1911	29	NA	NA
8.	1911-1912*	NA	NA	NA
9.	1912-1913	581	21.2	9.04
10.	1913-1914	817	49.6	15.0
11.	1914-1915	1088	52.7	19.3
12.	1915-1916	1298	59.4	22.6
13.	1916-1917	1429	66.3	24.7
14.	1917-1918	1724	72.4	33.2
15.	1918-1919	2213	79.2	39.0
16.	1919-1920	3011	96.0	45.7
17.	1920-1921	3580	107.5	57.8
18.	1921-1922	4261	128.4	79.5
19.	1922-1923	4962	164.1	105.2
20.	1923-1924	5616	181.2	138.5
21.	1924-1925	7220	212.6	280.0
22.	1925-1926	8263	226.6	289.6
23.	1926-1927	8264	239.0	475.8
24.	1927-1928	8587	254.7	502.3
25.	1928-1929	9188	267.1	565.1
26.	1929-1930	9316	273.1	582.1
27.	1930-1931	9404	266.5	279.1
28.	1931-1932	9303	274.0	587.0
29.	1932-1933	9054	271.1	571.4
30.	1933-1934	8112	145.2	415.5
31.	1934-1935	6108	112.5	219.0
32.	1935-1936	2152	74.1	102.2
33.	1936-1937	2154	74.2	98.3
34.	1937-1938	2704	105.8	114.5

(Contd.....)

(Table—3.8 Contd...)

Sl. No.	Year	No. of societies	No. of members (in thousands)	Working capital (in lakhs)
35.	1938-1939	2715	105.8	132.0
36.	1939-1940	2726	109.0	129.0
37.	1940-1941	2718	110.8	124.6
38.	1941-1942	2789	116.1	125.1
39.	1942-1943	2851	121.6	128.2
40.	1943-1944	2965	134.0	131.4
41.	1944-1945	3057	144.8	139.8
42.	1945-1946	3061	165.2	153.0
43.	1946-1947	3061	176.0	240.8
44.	1947-1948	3412	192.6	223.4
45.	1948-1949	3493	197.2	311.4
46.	1949-1950	4362	268.1	363.3
47.	1950-1951	5145	294.7	429.69

* During these years the Annual Reports of the Co-operative Societies were not prepared by the Government of Orissa.

Source : Complied from Annual reports on the working of co-operative societies in North Orissa and South Orissa, Cuttack for the years (from 1912-13 to 1936-37), pp. 1-5 and Annual Administration Report on the Co-operative Movement in Orissa, RCS, Bhubaneswar for the year from 1937-38 to 1950-51, pp. 1-3.

urban areas through the marketing co-operative societies.[23] But due to lack of adequate staff, liquidation of old dues, natural calamities and failure crops, the progress in the movement of co-operatives was slowed down. During 1946-47, there were 3061 co-operative societies with 1.7 lakh members and Rs. 2.4 crores of working capital. Due to the keen interest of the State and Central Government, the rate of growth of co-operative societies continued till 1951. The number of agricultural co-operative societies increased to a considerable extent after the attainment of independence. In 1946-47, the number of co-operatives which was 3,061 increased to 5145 in 1950-51. The number of members and working capital increased to the extent of 2.94 lakhs and Rs. 4.29 crores respectively (Table 3.8).

Table 3.8 reveals that during 1912-13, there were 581 co-operative societies in Orissa. But the same was increased to 5145 during 1950-51. Similarly the number of members was 21.2

thousands during 1912-13 and the same was increased to 294.7 thousands in 1950-51.

Co-operative Development in Orissa During Plan Period

First Five Year Plan

After the introduction of Five Year Plans, the Government of Orissa adopted a strategy for a new economic development of the state. In the First Plan, the economic development in all the spheres in a phased manner was envisaged. The First Five Year Plan which was introduced in the year 1950-51 made a provision of Rs. 5.13 lakhs for the development of co-operatives.[24] The provisions for finance, grants, subsidies to central co-operative banks and co-operative societies were emphasized during the First Five Year Plan. In order to increase the efficiency in the operations of the co-operative societies, different training programmes were introduced. The provision for propaganda, publication in journals and magazines, organisation of conferences for strong motivation, provision of subsides to the state co-operative banks, multi-purpose co-operative societies etc. were envisaged in the First Plan. Some steps were taken for the growth of coir industries under the co-operative schemes. On the basis of recommendations of the Indian Oil Seeds Committee, subsidies were given to the co-operative societies to compensate the losses due to fall in the price.[25]

The First Five Year Plan gave much emphasis on the development of rural and backward areas. The short term-training programmes were introduced to bring the rural people to the co-operative fold and acquaint them with the rules and principles of management of the co-operatives. In the year 1954-55, a non official summer training school was established to impart a short term training course of 150 trainees every year by the Orissa Co-operative Union. During 1955-56, there were 8,623 co-operative societies with 65 lakhs of member and Rs. 72 crores of working capital.

Second Five Year Plan

During the second Five Year Plan, out of total plan expenditure of Rs. 86.59 crores, Rs. 0.97 crores was earmarked for the development of Co-operatives.[26] (Appendix-VII) The plan was comprehensive in character. As the recommendations of the All India Rural Credit Survey Committee (AIRCSC) were accepted by the Government of Orissa, the existing state Co-operative Banks, Central Land Mortgage Banks, State Co-operative Marketing Societies were recognised under the district participation of the state. The share capital, cost of management, cost of construction of godowns for apex marketing societies was contributed by the State Government. The distribution of fertilisers was effected by the state apex marketing co-operative society through affiliated societies. The number of Central Co-operative Banks which was previously 25, reduced to 17 during this plan period.[27] There was amalgamation of the weak co-operative societies with 17 economically strong and viable Central Co-operative Banks. The amalgamation scheme was introduced as per the recommendations of the Registrar of Co-operative Societies with an objective of making a strong and viable co-operative base in the state.

During Second Five Year Plan, besides 50 pilot societies, 500 large co-operative societies were also organised. Due to sanction of adequate funds, 180 godowns were constructed. During this period, thirty Regional Co-operative Societies were also organised and considerable progress was made in the co-operative sector.[28] The credit requirements of the small farmers were fulfilled to a large extent and the exploitation of the money-lenders was reduced substantially. The Regional Marketing Co-operative Societies (RMCS) took a very important role in the distribution of fertilizer and helped a lot for the development of agriculture. In order to accelerate the co-operative movement in different fields, such as in processing, farming, sugar factories under large and medium industries scheme, co-operative farming for the resettlement of landless workers, weaker sections and backward people, various steps were taken during this plan period. Due to the necessity of more trained personnel, another training institute was also established at Sambalpur. Some steps were also taken by the Orissa State Co-operative Union for educating the mass about the Co-operative principles.[29] At the end of Second Five Year Plan, there were 11,206 societies with a membership of 11 lakh and working capital of Rs. 25.6 crores.

Third Five Year Plan

In order to increase the productivity and agricultural production, the Government of India, during the Second Five Year Plan, invited a team of experts of Ford Foundation to give suggestions regarding the means achieving this objective. This step was necessary due to stagnation in food production, while the demand for agricultural products was increasing rapidly. So during the Third Plan, a major programme was chalked out for the development of agriculture. The priority was given similarly in the Co-operative sector for the development of agriculture. In order to strengthen and revitalise the agricultural sector as well as the co-operative movement in Orissa at the primary level, proposal was also given to cover 75 per cent of agricultural population.[30] For the purpose of increasing production and processing, facilities for credit in a substantial measure was also created. In the co-operative sector, Rs. 2.37 crores was spent during the plan period. For the recognisation of credit co-operative societies, an action programme was taken up. Before the implementation of this action programme, the panchayat samities, central co-operative banks were also consulted. After this, in the year 1962-63, the small, inefficient, defunct, dormant and liquidated societies were amalgamated.[31] During this plan, 1,580 co-operative societies were amalgamated and 198 co-operative societies were reorganised. Societies numbering 2359 were also closed during this period. In order to meet the contingencies of the staff, subsidies were also provided.

Due to the policy of the RBI, the credit facilities for short-term and medium-term was reduced from the original target of Rs. 3 crores to Rs. 2 crores.[32] Three special programmes were sponsored and financed by the State Government for the purpose of plantation, orchard and lift irrigation schemes. Although there was a target to establish 32 branches of the Central Co-operative Banks, by the end of 1964-65, only 24 branches were establushed.[33]

The state marketing co-operative society was vested with the monopoly powers to distribute chemical fertilizers through the Regional Marketing Co-operative Societies (RMCS). In order to procure agricultural commodities as per the instructions of the State

Co-operative marketing society, 12 RMCS were organised in the field of marketing. A Price Fluctuation Fund (PFF) was created by a provision of Rs. 1.50 lakhs for the protection of the interests of the selected RMCS. Some other co-operative societies were also formed in the field of marketing. During this plan, the Aska Co-operative Sugar Factory was established. Thirteen pilot projects were envisaged during this period and one project consisting of 10 societies was to be organised in each undivided district in the field of farming. For providing employment opportunities, Labour Contract Co-operative Societies were organised. Two hundred fifty co-operative societies were established for the purpose with Government share of Rs. 2,000 and managerial subsidy of Rs. 1,200.[34] It was also proposed to organise consumer co-operative societies in different towns along with four wholesale stores at Cuttack, Berhampur, Puri, Sambalpur.

During this plan period, against a target of membership of 18 lakhs with a coverage of 75 per cent of agricultural population, about 16.9 lakh members with a coverage of 50 per cent of agricultural population was achieved. As many as 9,286 co-operative societies with working capital of Rs. 63.5 crores were functioning during the end of this plan period. (Table 3.9)

Fourth Five Year Plan

During this plan period, a new developmental dimension was envisaged in the field of co-operatives. The quantitative and qualitative growth in the field of co-operatives was intended in this plan. Besides these, steps were taken for diversification of co-operative activities to other fields in addition to agriculture. Marketing of minor forest produces, processing activities, urban consumers, labour contracts, house building etc. were the new areas of co-operative programmes. But priority was given to the co-operative activities in the rural areas, backward areas and weaker sections during this plan period.[35]

The structure of co-operative credit movement was streamlined and it was considered as another important achievement during this plan period. Because of this, in the year 1968-69, short-term credit increased to Rs. 11.87 crores from Rs. 4.29 crores.[36] In order to look into the credit sector programmes like managerial subsidy, subsidy to key personnel of Central Co-operative Bank located in backward areas, subsidy to new branches, special bad debt reserve and subsidy to Land Development Banks (LDB), a strong and viable primary society was undertaken at the bottom of this credit structure.[37] In order to cater to the credit needs of small and marginal farmers and to work as a catalytic agent of agriculture, the Co-operative Land Development Banks were proposed to work. During this plan, some important steps were taken in order to spread the marketing activities of the RMCS. The purchase, sale and fair price schemes introduced by the Government of Orissa in the T & RW department during the third plan period was transferred to Orissa State Tribal Development Co-operative Society (OSTDCS) during the year 1973.[38]

During the plan period, the price of the commodities was increased due to China-India war. The consumer co-operative societies were encouraged to solve these problems. Different co-operative pragrammes were also taken for a sustained growth of the co-operative sector. The establishment of more RMCS, co-operatives in new disciplines, creation of common cadre fund and opening of new branches in rural areas were other achievements of this plan.[39] At the end of the year 1973-74, there were 7,001 co-operative societies with a membership of 24.1 lakhs and working capital of Rs. 194.7 crores (Table 3.9).

Fifth Five Year Plan

In order to distribute essential commodities among the consumers in rural and urban areas, organisation of 422 consumer stores in urban areas, 57 RMCS, 30 Forest Marketing Co-operative Societies (FMCS), along with the Agency Marketing Co-operative Society (AMCS), Tikabali was undertaken during the fourth plan period.[40]

During the Fifth Five Year Plan, greater attention was focused on the credit structure of PACS, and Central Co-operative Banks, subsidy for mobilisation of deposits, schemes for rehabilitation of weaker central banks, share capital contribution to co-operative credit institutions and subsidy to LDBs for creation of cadre of key personnels.[41] Besides these, proposal for establishment of 20 marketing co-operative societies was also made to help directly through share capital in the field of marketing. According to the turnover of the marketing co-operatives, additional finance was also provided. Fours per cent subsidy was allowed to the FMCS irrespective of their turnover at the primary level. For the purpose of strengthening the FMCS and its activities, an amount of Rs. 10 lakhs was proposed during this plan.

Table—3.9 Co-operative development in orissa from 1951-52 to 1998-99

Sl. No.	Year	No. of societies	No. of members (in lakhs)	Working capital (in crores)
	(1)	(2)	(3)	(4)
1.	1951-52	5,543	3.2	4.7
2.	1952-53	6,022	3.4	4.7
3.	1953-54	6,544	3.6	6.2
4.	1954-55	7,764	4.8	7.2
5.	1955-56	8,623	6.5	7.2
6.	1956-57	9,166	7.7	12.8
7.	1957-58	9,948	9.1	14.5
8.	1958-59	10,364	10.3	17.1
9.	1959-60	10,876	12.3	NA
10.	1960-61	11,206	11.2	25.6
11.	1961-62	11,507	13.3	30.3
12.	1962-63	11,009	14.2	39.2
13.	1963-64	11,246	14.9	47.8
14.	1964-65	NA	NA	NA
15.	1965-66	9,286	16.9	63.5
16.	1966-67	8,965	17.5	70.2
17.	1967-68	8,712	18.2	79.2
18.	1968-69	8,117	19.1	79.3
19.	1969-70	7,877	20.3	94.1
20.	1970-71	7,415	21.2	100.3
21.	1971-72	7,088	22.0	150.9
22.	1972-73	6,914	23.0	181.1
23.	1973-74	7,001	24.1	194.7
24.	1974-75	7,102	25.7	253.9
25.	1975-76	7,193	29.1	294.0
26.	1976-77	5,837	30.2	323.6
27.	1977-78	5,793	30.6	374.1
28.	1978-79	5,810	31.4	477.7
29.	1979-80	5,748	32.6	584.1
30.	1980-81	5,756	34.4	699.1

(Contd.....)

	(1)	(2)	(3)	(4)
31.	1981-82	6,021	35.7	790.1
32.	1982-83	6,876	40.0	1006.1
33.	1983-84	6,220	40.1	1060.6
34.	1984-85	7,108	44.6	1264.5
35.	1985-86	6,329	46.0	1196.4
36.	1986-87	6,333	46.3	2136.5
37.	1987-88	6,448	47.5	1254.4
38.	1988-89	6,516	48.2	1475.7
39.	1989-90	6,491	48.7	1581.4
40.	1990-91	6,563	49.1	1455.0
41.	1991-92	6,686	49.9	1588.5
42.	1992-93	6,691	51.4	1655.3
43.	1993-94	4,511	50.8	844.8
44.	1994-95	4,393	50.4	1066.1
45.	1995-96	4,293	54.0	1184.1
46.	1996-97	4,424	52.0	1413.4
47.	1997-98	4,553	52.3	1389.1
48.	1998-99(p)	4,345	47.7	1685.7

NA : Not Available

Source : Compiled from Statistics on Co-operatives, RCS, Government of Orissa, Bhubaneswar, and Co-operative Movement in Orissa. (For the years 1951-52 to 1988-99).

For imparting co-operative education and training to the members, the capacity of the existing co-operating training colleges at Gopalpur and Bargarh was proposed to be increased. In the scheduled areas having more than 50 per cent tribal concentration, the strategy of sub-plan was introduced. The tribal sub-plan programmes were framed to suit the needs of the tribals. It was realised by the Tribal sub-plan (1974-79) that the economic plight of indebtedness, exploitation by outsiders, land alienation, problem of subsistence economy adversely affected the economic development of tribal areas.[42] The selection of the right type of co-operative structure according to the natural inclination of the tribals was necessary due to the production and consumption needs, agriculture inputs, marketing of tribal SAPs and MFPs.[43]

In 1971, a committee under the chairmanship of Sri K.S. Bawa was appointed by the Government of India in the Ministry of

Agriculture to study the structure of co-operatives in the tribal development project areas. The state of affairs of the tribals in Srikakulam of Andhra Pradesh, Singhbhum of Bihar, Bastar of M.P., and Ganjam, Koraput of Orissa was examined by the committee.[44] The recommendations of the committee consisted of several measures including a package of services in tribal areas. The credit (both consumption and production), supply of seeds and other agricultural inputs, marketing of SAPs and MFPs and supply of consumer goods were the major components of services in tribal areas.[45] The committee made suggestions that integrated credit and other services should be provided to provide financial assistance and to reduce exploitation of the tribal people. The establishment of the large sized multi-purpose societies (LAMPS) at block levels with number of branches at Gram Panchayats and hat centres was one of the important recommendations of Bawa Committee.[46] In order to meet the production, consumption and credit needs of the tribals, Tribal Development Co-operative Societies (TDCS), and Regional Co-operative Marketing Societies (RMCS), were established in tribal areas.[47]

The primary societies in sub-plan areas were assigned the task of providing 60 to 70 per cent of loans to the tribals. The Committee also suggested that the amount of overdues outstanding against tribal members should be treated as medium term interest-free loans repayable within five annual instalments. The interest subsidy to apex bank at the rate of 4.5 per cent would be provided by the TDA. This proposal was suggested by the Appu Committee to relieve the tribals from the clutches of dishonest moneylenders.[48] The Bawa Committee recommended that with the scheme of financial assistance, one supervisor should be posted in LAMPS. For the purpose of marketing of minor forest produces, finance should be provided to the tune of Rs. 5 lakhs to the TDCC's in the form of loans to the TDA's. In order to purpose vehicles for the handicaps, Rs. 20 lakh were provided by the Government to the TDCC.[49]

At the end of the Fifth Plan (1978-79), there were 5.8 lakh societies with a membership of 31.4 lakhs and working capital of Rs. 477.7 crores excluding LAMPS and OSTDCS (Table 3.9).

Sixth Five Year Plan

During the Sixth Five Year Plan, the consumer co-operative Societies were given priorities in the field of distribution of essential commodities to the needy people at a fair price. The marketing co-operative societies were also given sufficient financial assistance to work in tribal sub-plan areas. The credit, marketing and processing activities were also strengthened. The co-operative movement proposed to establish an egalitarian society. The PACS were reorganised to serve the small and marginal agricultural labourers, other underprivileged and backward communities belonging to ST and SC categories. In order to fulfil the credit needs of rural people, emphasis was given on the rehabilitation of weaker primary agricultural credit co-operative societies.

During the sixth plan, Central Co-operative Banks provided sufficient loan facilities to the PACS. The creation of stabilization fund, technical cells in apex LBDs rehabilitation of urban banks, employment of rural employed labour force, development of warehousing facilities and marketing co-peratives were also envisaged.[50] In order to protect the interest of the weaker sections in the distribution of fertilisers and pesticides, marketing co-operative societies were also streamlined. For the welfare of the small marginal farmers and tribals, the dug well programme was implemented through central co-operative banks, PLDBs and commercial banks which utilised the ground water resources properly.[51]

Towards the end of this plan (1984-85), there were 7,108 societies with 44.6 lakh members and Rs. 1,264.5 crores of working capital (Table 3.9). The progress of co-operative movement during sixth plan period was more prominent than the fifth plan.

Seventh Five Year Plan

During Sixth Five Year Plan, about 70 per cent of the total agricultural loans were distributed to the weaker sections. The number of agricultural families brought under the co-operative fold was 3762 lakhs. All the Gram Panchayats were covered under co-operative outlets and 221 LAMPS were organised in tribal areas.[52]

The increase in production and productivity, creation of adequate job opportunities in rural areas were emphasized during the Seventh Plan period. The achievements of the following objectives were envisaged in the programmes of the Seventh Plan:[53]

(*a*) For consolidation and strengthening the co-operative movement in general and credit movement in particular;

(*b*) To strengthen the LAMPS in marketing of SAPs and MFPs from the tribals;

(*c*) To increase in credit flows to the small and marginal farmers, rural artisans, SCs and STs and agricultural labourers;

(*d*) To reduce mounting of overdues by effective supervision and a recovery campaign;

(*e*) For streamlining and strengthening the consumer markets both in rural and urban areas to play a vital role in PDS;

(*f*) For the organisation of more processing units;

(*g*) Identification of training and education programmes of co-operative personnel to expand the co-operative movement.

In order to achieve these objectives, the allotment of Rs. 6.6 lakhs was proposed during this plan period. Out of this Rs. 2.3 lakhs i.e. 35 per cent of the total allotment was earmarked for the sub-plan area. There was introduction of a restructure system in the programmes of the co-operatives for quick and prompt repayment of overdues. Under 20-point economic programmes, housing scheme was also introduced through the co-operative societies. During this plan period, development of marketing co-operatives, co-operative storage, processing co-operatives and consumer co-operatives in the state was proposed. Some steps were also taken for the economic development of the scheduled caste and scheduled tribe people. There was also a programme for the upgradation of the co-operative education and training in Orissa. Due to acute poverty, the members belonging to scheduled tribes could not be able to provide share capital of 5 per cent of the loan. So the sanction of Rs. 2.52 crores to help 5.62 lakhs of tribal families for availing of the loan facilities from central plan assistance was emphasized in the proposal during this plan period.

There was also a proposal to subsidise the rate of interest for the tribal beneficiaries through the financial institutions out of central assistance. For the effective procurement and marketing of MFPs, SAPs and distribution of consumer goods, establishment of link between LAMP and TDCC was also proposed.[54] During this plan period, the co-operative societies provided loans to the weaker scheduled caste and schedule tribe families at a lower rate of interest.

At the end of the Seventh Plans (1989-90), there were 6,491 Co-operative Societies with 48.7 lakh members and Rs. 1581.4 crores of working capital which is explained in the table 3.9.

Eighths Five Year Plan

During the Eighths Five Year Plan, extensive packages of services and schemes were proposed to be implemented in various economic sectors like agriculture and industry. The plan had the following important objectives:[55]

(*i*) revitalisation of the entire co-operative structure in Orissa for providing better services to the weaker sections;

(*ii*) strict and effective supervision of the rural credit and to tap more rural deposits, ensuring increased trend of credit flow to the needy farmers;

(*iii*) streamlining and strengthening the consumer co-operatives in rural and urban areas;

(*iv*) organisation of labour-intensive agro-processing units; and

(*v*) intensification and upgradation of co-operative education and training facilities in the state.

In order to serve in a better manner, the Eighth plan revitalised the economic base of the targeted group through the credit co-operatives. Out of the total allotment of funds of Rs. 77 crores, Rs. 12 crores was for the tribal sub-plan areas. The farmers were exempted to repay the loan amount of Rs. 10,000 due to implementation of Orissa Agriculture and Rural Debt Relief Scheme by the Government. During this plan, the marketing Co-operatives were restructured in order to give more attention to the RCMS for development of agriculture procurement of SAPs and distribution of consumer goods. The co-operative societies played a vital role in the socio-economic development of tribals. They worked as a first line of defence regarding the marketing activities with three important objectives:[56]

(*i*) to provide adequate credit facilities to the members of tribal community at the time of necessity for the development of their economic conditions;

(*ii*) to procure SAPs and MFPs at a reasonable price and provide necessary marketing facilities;

(*iii*) to supply essential consumer goods at a reasonable price. The objectives to be achieved through the programmes of this plane were as follows:[57]

(*a*) Consolidation and strengthening of the co-operative movement and credit structure in Orissa to provide the basic needs of the weaker sections effectively;

(*b*) Strengthening and improvement in the normal functioning of the LAMPS for the provision of better credit, marketing and consumer service facilities to the tribals more effectively through tribal participation in decision-making;

(*c*) Strict and effective supervision of credit through organisation of recovery campaign for the reduction of mounting overdues;

(*d*) Organisation of more and more processing units;

(*e*) Intensification of the training and educational programmes in order to meet the growing needs of the co-operative perwsonnel in the rapidly expanding co-operative movement and establishment of trained cadre at the appropriate levels.

During Eighth Plan period, Rs. 4.368 lakh was invested for development of co-operatives and many tribal families were brought under co-operative fold. It helped to increase flow of credit to the tribals from different co-operative credit institutions in sub-plan areas. Nine Central Co-operative Banks, 224 LAMPS, 20 Primary Land Development Banks, 10 Urban Co-operative Banks worked in different areas. Many institutions like 6 RCMS, 100 PACS, 4 oil mills and rice mills, 35 godowns, 7 cold storages, 350 outlets, 20 students consumer stores, 3 integrated cotton and oil seed growers society were strengthened. For the purpose of helping the tribals and improving their standard of living, the AMCS, Tikabali was provided with necessary funds to encourage agro-based labour intensive industrial units in the tribal areas.[58] There was a proposal for the organisation of some forest labour contract societies in the potential areas to save the forest labourers from exploitation and ensure them fair wages.[59]

In Orissa, density of population in plain areas is very high. Seventy-seven per cent of the people in the state live on agriculture. Due to uncertain climatic conditions and uneconomic land holding in the state, productivity of land is less than the national level. So in order to make the agriculture a profitable occupation, the co-operative societies have a significant role, particularly in the field of agricultural credit.

During different plan periods, the direct interference of the State Government and diversification of activities helped the growth of co-operative movement to significant extent. It was noticed that co-operatives failed in some aspects and special efforts were made to remove the shortcomings to cater to the needs of the societies and weaker sections. From the table 3.9, it is revealed that the number of co-operative societies was 5543 at the beginning of first plan period in the state of Orissa, but it was reduced to 4553 at the beginning of ninth plan period. Similarly there were 3.2 lakhs of members in first plan but the same has increased to 52.39 lakhs at the beginning of ninth plan (1997-98).

Ninth Five Year Plan

During ninth plan period, much emphasis was given to develop not only production but also creation of sufficient job opportunities in rural areas. The programmes of the ninth plan were to achieve the following objectives:

(*a*) to strengthen the LAMP in marketing of SAPs and MFPs of the tribals;

(*b*) Intensification of training of educational programmes of co-operative personnel to expand the co-operative movement;

(*c*) To provide timely and adequate credit to the tribals for improving their economic conditions;

(*d*) To streamline and strengthen the consumer co-operatives in rural and urban areas;

(*e*) To organise labour intensive, agro-processing units.

During ninth plan, it was programmed to bring more tribal families under co-operative fold and to increase credit flow to them from the co-operative credit institutions in sub-plan areas. During 1997-98, Rs. 20.11 crores was spent on co-operatives. But in the year 1998-99, the amount of funds allocated for the development of co-operative sectors was reduced to Rs. 9.68 crores. During this plan, the Central Co-operative Banks introduced "Kissan Credit Card" sponsored by the Reserve Bank of India and NABARD for providing timely and adequate credit to the farmers of Orissa. Under the scheme 3,55,764 "Kissan Credit Cards" have already been distributed by 25th June, 1999.

During this plan period, average number of societies per 100 sq. km. comes to 4. With regard to average membership per society, it was 880 and the average working capital and average loans advanced per PACS was Rs. 21,12,000 and Rs. 8,04,000 respectively. During the ninth plan, average loans advanced per borrowing member of PACS was Rs. 4,576. The percentage of population covered by co-operatives and percentage of population covered by PACS was 83 and 63 respectively.

During ninth plan, 46 co-operative societies with 1,08,000 members and Rs. 8.8 crores as share capital were operating in Kandhamal district as on 31-03-2001. The number of RCMS and sepecialised commodity marketing co-operative societies operating in the district was 1 and 4 respectively. Thus during this plan period, co-operative societies did not progress much in Orissa in general and in Kandhamal district in particular.

REFERENCES

1. Bedi, R.D., 'The Theory, History and Practice of Co-operation, Loyal Book Depot, Meerut, 1977, p. 192.

2. Report of the Committee on Co-operation in India (1912), p. 4.
3. Review of the Co-operative Movement in India, 1930-40, Reserve Bank of India, p. 7.
4. Review of the Co-operative Movement in India, 1939-46, p. 2.
5. Review of the Co-operative Movement in India 1939-46, p. 11.
6. Draft Fifth Five Year Plan, Planning Commission, Government of India, p. 78.
7. Sen, K.K., "Indian Economics", New Delhi, Sultan Chand and Company, 1992, p. 270.
8. "Census of India, 1991, (Series-I), Census Commissioners of India, New Delhi, 1992, p. 92.
9. "Orissa Co-operative Congress", Souvenir, 1984, Bhubaneswar.
10. Sahu Swaroop, "Management of Co-operative Banks in India", New Delhi, Anmol Publication, pp. 1-5.
11. "Annual Report on the Working of Co-operative Societies in North Orissa", Patna Govt. Press, 1926-27, p. 1.
12. "Annual Report on the Working of Co-operative Societies in South Orissa", Cuttack Govt. Press, 1937, p. 1.
13. "List of Societies in the RCS, Bhubaneswar, Orissa."
14. Samal, P., "Co-operation in Orissa", (Memio), Office of the R.C.S. Orissa, Chapter-V.
15. *Ibid*.
16. "Annual Reports, Bihar-Orissa", 1914-15, pp. 1-2.
17. "Annual Reports", *op. cit*., 1918-19, p. 2
18. *Ibid*, pp. 3-4.
19. "Review of Co-operative Movement in India", 1939-40, RBI, p. 2.
20. Annual Reports of the Co-operative Societies in Orissa, Cuttack, 1938-39, Chapter I, p. 1.
21. *Ibid*., p. 2.
22. "Orissa Co-operative Congress", 1984, Co-operative Union, Bhubaneswar.
23. "Annual Report on the Working of the Co-operative Societies", 1939-40, Govt. of Orissa, pp. 1-4.
24. "First Five Year Plan", Govt. of Orissa, Planning Dept., 1952, pp. 53-55.
25. *Ibid*., p. 55.

26. "Co-operative Movement in Orissa, A Profile", 1990-91, Registrar of Co-operative Society, Bhubaneswar, p. 20.
27. "Second Five Year Plan", Govt. of Orissa, pp. 26-28.
28. *Ibid.*, pp. 27-28.
29. *Ibid.*, p. 20.
30. "Third Five Year Plan", Planning and Co-ordination Dept., Govt. of Orissa, pp. 66-70.
31. *Ibid.*, pp. 66-70.
32. *Ibid.*, pp. 66-70.
33. *Ibid.*, pp. 66-70.
34. *Ibid.*, p. 70.
35. "Fourth Five Year Plan", Govt. of Orissa, Planning and Co-ordination Dept., pp. 97-115.
36. *Ibid.* p. 99.
37. *Ibid.*, pp. 100-105.
38. " A brochure on the activity of the OSTDCS", Bhubaneswar, p. 2.
39. "Fourth Five Year Plan", *op. cit.*, pp., 110-115.
40. "Fifth Five Year Plan", Orissa (Draft), Planning and Co-ordination Dept., Govt. of Orissa, Bhubaneswar, 1973, pp. 273-281.
41. *Ibid.*, p. 280.
42. "Tribal Sub-plan for Tribal Regions of Orissa", 1974-79, (Draft)., T & RW Dept., Orissa, Bhubaneswar, 1975, p. 29.
43. *Ibid.*, pp., 28-29.
44. Bawa, K.S., "Summary Report of the Study Team on Co-operative in Tribal Development Project". Govt., of India, New Delhi, p. 32.
45. *Ibid*, p. 33.
46. "The Role of Co-operative in Tribal Development", Singh, B., "Adivasi" Tribals Harijan Research-cum-Training Institute (THRTI), Vol. -XV, 1973-74, p. 5.
47. "Sub-Plan for Tribal Regions" (1974-79), *op. cit.*, p. 29.
48. *Ibid.*, pp. 78-80.
49. *Ibid.*, p. 80.
50. "Sixth Five Year Plan, 1980-85", (Draft), Orissa, pp. 167-176.
51. "Annual Administration Report of the working of the Co-operative Society in Orissa", Bhubaneswar, Agriculture and Co-operative Dept., 1979-80, p. 6.

52. "Seventh Five Year Plan", (1985-90), Govt. of Orissa, P & C Dept., pp. 185.
53. *Ibid.*, pp. 186-187.
54. *Ibid.*, pp. 188-189.
55. "Eighth Five Year Plan", 1990-95, Vol. I, Govt. of Orisssa, P & C Dept., Bhubaneswar, pp. 65-67.
56. "Tribal Sub-Plan (Draft) for Eighth Plan (1992-97)", Government of Orissa, H & TW Dept., 1991, p. 152.
57. *Ibid.*, pp. 152-153.
58. *Ibid.*, p. 158.
59. "Report of the Committee on Forest and Tribals in India". Govt. of India, Ministry of Home Affairs, Tribal Development Division, New Delhi, 1982, pp. 12-13.

4

Approach and Strategies for the Development of Co-operative Marketing

Introduction

Organised marketing is of considerable significance to the economy of a country. This is because the imperfections in the marketing system constitute a major constraint on production. Marketing is the crux of the whole food and agriculture problem. It would be useless to increase the output of food, it would be equally futile to set up optimum standards of nutrition, unless means could be found to move from the producer to the consumer at a price which represents a fair remuneration to the producer and is within the consumer's ability to pay.[1] Marketing thus begins at the farmer's field. It includes all such activities as (*i*) collection of surplus from the individual farmers, (*ii*) transport to the nearest assembling centre, (*iii*) grading and standardization, (*iv*) pooling, (*v*) processing, (*vi*) warehousing, (*vii*) packing, (*viii*) transport to the consuming centres, (*ix*) bringing the buyers and sellers together, and (*x*) sale to ultimate consumer. All these functions require capital and also involve risks due to fluctuation in prices, losses and deterioration in quality, etc. The arrangements made for raising the requisite finance for the above activities bearing the market risks at various levels, also therefore form part of the marketing functions.[2]

Agricultural marketing has certain special characteristic features[3] (*i*) Agricultural produce in most cases is bulky for its value in comparison with many manufactured goods. The demand, it makes on storage and transport facilities, is heavy and specialised resulting in heavy costs, (*ii*) the farming output is seasonal in character. The demand for it by consumer is spread over the whole year. The market system has, therefore to balance suitably the seasonal outflow of the producer from the farm with the relatively steady and continuous consumer demand, (*iii*) In view of the small size of the individual marketable lots, the collection of the produce becomes a complicated process particularly as the consumers are generally concentrated in urban areas, (*iv*) Most of the farm produce suffers loss and deterioration in quality during storage and transport. For certain commodities like plantation crops where production is highly localised and consumption is widespread, their marketing becomes more difficult.

It is difficult for the small and medium-scale producers individually to undertake most of these functions. Because of his weak position, most of these functions are usually in the hands of intermediaries or middlemen.

The need for an organised marketing system for agricultural produce has been repeatedly emphasized by most of the committees and commissions set up for re-organisation of economic system in the country. As early as 1915, the Maclagan Committee on cooperation made a reference to co-operative societies for the sale of agricultural produce. The same spirit was reiterated by the Royal Commission on Agriculture in 1928.

In 1931, a team of foreign experts attached to Central Banking Enquiry Committee emphasised that the question of organised marketing was of far greater national importance than that of credit.

The Dantwala committee on co-operative marketing observed that "the main object for which growers organise a co-operative marketing society is to enable them to market their produce to their best advantage and for this purpose to streamline the whole process of movement of goods to the consuming markets".[4]

Till the end of 19th century, the problem of marketing was not a vexed one in India as our economy was largely a subsistence economy, when farmers produced crops for self-consumption rather than with a view to dispose them of in the market. Life was simple, calm and contented; no complicated problems of marketing were involved in the rural economy. But the entire economic fabric has since undergone a very great change, almost revolutionary in character, and India, in common with the rest of humanity is faced with its own intricate problem of distribution. Marketing has come to the forefront and it is universally recognised as the crux of the economic problem. Orderly and efficient marketing should indeed be treated as, the basic essential for agricultural prosperity.

It is a well-known fact that the prices received by the agriculturists in India are wholly inadequate and have no relation with the actual prices paid by the consumers. A large chunk of them is swallowed by a host of middlemen whose charges are wholly incommensurate with the services actually rendered by them. Describing the powerful position of the trader-cum-money-lenders, the All India Rural Credit Survey Committee remarked that:

Often enough, the cultivator's position is that of having to bargain if he can, with someone who commands the money market and commands the credit, commands the market and commands the transport.[5]

The committee on State Trading in its report says, "The vast majority of agricultural producers in the country are usually at the mercy of traders. Ignorance and lack of resources compel them at harvest time to part with the products of their soil at relatively low price and any rise in prices occurring subsequently during the season goes only to the middlemen."[6]

Due to the small and scanty output of our farmers, it is difficult as well as expensive to sell any commodity in small lots. Secondly, the smaller the amount of produce for sale, the larger will be number of hands through which it will pass, which if not unproductive is surely uneconomical.

The need for co-operative marketing does not depend upon the fact that it will assist in the removal of various malpractices. It is envisaged that the co-operative marketing of agricultural produce, if efficiently carried out, should help reduce the price spread between the producer and the consumer and thereby ensure a better return to the primary producer. In 1947 the prices subcommittee stated. "The ultimate interests of the cultivator, however, lie in the development of co-operative marketing. It is only when cultivators join hands, pool their produce, and grade and process it before sale, that they can obtain a fair return.[7]

Co-operative marketing is needed to strengthen the bargaining position of the cultivator at the first stage of marketing from the farm to the wholesale market. It can add to the withholding power of the cultivator by giving him a loan or advance payment to meet his immediate needs. The co-operative can keep his produce in storage along with that of other members until it can be sold at a fair price. The very fact that this produce is held from the market acts as a stabilizing and price strengthening factor because concerted action is being taken. If the quantities involved are substantial in amount, the co-operative acquires a position of strength in dealing with traders and, therefore, it can sell to advantage. Also the process of storing, grading, cleaning and quality control become more feasible and economical for large quantities.[8]

If the problem of marketing, however complicated and bewildering is not properly or adequately solved, the prospect of the co-operative credit movement itself would continue to remain dim in spite of all that is being done. Its equitable solution would be a boon to the hard-pressed, much exploited sons of the soil. The report of the Technical Meeting on Co-operatives in Asia and the Far East, organised by the Food and Agriculture Organisation of the United Nations (F.A.O) at Lucknow in India in 1949, emphasised that :

Well organised marketing institutions would confer even greater benefits on the agricultural producer than do the credit institutions. The latter by supplying cheap credit may reduce interest charges to the agricultural borrower, but a greater drain on his income than the exorbitant interest that the village moneylender charges his exploitation by the trader who gives the producer an inadequate share of the prices of his produce. Moreover, the existence of the chain of middlemen in the marketing of agricultural goods considerably reduces the return to the producer. If such middle men could be eliminated and a fair share of the price secured to the farmer, the additional income he would receive thereby would be of far greater benefit to him than a reduction of interest. Such additional income would also help him to pay debts to the society more rapidly, and thus strengthen credit institutions.[9]

If the entire trade of a country is left in the hands of marketing community, the economy of the country is very likely to be thrown into great jeopardy, The result is that, "prices keep sky-rocketing and the market becomes the favourite hunting ground for sharks.[10]

Co-operative marketing is now considered to be a logical corollary of co-operative credit and the one without the other is incomplete and imperfect. A credit co-operative in which marketing has not been linked or left out would be like Hamlet without the Prince of Denmark. In 1948, the Dewan Behadur H.L. Jaji, a champion of co-operative Movement, said "the future of co-operative lies in the development of marketing more than in any other direction."

The imperative necessity of co-operative marketing in India arises because market conditions often deviate from healthy practices and various forms of speculations are resorted to. In such cases the profit motive on the part of middlemen leads to price manipulation and the consequent fluctuation of prices. The co-operative marketing of agricultural produce and forest produces if developed on a large-scale in India, can help in the stabilization of prices.

It may thus be noted that the importance of co-operative marketing lies not only in its efficiency as a system best suited to ensure the cultivator a fair return for his produce but also as *sine qua non* for largescale expansion of co-operative production credit. It has been recognised that the large scale expansion of co-operative credit in recent years has not been accompanied by corresponding increase in co-operative marketing and processing and the future expansion of co-operative credit requires an expansion of marketing and effective linking of credit with marketing.

History and Growth of Co-operative Marketing in India

The initial impulse for organising the co-operative system in India was not marketing. In the early years of twentieth century, co-operative aimed at providing credit facilities to agricultural households in the early years of this century. At that time the concern for credit was paramount because a large number of agricultural households were head and ears in debt and under the usurious clutches of private moneylenders. The crux of the problem then was to rescue the peasantry from indebtedness. On Frederic Nicholson's recommendation, the Government of India passed Co-operative Credit Societies Act in 1904, for organisation of Co-operative Credit

Societies in villages to provide credit to fulfil the needs of the peasantry.

After the 1904 Act was passed for the organisation of co-operative credit societies, it was realised that co-operative societies for other activities would also be beneficial for the people. So in 1912, a more comprehensive Act was passed to help for the formation of non-credit societies including marketing societies. In spite of legal provisions to this effect, except for some sporadic effects, co-operative marketing societies did not catch attention of the farmers or the Government. However, all the important commissions or committees appointed for the development of agriculture and banking stressed the need for the development of agriculture and banking stressed the need for the development of co-operative marketing. As early as 1915, the Maclagan Committee on Co-operative made a reference to Co-operative Societies for the sale of agricultural produce.

"Among the agricultural societies, for purposes other than credits, the outstanding types are those for the role of produce. A co-operative marketing society by elimination of unnecessary middlemen made available the profit from agricultural merchants and the consumer. The removal of such elements as are merely parasitic will mean more business, a quicker turnover and better understanding between the wholesale purchaser and the producer of the crop."[11]

The same spirit was reiterated by the Royal Commission on Agriculture in 1928: "Group marketing must be more efficient than marketing by individuals especially in conditions such as those which exist in India where the individual producer is such a small unit. The ideal to be aimed at, is therefore, co-operative sale societies which will educate the cultivator in production and preparation for market of his produce and will provide sufficient volume of the produce to make efficient grading possible and will bring the producer into direct touch with export market and with large consumers in the country."[12]

In the year 1931, a team of foreign experts attached to the Indian Central Banking Enquiry Committee emphasised that the question of organised marketing was of far greater national importance than that of developing rural credit. To supply the credit requirements of the ryot was no doubt important, but not so much as it was to cure the diseases from which the indebtedness of the ryots arose. One of the malaises from which the farmers suffered was the lack of opportunities to ,ell profitably the produce raised by them and consequently there was no stimulus to greater production."[13]

The importance of co-operative marketing was also recognised by the Reconstruction Committee (1945) of the Viceroy's Executive Council in their Report on Reconstruction Planning as "The Co-operative movement has hitherto been a predominantly credit structure designed to relieve rural indebtedness and provide the agriculturists with cheap and timely finance. It has, however, only touched the fringe of the problem of agricultural credit and it is necessary to link it up more actively with production, marketing, distribution and consumption. The societies should also take steps to encourage thrift and savings among their members. This linking of production and consumption through marketing of agricultural produce lends itself peculiarly to treatment by co-operative means"[14]

In spite of these recommendations, however, co-operative marketing continued to remain a neglected subject for a long time, the government and the co-operators being preoccupied with the development of co-operative credit only. Co-operative marketing of agricultural products, had however, made some progress in India prior to 1947, chiefly in the then states of Madras, Bombay, United Provinces, Punjab and to a limited extent in Central Provinces and Berar, Bengal, Coorg, Baroda and Mysore.

At the end of 1943-44, there were in the then composite Madras State, 181 primary marketing societies, 5 marketing federations and a provincial marketing society. These societies issued loans to the extent of Rs. 139.18 lakhs on the pledge of produce and sold produce such as paddy, groundnut, cotton, potatoes etc, worth Rs. 147.02 lakhs during 1943-44. The state government encouraged the marketing societies and rural co-operative credit societies to construct their own godowns by offering long-term loans to the extent of seventy-five per cent of the cost and grants to the extent of twenty five per cent. At the end of 1943-44, 28 marketing societies owned 37 godowns.[15]

At the end of 1942-43, there were 142 co-operative sale societies and a provincial marketing society in the erstwhile Bombay state which were dealing in cotton, fruits, vegetables, chillies, areca nut, paddy etc. These marketing societies sold commodities worth of Rs. 281.5 lakhs of which the cotton sale societies at Gadeg, Hubli and those in Surat and Broach districts accounted for Rs. 68.41 lakhs.

In 1942-43, there were 116 marketing unions and a federation for the sale of wheat, barley, pulses, oil-seeds, hemp, tobacco, etc. in Uttar Pradesh. Ghee worth Rs. 3.54 lakh was handled by 727 ghee marketing societies and 8 unions. Regarding marketing of sugarcane, spectacular achievement was made. Eighty-six central cane unions and 1, 117 primary societies covering 17,325 villages were operating. These unions and societies supplied about 13 crore maunds of sugarcane to the sugar factories situated in these areas.

In Bihar, cane development and supply societies were functioning exactly on the same lines as in the United Provinces. In 1942-43, 90.36 lakh maunds of sugarcane was marketed by these societies.

In Punjab, there were 37 sale societies and commission shops in the year 1943-44. During that year, agricultural produce worth Rs. 78 lakh was sold by these societies.

Co-operative marketing had also to a limited extent made progress in other provinces like the central provinces and Bengal and also Coorg, Baroda and Mysore.

In 1945, the Co-operative Planning Committee recommended that within ten years, 25 per cent of the total annual marketable surplus should be sold through co-operative organisation and that for this purpose a marketing society should be organized in each of the then 2000 'mandis' in the country, roughly at the rate of one society for a group of 200 villages to undertake grading, pooling, processing whenever necessary and sale of agricultural produce to the best advantage of the growers. The committee also emphasized the need for an effective link between co-operative credit and marketing and also for government subsidies to the marketing societies for the first five years to meet their managerial cost.[16] No planned effort however, seems to have been made to implement these recommendations.

In 1951, the All India Rural Credit Survey committe found the position in regard to co-operative marketing extremely unsatisfactory. Though the number of all types of marketing societies registered in 1951-52 was over 10,000 which included 21 state co-operative marketing societies, 1885 marketing unions and more than 8,000 primary societies, its total effect on the economy was insignificant. The committee found that in only five out of 75 districts surveyed by them, did the produce sold through co-operatives exceed one per cent of the total sale through all agencies. The private trader dominated the rural economy. The survey committee stated :

"A few, very few successful co-operative marketing societies do exist in India, some of these may be significant pointers to the lines on which future progress is possible; but as a present contribution towards bringing about a system in which marketing is by the cultivator and for the cultivator, the part which they occupy in the total picture is wholly insignificant. All the co-operative marketing societies of India put together still fail to catch one's attention as anything important, lacking in this respect, even that purely numerical impressiveness which, on paper, credit societies manage to marshal among themselves.

E.M. Hough, an authority on co-operative movement in India, regretted that "marketing has occupied a far smaller place in the co-operative picture in India than in many countries.

By the end of June, 1050, there were 6907 primary marketing societies having a membership of about 13 lakhs. The value of goods sold by those societies amounted to Rs. 25 crores. There were 1805 marketing unions and federations of which 1,693 were development unions and care unions in Uttar Pradesh. Their paid- up share capital amounted to Rs. 102.24 lakhs and they issued loans totalling Rs. 608.11 lakhs during 1949-50.[17]

Co-operative Marketing Through Five Year Plans

First Five Year Plan

During the first plan, the co-operative movement was accorded considerable importance. However, in respect of co-operative marketing, though the plan envisaged that it should be encouraged in all possible ways, no specific targets were formulated for its expansion. The Dantawala Committee an Co-operative marketing has stated : "During most of the First plan period, co-operative marketing continued to remain more or less a neglected field.[18] The Committee on Co-operative Credit also stated : "No special efforts appear to have been made, therefore, to strengthen or expand co-operative marketing during the period of the plan.[19] The value of agricultural produce marketed by all co-operatives during the year 1955-56 was thus only Rs. 53 crores as against Rs. 47 crores during 1950-51.[20]

The position of the co-operative marketing societies as on 30th June, 1956 is explained in Table 4.1.

Table—4.1 Progress of marketing societies in India on 30th June, 1956

(Rs. In lakhs)

Sl. No.	*Particulars*	*State*	*Union & Federation*	*Primary*
1.	No of societies	19	2,354	9778
2.	Membership (in thousands)		1803	1014
	(a) Individuals	4.0	1803	1014
	(b) societies	3.5	45	6
3.	Paid up capital (Rs.)	28	220	206
4.	Value of goods			
	(i) Distributed (Rs.)	834	4566	747
	(ii) Marketed (Rs.)	17	268	1631

Source : Review of the Co-operative Movement in India, R.B.I. 1955-56 p. 82

Commenting on the position of co-operative marketing societies, the Reserve Bank's Review of the co-operative Movement in India (1954-56) stated :

The long period of controls, procurement and distribution of essential goods, as well as the process of transition from a controlled to a decontrolled economy had virtually come to an end at the commencement of the period under review, thus making it possible for the marketing societies in the country to function once again under comparatively normal conditions. The regime of strict controls and austerity measures, although it helped the country to weather a period of acute scarcity in essential goods had left certain undesirable effects on the working of the marketing societies. In general, the societies had concentrated their energies on the supply and distribution of food grains, cloth and other consumer goods, to the neglect of the marketing of the members' produce, which was the proper function. The commission earned by the societies on the supply business was not always utilized to build up reserves and develop the marketing aspect proper. Many marketing societies, therefore, which had flourished in the periods of controls, emerged out of that period as small and weak units.[21]

Second Five Year Plan

In pursuance of the recommendations of the Rural Credit Survey Report, considerable emphasis was laid on the development of co-operative marketing in the second plan. The Planning Commission observed :

"The primary consideration for the development of agricultural marketing is to re-organise the existing system so as to secure for the farmer his due share of the price paid by the consumer and subserve the needs of planned development. To achieve these objects, malpractices associated with buying and selling of agricultural products have to be eliminated, arrangements made for the efficient distribution of marketable surpluses from producing to consuming areas and co-operative marketing has to be developed to the maximum extent possible. Rural marketing and finance have to be integrated through the development of marketing and processing on co-operative lines."[22]

The plan envisaged the organization of 1800 primary marketing societies in important 'mandies' and an apex marketing society in each state as a central organisation. To co-ordinate the activities of the primary societies, it was also envisaged that cooperatives would be able to handle about ten per cent of the marketable surplus to the end of the plan. Financial assistance from the Government by way of (*a*) state participation in share capital, (*b*) subsidy towards the cost of managerial staff in the initial stages was also provided to the marketing and processing societies under the plan.

During the second plan period, 1869 primary marketing societies were either organised or recognised and apex marketing societies were set up in all the states, except in Jammu and Kashmir. A National Agricultural Co-operative Marketing Federation was also set up to promote inter-state and all on trade and to co-ordinate the activities of apex marketing societies and also to provide market intelligence to them. In addition, a number of marketing societies come into being outside the plan programmes, most of which were specialised single commodity societies, such as for fruits and vegetables, plantation crops, etc.

The position with regard to the working of marketing societies at various levels at the end of second plan (1960-61) is shown in Table 4.2.

Table—4.2 Position of co-operative marketing societies as on 10th June, 1961

(Rs. in lakhs)

Sl. No.	*Particulars*	*State*	*Central*	*Primary*
1.	No of societies	24	171	3,108
2.	Membership			
	(i) Societies	5,181	16,277	74,635
	(ii) Individuals	367	73,499	13,92,287
3.	Working capital	908.65	1,034.395	2,821.33
4.	Value of agricultural produce sold	2,770.14	887.40	5,062.83
5.	No. of societies at profits	16	106	1,665

Source : Statistical statements relating to co-operative movement in India, R.B.I, 1960-61, pp. 179 to 184

Table 4.2 reveals that by the end of the second plan, there were 3108 primary marketing societies in the country. As far as organization of marketing societies was concerned, the target of the second plan was exceeded and at the end of the plan, there was a network of primary marketing societies at the mandi level, apex marketing societies at the state level, and a National Federation at all India level besides district/regional marketing societies in a few states.

Commenting on the progress of co-operative marketing societies during the second plan, the Committee on Co-operative Marketing (1966) stated :

Though by itself, this figure may be impressive and represents a substantial increase in the marketing operations of co-operatives during the second plan period, yet the progress cannot be said to be satisfactory, as nearly 50 per cent of the total value of agricultural produce marketed was represented by sugarcane which is marketed under a legal compulsion. Further, we are not sure as to how far has been avoided in arriving at this figure. Even taking the entire figure of Rs. 174 crores, it represented only a negligible fraction of the total marketed surplus of agricultural produce.[23]

Third Five Year Plan

During the Third plan, the co-operative movement was accorded a crucial role in implementing the scheme of economic development. A rapidly growing co-operative sector, with special emphasis on the needs of the peasant, the worker and the consumer was considered to be vital factor for social stability for expansion of employment opportunities and for rapid economic development. It stated that "co-operation should become progressively the principal basis of organisation in branches of economic life, notably agriculture, minor irrigation, small industries in processing, marketing, distribution, rural electrification, housing and construction, and the provision of essential amenities for local communities. Even the medium and large industries and in transport, an increasing range of activities can be undertaken on co-operative lines. "Development of co-operative marketing was given a plan of special importance in scheme of integrated rural credit envisaged in the Third Plan not only because it was desirable as such but because it was an essential prerequisite for the envisaged large-scale expansion of co-operative credit and agricultural production. The success of the co-operative credit programme would to a very large extent, depend on the development of marketing societies, which will not only act as the channel for the recovery of credit extended by the service societies but will also enable the farmer to get a better return for his produce and to plough back the surplus for increased agricultural production.

During the Third plan, the main task was firstly to place the marketing societies on a sound basis, link them effectively with village societies and to enlarge their total business, and secondly to set up marketing societies in areas not provided with co-operative marketing facilities during the second plan.[24] Towards achievements of these objectives, the Third Plan envisaged the organisation of 544 new marketing societies. It also fixed a target of marketing of agricultural produce worth Rs. 360 crores through co-operatives in last year of the plan, which meant roughly doubling of their performance. Targets for the establishment of 980 additional godowns were also laid. Arrangements were also made for providing financial assistance to marketing societies by way of share capital contribution, loans and subsidy for construction of godowns, loans for establishing cold storage, subsidies for managerial cost and setting up of grading units, etc.

As a result of the progress made in this direction, all important secondary markets were, by and large, covered by marketing societies by the end of the Third Plan. During the Third Plan, 452 additional primary marketing societies were organized and state partnered, thus bringing the total number of state partnered society to 2321 at the end of June, 1966. The overall position of co-operative marketing societies in India as on 30th June, 1966 is shown in Table 4.3.

Table 4.3 reveals that the total number of marketing societies (State, Central and Primary) in the country as on 30th June, 1966 were 3374 of which 3198 were primary marketing societies. Of

Table—4.3 Position of marketing societies in India as on June, 30, 1966.

(Rs. in lakhs

Sl. No.	*Particulars*	*State*	*Central*	*Primary*
1.	No. of societies	21	155	3198
2.	Membership			
	Societies	5667	27627	139823
	Individuals	1235	54687	2140644
3.	Working capital	4807.21	1728.24	6371.57
4.	Value of Agricultural Produce sold:			
	As Owners (Rs.)	6164.40	792.32	3965.81
	As Agents (Rs.)	1188.05	370.18	9395.22
5.	Consumer goods sold			
	As Owners (Rs.)	2730.88	2834.00	10269.92
	As Agents (Rs.)	1080.69	204.79	1144.06
6.	No. of societies working at profit	16	121	2017

Source : Statistical statements relating to co-operative movement in India, R.B.I part II, Non-credit 1965-66.

the latter, 2729 societies were general purpose societies and the remaining were dealing in commodities like cotton, arecanut, tobacco, fruits and vegetables etc. One of the important activities undertaken by the marketing societies in several states during the period under review was the procurement of foodgrains on behalf of state governments and the supply of farm requisites especially chemical fertilizers. Co-operatives were appointed as the sole distributors of chemical fertilizers in many of the states.

Fourth Five Year Plan

The essential features of the co-operative marketing programme in the Fourth Plan are as follows:

(1) Steps will be taken to strengthen the existing co-operative marketing structure especially at the primary level;

(2) The apex federations at the state and national levels will be strengthened to enable them to reach optimum efficiency;

(3) Efforts will be made to introduce grading and pooling and other improved techniques in as many co-operatives as possible;

(4) The schemes initiated in the previous years for establishing grading units with equipment and suitable personnel will be continued;

(5) The scheme for maintenance of price fluctuation funds which enable the societies to make outright purchases will also be continued.

Physical Targets

Co-operatives will aim at handling in the last year of the Fourth plan, 8 million tonnes of foodgrains, 36 million tonnes of sugarcane, 0.6 million tonnes of groundnut, 10,000 tonnes of fruit and vegetables and 1. 8 million bales of cotton. At current prices, the value of agricultural produce likely to be handled by the agricultural and processing co-operatives is expected to be of the order of Rs. 900 crores in 1973-74. Co-operatives are also expected to handle agricultural commodities worth Rs. 25 crores in inter state trade and Rs. 10 crores in the export trade.[25]

The co-operative marketing movement made significant progress during last five years ending June, 1971. At the beginning of 1971-72, the co-operative marketing structure consisted of 3261 primary marketing societies, 159 district marketing societies, 21 state level marketing societies besides a National Federation at the apex. In addition, there were 3 state marketing federations for special commodities, one each in Delhi and Gujarat, for fruits and vegetables, and one in the Union Territory of Laccadives for coconut. There was also an inter-state Federation for marketing arecanut in Mysore state. The number of state partnered primary marketing societies was 2512, representing 77 per cent of the total number of such societies. During 1971-72 attention was largely devoted to stimulate the co-operatives in areas with large potential for growth, promotion of integrated marketing system, coordination of activities between marketing and consumer co-operatives, etc.

Achievements During Fourth Plan

The target of handling Rs. 900 crores worth of agricultural produce is likely to be achieved by the end of Fourth Plan, even though the achievement in 1970-71 was only Rs. 655 crores. This optimism is based on several new factors and fresh efforts are being made. About 400 selected marketing societies are being further strengthened by share capital assistance under the recently approved central sector scheme. It is expected that the assisted societies will double their turnover during the next 2-3 years. Further marketing societies are being increasingly involved in the procurement operations of the Cotton Corporation, Jute Corporation and Food Corporation of India, with whom working arrangements have been/are being made.

The Fourth Plan target of Rs. 25 crores for inter-state trade has already been achieved in the first two years of the plan. In fact, during 1970-71, inter-state trade by co-operatives was of the order of Rs. 63 crores. In the field of exports, the co-operatives handled agricultural produce worth Rs. 6 crores during 1970-71 and it is expected that the target of Rs. 10 crores would be achieved by the end of the Fourth Plan.

In the field of agricultural supplies, co-operatives distributed fertilisers worth Rs. 250 crores during 1970-71 through a network of over 36,000 retail depots and 2000 sub-wholesale centres. During 1973-74, the value of fertilisers to be distributed by them is expected to be of the order of Rs. 450 crores. In terms of nutrients co-operatives are expected to handle about 2.1 million tonnes accounting for about 55 per cent of the total consumption of chemical fertilisers. The value of other agricultural inputs, such as, improved seeds, agricultural implements, pesticides and others handled by co-operatives during the first 2 years of the plan was around Rs. 50 crores each year, of which seeds accounted for Rs. 24 crores, pesticides and others accounted for Rs. 20 crores and agricultural implements Rs. 6 crores. This is likely to go up to Rs. 100 crores during 1973-74 as against a target of Rs. 115 crores set in the plan.

Fifth Five Year Plan

The objectives in the Fifth Plan was to consolidate and strengthen the co-operatives as a democratic and viable structure responsible to the needs of the peasants, the artisans, the workers and the consumers. The co-operative movement was important for implementing the national policy of growth with social justice.

Agricultural marketing including supply of agricultural production requisites, and processing would continue to be assigned a central position in the strategy of co-operative development.

The principal aim in the sphere of agricultural marketing would be to nationalise, consolidate and suitably strengthen the co-operative marketing structure, so that it can adequately support and service the programmes of increased agricultural production in the best interests of the producer and the consumer.

Social attention was given to removing regional imbalance in the field of co-operative marketing such as have been experienced in the last few years, and appropriate measures would be taken to that end.

Co-operatives would continue to diversify their marketing operations, and increasingly undertake the purchase of cash crops and oil seeds with a view to stabilising the prices both at the producer and the consumer end while the co-operative marketing societies would closely co-ordinate their activities with the public sector commodity corporations, the latter also would need to give necessary trade support to the co-operatives and also fully include them in their price support and commercial procurement operations.

It was estimated that about 100 new marketing primaries were to be organised during the Fifth Plan.

It was envisaged that, during the last year of the Fifth Plan, cooperatives would handle agricultural produce of the value of Rs. 1,900 crores, consisting of foodgrains worth Rs. 800 crores, sugarcane worth Rs. 600 crores and the balance of other crops. Inter-state trade by co-operatives was envisaged to be of the order of Rs. 80 crores annually by the end of Fifth Plan. In the field of exports, co-operatives were expected to step up their operations to Rs. 15 crores by 1978-79. During the Fifth Plan, the built-up storage capacity with the co-operatives would be raised to 6.8 million tonnes by 1978-79.

By the end of 1976-77, there were 3,370 co-operative marketing societies, out of which 2,810 were functioning for the marketing of general commodities and 560 were meant for the marketing of specific commodities. The membership of those co-operatives was 33.49 lakhs. Their total working capital, on June 30, 1977 was Rs. 311 crores. The value of agricultural produce marketed by those co-operatives during 1976-77 was Rs. 1,073 crores while in 1976-77, these co-operative societies marketed foodgrains worth Rs. 540 crores. The total value of agricultural produce handled by marketing co-operatives amounted to Rs. 1,797 crores in 1978-79.

Sixth Five Year Plan

The framers of the Sixth Plan observed:

"Co-operative marketing infrastructure has come to cover almost all important secondary and tertiary markets. The co-operatives have attained sufficient growth in business operation and have diversified their activities manifold. Yet the total share in the market still continues to be small and has not kept pace with rapidly growing output and volume of agricultural produce. The value of agricultural produce marketed by them was only Rs. 1750 crores in 1979-80 mainly of sugarcane, cotton and foodgrains and largely limited to only five states, namely Punjab, Haryana, U.P., Kerala and Madhya Pradesh. Co-operatives had yet to enter the field of fruits and vegetable marketing."

The Planning Commission indicated that co-operative marketing system was not able to give satisfactory performance due to weak primaries. It was noted that co-operative marketing had made a remarkable processing of sugarcane and dairy marketing. Co-operative processing was also progressing in oil crushing, fruit and vegetable processing, cotton ginning and processing, jute bailing, spilling mill etc. However, except sugar other co-operative processing had not yet made any impact.

The Planning Commission provided for assistance to all marketing societies to build up their own storage capacity which with only 47 lakh tonnes was inadequate. It also provided for storage of potato, onion and fruits and vegetables. At the end of March 1980 co-operatives had only 125 cold storages with the capacity of 2.41 lakh tonnes.

During this plan period, the development of agricultural co-operative marketing, however, had been very uneven among different states. The agricultural produce marketed per hectare ranged from Rs. 8 in Rajasthan to Rs. 509 in Maharashtra. The six states of Gujarat, Haryana, Karnataka, Maharashtra, Punjab and U.P. contributed 81 per cent of the overall achievement. At the end of Sixth Plan the total number of marketing societies was 4,130. The value of foodgrains handled by these societies was Rs. 900 crores in 1984-85.

Seventh Five Year Plan (1985-90)

The seventh plan aimed at strengthening the primary marketing societies and making their activities broad-based. It was proposed to forge effective links between the marketing co-operatives and public sector commodity corporations such as the Food Corporation of India, Cotton Corporation of India and Jute Corporation of India. Close co-ordination would also be effected among the marketing co-operatives, consumer cooperatives, civil supplies corporations and public distribution system.

It was envisaged that by the end of Seventh Plan period, the cooperatives would undertake the retail sale of fertilizers to the extent of 8.3 million tonnes, with their share in the overall distribution of fertilizers rising from 47 per cent in 1984-85 to 55 per cent in 1989-90. The value of agricultural produce marketed by co-operatives is expected to increase to Rs. 5,000 crores in 1989-90.

There were 2,937 primary marketing societies and 3,920 special commodity societies for oilseeds, etc. on 30th June, 1987.[26] The total value of agricultural produce marketed by co-operative societies was estimated at Rs. 4,014 crores in 1986-87. The value of agricultural produce marketed by co-operatives was, however, 4,193 crores of rupees in 1985-86. There were nearly 67,000 co-operative retail outlets for fertilizers. During 1986-87, these outlets were estimated to have distributed around 30 lakh tonnes of fertilizers, nutrients, representing over 35 per cent of the fertilizers distributed in the country.

Eighth Five Year Plan

The emphasis on developments of co-operative marketing was reiterated in the 8th Plan thus:

"Co-operatives are expected to play a major role in the distribution of inputs and services to the farmers on the one hand and in assisting marketing and processing of agricultural produce on the other."

It is noted that NAFED had undertaken price support operations for oilseeds, coarse grains, pulses, potatoes and onions. It noted with satisfaction that NAFED's export of 3,60,220 tonnes of onion had helped maintain stabilisation of onion prices in domestic market. It was noted that 114.47 tonnes of storage capacity had been created under co-operative sector. There were 229 cold storages with 6.35 lakh tonnes capacity. The Eighth Plan acknowledged that "It had emerged as an important countervailing factor to the private traders for the benefit of both producers and consumers. It has been pointed out that given adequate freedom of action in their management, co-operatives can emerge strong and efficient."

The Eighth Five Year Plan re-emphasized its concern for strengthening co-operative structure for fulfilment of Eighth Plan objectives: " In order to equip the co-operatives with adequate godown facilities for providing distribution of inputs and consumer goods and to facilitate marketing of agricultural produce, efforts would be made to provide each viable PAC and primary marketing society with a godown of its own and storage capacity of 21 lakh tonnes and 70 cold storages with a capacity of 3 lakh tonnes would be created."

Ninth Five Year Plan

The Ninth Plan placed considerable emphasis on the development of co-operative marketing. Efforts were also envisaged to be taken to strengthen the existing marketing societies at the primary level. The main emphasis in the ninth plan in the sphere of co-operative agricultural marketing was on the consolidation and strengthening of existing societies. It is proposed to forge effective links between the marketing co-operatives and public sector commodity corporations such as the Food Corporation of India, Cotton Corporation of India and Jute Corporation of India.

It was envisaged that by the end of ninth plan period, the co-operatives would undertake the retail sale of fertilizers to the extent of 10.5 million tonnes, with their share in the overall distribution of fertilizers rising from 52 per cent in 1997-98 to 56 per cent in 2001-2002. The value of agricultural produce marketed by co-operatives is expected to increase to Rs. 7,5000 crores in 2001-2002.

On 30th June, 2001, there were 2,958 primary marketing societies and 3,340 special commodity marketing societies for oilseeds etc. The total value of agricultural produce marketed by co-operatives was Rs. 6,235 crores in 2001-2002.

REFERENCES

1. Report of the Marketing Sub-Committee of the United Nations Conference on Food and Agriculture (1946), p. 2.
2. Report of the Committee on Co-operative Marketing (1966), p. 6.
3. *ibid.*
4. Report of the Committee on Co-operative Marketing (1966). p. 16.
5. All India Rural Credit Survey Report (1954) p. 102.
6. Dr. Mathur B.S "Co-operation in India", (Sahitya Bhawan, Agra 1990), p. 288.
7. Report of the Prices Sub-committee (1947), p. 165.
8. Report on India's Food Crisis and Steps to Meet It 1959 pp. 89-99.
9. FAO Agricultural Development Paper No. 34 p. 40.
10. Iyenger, A Study in the Co-operative Movement in India, p. 90.
11. Jha Dibakar, "A Prospective on Co-operative Marketing" (Vikas Publishing House Pvt. Ltd., 1997), p. 75.
12. *ibid*, p. 75.
13. Report of the Central Banking Enquiry Committee (1931), Foreign Experts Report, p. 26.
14. Marketing Sub-committee (1946) p. 53.
15. Report of the co-operative planning committee (1946) pp. 61-62.

16. *Ibid* pp. 64-65.
17. Review of the Co-operative Movement in India 1948-50, Reserve Bank of India, p. 83.
18. Report of the Committee on Co-operative Marketing (1966) p. 23.
19. Report of the Committee on Co-operative Credit (1960) pp. 1-67.
20. Report of the Committee on Co-operative Marketing (1966) pp. 2-3.
21. Review of the Co-operative Movement in India 1954-56, R.B.I., p. 82.
22. Second Five Year Plan, Planning Commission pp. 267-277.
23. *Ibid* p. 27.
24. Third Five Year Plan, p. 165.
25. Fourth Five Year Plan 1969-74, Planning Commission. p. 222.
26. Mathur, B.S. "Co-operation in India", Saahitya Bhavan, Agra, 1990, p. 265.

5

History and Development of Agency Marketing Co-operative Society (AMCS), Tikabali

Introduction

The district of Kandhamal is endowed with vast forest resources. It is divided into two forest divisions, viz, Balliguda and Phulbani. Each year the lease of forests in respect of both the forest divisions was given for collection and marketing of minor forest produce. Till the year 1950, the lease was being given to private businessmen. As there is no institution to undertake business in those items, the private lease holders always exploited the tribals.[1] The innocent tribals were often beguiled into weight and payment. Turmeric is widely cultivated in the hilly areas by the tribals. There was no proper communication between the villages in the district before independence. The businessmen of the neighbouring districts such as Ganjam and Puri came to the district to do business in tribal products. They purchased turmeric, ginger, tamarind, siali plates etc. From the tribals in exchanges of salt, dry fish, cloth, utensils, ornaments, bidi, match-box and other necessary products. The traders obtained huge amount of profits by carrying on turmeric business and exploited the tribals to a large extent. After 1947, the government of independent India considered the sufferings of the tribals seriously and took many steps for the welfare and upliftment of the tribals.

The establishment of co-operative societies was one of the important measures taken by the government to save the tribals from the exploitations of the businessmen and to increase their standard of living. Late S.C. Roy, the then Registrar of Co-operative Societies posted Mr. Prabhakar Pattnaik as the senior inspector of the non-credit society of Berhampur circle to organise a co-operative society in Kandhamal district.[2] He is considered to be the pioneer of co-operative movement in the district. After survey of the tribal villages, he felt the importance of an organization of the co-operative society for the turmeric growers in order to provide them with a supplementary and perennial source of income. Tikabali, one of the leading trading centres of the district—was chosen by him.[3] Due to the sincere efforts of Mr. Pattanik, Agency Marketing Co-operative Society, Tikabali was established. For the formation of the society, some local members namely Sri Dinabandhu Pradhan, Sri Pada Mallick, Sri Dinbandhu Panda, Sri Bharat Chandra Bhoi and Sri Bhagaban Sahu co-operated with the movement of Mr. Pattnaik. Although some scheduled caste people were very much jealous of the movement and revolted against it, he could be able to tide over their obstacles and succeeded in his efforts to materialise a society at Tikabali. Therefore Mr. Pattnaik could be regarded as the founding father of the AMCS, Tikabali, Orissa.[4]

In order to help the tribals for production and marketing of turmeric and other local agricultural products, Turmeric Growers Marketing Co-operative Society, Ltd. Tikabali was registered under the Madras Co-operative Society Act of 1932 and deemed to have been registered under the Orissa Co-operative Society Act of 1962 (Act II of 1963), bearing No. J-711 with 11 (eleven) members[5] on 19th November, 1947. As the first president of the Society, Sri Pyari Mohan Samantray, Deputy Tahasilder of G. Udaygiri, was nominated and worked for its development.[6] In 1950, one person from the tribal community named Mr. Dinabandhu Pradhan of Raibanza village was elected as the President of the society. He worked efficiently and enthusiastically which generated confidence among the tribals in favour of the society.

For the assistance of the tribals and non-tribals, a scheme was proposed by Sri S.H. Khalndar, the then Assistant Registrar of Co-operative Society, Berhampur Circle. It was initiated during the first part of 1948 under which the crop loan was sanctioned on the personal security and turmeric standing in land.[7] The payment of loan was acceptable either in cash or in kind after harvesting.[8] This scheme was very much popular among the tribals and created confidence in their minds. During the same year, two more procurement centres at Linepada and Sankarakhole were established for the purpose of the growth and expansion of the business of the society.[9] Due to the keen competition of the private traders in the business of tribal products, the society had to face difficulties during the initial stage of progres.[10] Sri Prabhakar Pattnaik, the then secretary of the Society in the year 1949, could be able to take some steps for the growth of the business of the society. His success in this field was also due to strong support by Sri Gangadhar Mishra.[11] In order to propagate and spread the aims and objectives of the society, they sought the help of the growers of the district. The expansion of the business of the society required more godown space. So the Assistant Registrar of the Co-operative Society, Berhampur established 9 godowns at Tikabali for keeping of stock of turmeric.[12]

The scheduled caste people were more educated than the tribals in the district. The tribals had faith in the legal advice of the scheduled caste people in the matters of business. Due to the intimate relationship between the scheduled caste and scheduled tribe people, the private traders appointed scheduled caste people as their business agents on commission basis for the negotiation of the turmeric business.[13]

For the expansion of the turmeric business, the officials of the Turmeric Grower's Society engaged the scheduled caste people as agents to explore their turmeric business in the district[14]. Due to the involvement of the scheduled caste people in turmeric business contact with the tribal people of the interior parts of the district could be possible. Thus the society looked after the interest of the tribal and scheduled caste members, established good contact with the interior areas and gained the support of the tribals.

The society had to go through a very difficult period due to the inadequacy of funds during the initial state.[15] But after some time the society could raise a large amount of share capital by increased number of tribal and non-tribal members by creating strong confidence among them.[16] Gradually large number of tribals were interested to become members of the society which helped it to increase the amount of working capital.[17]

At the initial stage the society was carrying on business of purchasing and selling of turmeric. It also advanced loans to the tribals for the purpose of agriculture work. During that period the society could not render services to the tribals regarding the sale of minor forest produces. So the tribals, after collecting minor forest produces, were bound to sell the products to the private traders at a throwaway price.[18]

Due to lack of government agencies for the purchase, the tribals were being exploited by the private businessmen. So in order to save them from the clutches of private traders' exploitation, a meeting was organised at Chatrapur in the district of Ganjam in the year 1949, under the chairmanship of Sri Jagatbandhu Mohapatra, I.A.S., Registrar of Co-operative Society.[19] Mr. Prabhakar Pattnaik, the first Secretary of the society, other officials of Berhampur Co-operative circle and district level forest officers of Phulbani participated in the meeting. A resolution was passed in that meeting and Turmeric Growers' society was empowered to purchase minor forest produces from the tribals.[20] A lease has been accorded by the Forest Department to the Society on permanent basis since that period to procure minor forest produces. An amendment of the nomenclature was changed during the same year and the society was renamed as "Agency Marketing Co-operative Society, Ltd., Tikabali."[21] For the procurement of minor forest produces, some new procurement centres were established in the district. The Government of Orissa also provided assistance in the shape of materials for the growth of business of the Society.[22] The AMCS, Tikabali was affiliated to Boudh Central Co-operative Bank in the same year.[23]

Due to sincere efforts of Sri Prabhakar Pattnaik, the then Secretary of AMCS, and Sri Gangadhar Mishra, enrolment of large number of tribal members was possible which helped the Society for its growth and expansion.[24] During the year, total number of members increased to 312 as against 248 in 1949-50.[25] The AMCS, Tikabali, was considered as the second biggest co-operative organisation in the state as per the reports of the working of Co-operative Society in Orissa, published by the Registrar of Co-operative Societies, Cuttack in 1950-51. As an exporter of turmeric, the AMCS, Tikabali, extended its business activities to Madras, Nagpur, Calcutta and Tatanagar in the year 1952-53.[26] During 1954-55, the society launched new programmes and its operational dimension increased enormously.[27] Different incentives and facilities provided in the new programmes were production bonus, loan facility, training to tribal members, distribution of dividend to the shareholders, introduction of new weight and measure systems and better procurement prices. Due to the introduction of this new programme, confidence of the tribals in the activities of the society increased enormously.

During the period of Sri K.K. Chatterjee, the then Secretary of the AMCS from 1955-58, the Society suffered a heavy loss of Rs. 1,21,586 because of the slump in turmeric business and cut-throat competition in turmeric trade from the private merchants.[28] Due to the ineffective performance of the AMCS during Mr. Chatterjee's period, the private businessmen got an opportunity to carry on business in competition with the society.

After realising the difficult situation of the Society, the Government of Orissa deputed Mr. Gangadhar Mishra to work as the Secretary of AMCS in place of Mr. K.K. Chatterjee. The state government also provided financial assistance to the Society in order to overcome its financial crisis.[29] As Mr. Mishra, the Secretary of AMCS was in close contact with the Society for some years, he effectively managed the society. Thus the Society carried on its business successfully, acquired goodwill and regained its past glory. For the purpose of the expansion of the Society, the help of the tribals and traders of the locality was taken by Mr. Mishra. Sri K. Ramamurty, the then Registrar of the Co-operative Society, suggested to open sales centres outsides Orissa to sell the hill brooms at a higher price.[30] In the year 1957, Mr. Mishra, the Secretary of the Society, took the initiative in opening up a sales centre at Bombay.[31] The broom sticks produced at Narayan Prasad areas of Boudh, Kaligna and Tikabali areas of Kondhamals were sold at this centre profitably. Bombay sales center acquired goodwill for the Society in selling of good quality broom sticks.[32] During the tenure of Mr Mishra, the procurement centres of the AMCS was extended to the whole of Balliguda Forest division. A bone power mill was also established at Tikabali during this period. The AMCS, Tikabali achieved tremendous success during his tenure because of his effective administrative skill and leadership qualities. During this period, the recovery of heavy losses of past years could be possible due to huge amount of profits.[33] The private traders tried to make competition with the society by evil practices during the year 1960-61. But the business of the society was not affected due to effective management of the society.[34] In the year 1969-70, according to instructions of the Government of Orissa, a special scheme of expansion programme of purchase and sale operations was introduced by the AMCS, Tikabali.[35] In order to bring large number of tribal producers under the fold of co-operatives through outright purchase of turmeric from the tribals at a remunerative price and to relieve them from the exploitation of private traders[36], cash credit accommodation to the tune of Rs. 25 lakhs was made available from State Bank of India, Phulbani under hypothecation and government guaranttee.[37] During the tenure of Sri Sibram Rath, the then Secretary of AMCS in the year 1969-70, the society purchased turmeric worth Rs. 14.50 lakhs under the scheme paying a higher price to the tribals than the private traders to bring them into the co-operative fold. For the purpose of exporting, the turmeric was stored. In the meantime, the price of turmeric was reduced due to non-availability of wagons on account of war with Pakistan and troubles in Bangladesh.[38] Due to unhealthy competition of reduction of price by the private traders, the society had to sell the stock at a throwaway price in order to avoid further damage on storage and paying huge interest on the cash credit. It incurred loss to the extent of Rs. 6 lakhs on this account in 1971-72.[39] Due to the continuous loss of the society for a period of 4 years, it could not pay the cash credit loan and become ineligible to draw further fund under the cash credit system. The Banks also did not come to help because the audit of the society could not be done after 1967-68.

The National Co-operative Development Council (NCDC) visited the society in the year 1974-75 and recommended for more share capital contribution for operating on sound footing as otherwise the tribals would suffer.[40] The NCDC contributed a sum of Rs. 6.5 lakhs and Government of Orissa contributed Rs. 3.5 lakhs towards the share capital of the AMCS to help the society for expansion of its business and to clear the cash credit loan of State Bank of India, Phulbani. The reformation of the AMCS, Tikabali was started during the tenure of Sri S.K. Mohanty, the then Secretary of the Society in the year 1982-83.[41] Many tribal welfare activities in the district were initiated by the sincere efforts of Sri Mohanty.[42] The

AMCS, Tikabali gave financial assistance for the establishment of college at Tikabali to educate the people of the tribal community in this area. This is one of the greatest achievements of Sri Mohanty during his tenure as secretary of the Society.[43] Therefore the society conducted its business efficiently and achieved much success for about two deca-des till the year 1990-91. The AMCS, Tikabali could be able to earn goodwill for its good quality products and made business transac-tions with the traders of almost of big cities and towns in the country.[44]

Objective of AMCS

The objectives of the society as mentioned in the Bye-laws[45] are:

(*i*) to raise the economic standard of Adivasi members and landless forest labourers whose main occupation is collection of minor forest produces and working in forest crops;

(*ii*) to purchase MFP of members and arrange sale to their best advantage;

(*iii*) to educate the members in improved method of turmeric cultivation;

(*iv*) to borrow and advance loans to its members for growing turmeric on the security of crop standing on their fields or on the pledge of their produces sent for sale;

(*v*) to arrange for sale of turmeric and other produces of members to their best advantage and also purchase the above produces from them;

(*vi*) to take up pooling, grading, standardising and processing of MFP and other produces of the members wherever necessary to help the Adivasi members;

(*vii*) to rent own godowns and sale depots to facilitate storage of members' produces, grant loans to them, purchase and sale of their produces as well as arrange daily necessities of life;

(*viii*) to own plants and machineries and other equipments necessary for exploitation of MFP and processing of members' produces;

(*ix*) to purchase wholesale at reasonable rate of agricultural and domestic necessaries of members and non-members and such other commodities as are generally required by Adivasis for supplying to the same in retail;

(*x*) to take lease of forest produces to facilitate the business of the society on behalf of the members;

(*xi*) to act as an agent to the government on other recognised institutions in the field of procurement and distribution;

(*xii*) to produce such implements and tools necessary for the members for collecting MFP, SAP and attending work in forest crops;

(*xiii*) to disseminate among members the latest improvement in agriculture by arranging demonstration according to the advice of the Agriculture Department and also for the improvement of quality of MFP as per the advice of the Forest Department;

(*xiv*) to do all other things as are incidentally conducive to the attainment of the above objects;

(*xv*) to encourage thrift, self help and co-operation among members.

Membership

The number of members of the society was 201 in the first year 1947.[46] The membership increased to 64,371 by the end of the year 1998-99.[47] The members are classified into four categories:[48]

(1) Those Adivasi members who collect minor forest produces (MFP) or are engaged in cultivation work in forest as labourers are known as class members;

(2) The other non-Adivasi members who collect MFP or are engaged in cultivation or working in the forest as labourers are classified as 'B' class members. They are not entitled to cast their votes or participate in the Board of Management;

(3) The traders who have business transactions with the society are admitted as 'C' class members. They also have no rights to cast their votes and to take participation in the management or profits of the society;

(4) The Government, Panchayat Samities, Gram Panchayats and other local bodies are admitted as 'special class' members are explained in detail in table 5-1.

Table 5.1 reveals that during the year 1950-51, the membership of AMCS was only 200 but the same has increased to 64,371 during the year 1998-99. There was no special class member upto 1997-98. But during the year 1998-99, 23 special class members ('D' class) are found in the society.

Table—5-1 Category-wise members of AMCS, Tikabali from 1951-52 to 1998-99

Sl. No.	Decade	'A' Class members (ST)	'B' Class members (SC)	'C' class members (Trader)	'D' class members special class	Total
1.	1950-51	200	--	--	--	200
2.	1960-61	3,075	142	8	--	3225
3.	1970-71	7,679	200	16	--	7,895
4.	1980-81	13,200	1189	790	--	15,180
5.	1990-91	19,000	4650	1759	--	25,409
6.	1998-99	56,339	7924	85	23	64,371

Source : Figures compiled from Appendix-VIII and Annual Administration Report of AMCS, Tikabali, 1998-99, p. 2.

When a member of the society dies, his minor nominee, heir or legal representative can be a member through his guardian.[49]

The Board of Directors is vested with the power of admitting or refusal of a new member.[50] If a person is refused to be enrolled as a member, he shall be intimated by the Board of Directors within 7 days. A member cannot resign before the completion of one year of his membership. If a member dies, his membership is ceased. Each member of the society must be a resident of the operational area of the society. If he has no residence in this area, he can be permanently removed from membership of the society.[51] According to the bye-laws of the society, the share of the disqualified member can he transferred to a qualified member of the society. The Board of Directors may remove a member from membership of the society when it is proved that he deceives the society or drags the society into the court of law. Similarly, if any member becomes bankrupt or his general conduct necessitates his removal in the interest of the society or is convicted of an offence involving moral turpitude, then the Board of Directors removes him from his membership.[52] When the board removes a member, the decision must be communicated to him within 7 days. The Board of Directors is considered to be the final authority in the matter of admission or removal of a member.[53]

Management

The management of the society is vested in a Board of Directors consisting of ten members of which seven are elected and three nominated by the government[54]. The directors are elected for a period of 4 years by the 'A' class members in the general body meeting of the society from seven electoral zones. The other three government nominees are (1) Deputy Registrar of Co-operative Society or his nominee; (2) Conservator of Forests, Berhampur circle or his nominee; and (3) The Managing Director of Orissa State Tribal Development Co-operative Corporation or his nominee.[55]

Election of the Board of Directors is made by an election being conducted by the election officer of Co-operative Department appointed by the Government of Orissa. According to the Election rule of the Orissa Co-operative Societies, the President is elected from among the elected members of the Board of Directors.[56]

Electoral Zones

(*a*) Baliguda Zone covers Baliguda Block, Nuagaon Block, Daringibadi, Simanbadi and Dasingibadi area of Daringibadi Block.

(*b*) G. Udayagiri zone covers the whole of Raikia and G. Udayagiri Block.

(*c*) Belghar Zone covers the whole of Tumudibandh and Kotagarh Block.

(*d*) Jhingiriguda zone covers Katingia, Mahaguda, Godapur, Brahamnigaon and Jhingiriguda area of Daringibadi block.

(*e*) Phulbani zone covers the whole of Phulbani, Khajuripada, Phiringia, Harabhanga and Kantamal block.

(*f*) Sankarakhole Zone covers the whole of Chakapad block; and

(*g*) Tikabali Zone covers the entire Tikabli area. (See Map No.3)

The General Body has been empowered to remove any elected member or members of the Board of Directors through a resolution passed in the meeting.[57] If any member of the Board of Directors wants to resign from his office, he can do so at any time by a resolution addressed to the secretary of the society. The directors of the society met once in every two months or often if necessary. An Executive Committee consisting of five members including the president is elected by the Board of Directors in order to carry on the business of the society. If a state of emergency arises, the secretary of the society is empowered to get the consent of the Board of Directors or Executive Committee by circulation and such decision is required to be placed in the next meeting of the Board of Directors or Executive Committee for approval. If any difference of opinion among the

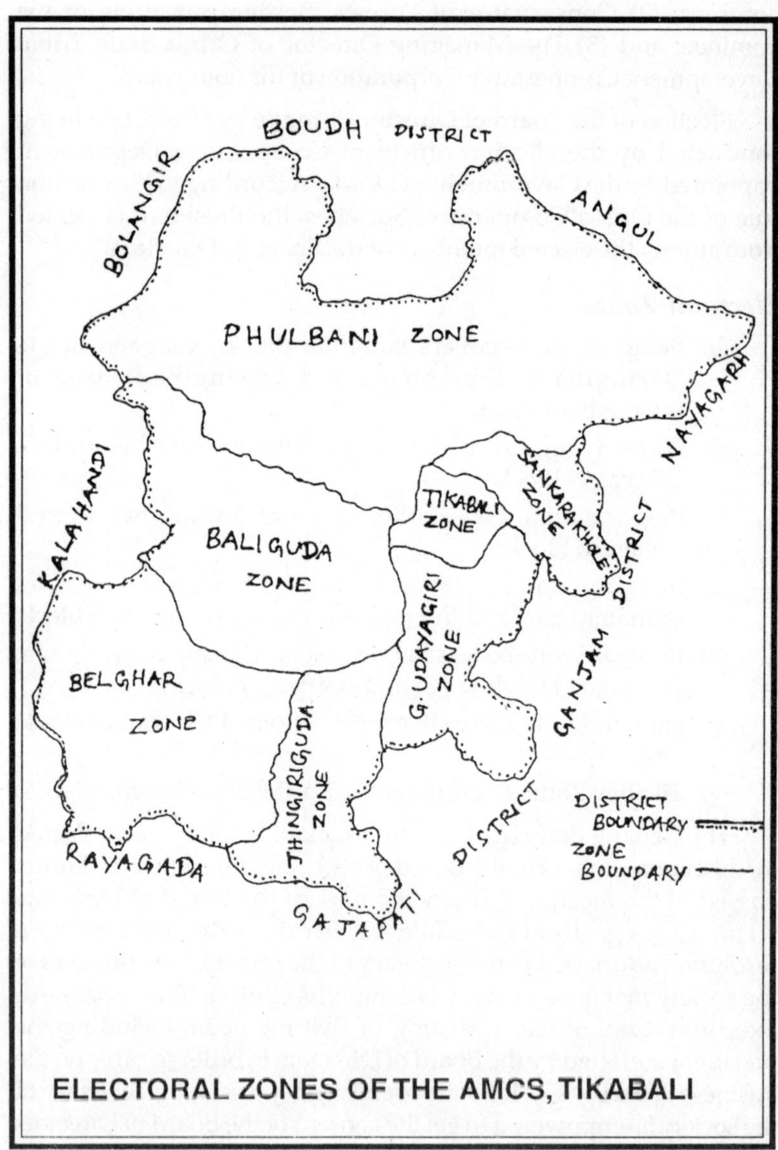

ELECTORAL ZONES OF THE AMCS, TIKABALI

members of Board of Directors or Executive Committee arises, those are placed in a meeting of the Board of Directors or Executive Committee as the case may be for taking decisions. If a director remains absent in the three consecutive meetings of the Board of Directors, his membership is ceased. His case for reinstatement may be considered if sufficient and satisfactory reasons are cited by him regarding his absence.

The following normal powers and duties are conferred on the Board of Directors as per the provisions of the Bye-laws.[58]

(*a*) Admission of members; (*b*) Borrowing from financial institutions and Government; (*c*) Investment of reserve and surplus funds of the society; (*d*) conducting of new lines of business with the approval of RCS, Orissa; (*e*) Appointment and dismissal of the staff; (*f*) placing all the directions of RCS; (*g*) Action against the defaulters; (*h*) Proposal for distribution of annual profits; (*i*) Proposals, agreements and contracts with the Government relating to procurement, sale of MFP and other commodities; and (*j*) The president shall preside over all the meetings or in his absence the committee may elect one member to preside over the meeting.

Secretary

The Government of Orissa gives appointment to the Secretary of the Agency Marketing Co-operative Society, Tikabali. Then his appointment is approved by the Board of Directors of the Society. He is a paid employee of the society. He attends all the meetings of the Board of Directors, Executive Body and the General Body of the Society. But he cannot cast his vote in these meetings. All the activities of the Society are executed by him.[59] All the documents of the society are prepared in the name of the secretary. He also deals with a lot of correspondence with the members, traders and Government agencies. He maintains all the accounts and registers of the society and records proceedings of all the meetings. As per the order of the Board of Directors, monetary transactions are handled by him. He takes necessary steps for the annual audit of the accounts of the society in time. Under his active supervision and guidance, the society makes progress. All other works assigned to him by the Board of Directors are performed by him. If the Secretary goes on leave, the Board of Directors may authorise another person to perform his routine activities.

The General Body

The meeting of the General Body generally takes place once in a year for the discussion on the conduct of business of the society. It has the ultimate authority in all matters relating to the administration of the society. The General Body can elect and remove directors. Annual audit reports of the society are presented in this meeting. The General body can amend or repeal existing rules mentioned in the bye-law of the society. The functions of the General Body also include resolution regarding distribution of profits, expulsion of members and other kinds of business which are not assigned to the Board of Directors. The meeting of the General Body is presided over by the President of the Society. If he is absent, a chairman may be elected from among the members to preside over the meeting. The resolution is taken on the basis of the support of majority of the members present and vote in the meeting. For convening meeting of the General Body, a notice is circulated to all the members before seven days by means of fixing of notices in conspicuous places or by beating of drums in the villages coming under jurisdiction of the society. Date, time, venue and the agenda of the meeting are clearly mentioned in the notice.[60]

Funding Pattern

The funds of the society are obtained from the following sources:

(*a*) Subscriptions received by issue of shares;

(*b*) Admission and other fees;

(*c*) Deposits from members and non-members;

(*d*) Loans and cash credit from SBI and other financial institutions. The borrowing of the society according to its bye-laws should not exceed 20 times of its reserve fund and paid up share capital;

(*e*) Government grants, donations and subsidies;

(*f*) Other resources from Panchayat Samities, Gram Panchayats and local bodies etc.

Out of the total share capital of Rs. 2 lakhs of the Society, 'A' and 'B' class shareholders contribute for 50,000 shares @ Re 1 per each share. 'C' class shareholders contribute for 500 shares @

Rs. 10 each per share and special class shareholders contribute for 145 shares @ Rs. 1,000 per each share.[61] Each member is required to pay 10 paise per share for admission fee which does not exceed Rs. 2 in any case. Admission fee is not paid by special shareholders. A member in the society cannot transfer his shares to another person without the sanction of the Board of Directors.[62] As per the decision of the Board of Directors, the society can receive deposits at the rate of 8 per cent interest from the members or other persons or institutions registered under Orissa Co-operative Society Act.

The AMCS is engaged in numerous transactions with the members of the society which may be in terms of cash or kind. The Society sanctions loans to its members only. Generally a member takes loan from the society for different objectives such as purchase of tools and equipments for collection of minor forest produces or to work in forest coups or to meet domestic expenses.[63] On certain occasions, the members may be advanced loans to meet the expenses for household, social and ceremonial needs for a specific period. The sources of funds of the society are represented in Table 5.2.

Table—5.2 Funding pattern of the AMCS, Tikabali (1950-51 to 1993-94)

(Figures in Lakhs)

Sl. No.	*Years*	*Share capital*	*Government subsidies*	*Working capital*
1.	1950-51	0.04	0.06	0.79
2.	1060-61	0.10	1.03	1.76
3.	1970-71	1.79	1.07	26.27
4.	1980-81	13.16	4.48	51.39
5.	1990-91	21.86	13.34	222.23
6.	1993-94	22.75	3.33	256.00

Source : Final Audit Report from the year 1950-51 to 1990-91 the AMCS, Tikabali. Figures complied from Appendix-xvi and subsidy Register of AMCS, Tikabali.

* Share Capital includes Government share and shares of 'A' and 'B' class members.

Table 5.2 shows that in 1950-51, the amount of share capital of the society was only Rs. 0.04 lakh which continuously increased to Rs. 22.75 lakhs in 1993-94. The amount of Government subsidy also shows a rising trend from Rs. 0.06 lakh in 1950-57 to Rs. 13.34 lakhs in 1990-91. As regards the working capital of the society, it can be said that the position is satisfactory. The amount of working capital was Rs. 0.79 lakh in 1950-51 which continuously increased to Rs. 256 lakhs in 1993-94.

Staffing Pattern

The Secretary of AMCS, Tikabali comes on deputation from Co-operative Department of Government of Orissa. He is the Chief Executive Officer of the Society who is not below the rank of an Assistant Registrar of the Co-operative Society (ARCS). In the AMCS, a group of ministerial staff are appointed for the prupose of assistance to the secretary in the matter of office administration and business management of the Society. Three Sub-Asst. Registrar of Co-operative Societies (SARCS) work in the Society. Two of them come on deputation from the offices of Government of Orissa and the other comes from the Co-operative circle. In the AMCS, two senior inspectors of Co-operative societies work who are below the rank of Sub.Asst. Regirstrars of Co-operative societies. For the purpose of office administration, an establishment officer designated as Accounts Officer is also appointed. The staffing pattern of the AMCS, Tikabali is shown in Table-5.3.

Area of Operation

The area of operation of the AMCS, Tikabali extends over the whole of the district of Kandhamal and some areas of Boudh district. It is divided into 7 zones for the purpose of procuring MFP and SAP items. The supervisors are appointed to supervise the procurement centres established under each zone. The MFP and SAPs collected and produced by the tribals of the district are delivered by them at the procurement centres of the society. They also get ready for cash payment of their products. The price of each forest product is decided beforehand in the Board and duly approved by the collector of the district.[64] (Appendix—IX). Price discrimination is eliminated due to this procedure of price fixation. After collecting the tribal products at different procurement centres, the society stores them in the local godowns till the products are despatched to the terminal points.

Table—5.3 Staff position of AMCS, Tikabali in 1998-99.

Sl.No	*Designation*	*Total Strength*
1.	Secretary	1
2.	Accounts Officer	1
3.	Zonal Officer	1
4.	Branch Manager	1
5.	Tamarind Plant Manager	1
6.	Accountants	2
7.	Ledgter Clerk	2
8.	Clerk	5
9.	Senior Supervisor	22
10.	Junior Supervisor	26
11.	Heavy Vehicle Driver	7
12.	Light Vehicle Driver	1
13.	Cleaner	1
14.	Peon-cum-watcher	46
15.	Tamarind plant driver	1
	Daily wage staff	
16.	Clerk	1
17.	Supervisor	9
18.	Light vehicle driver	3
19.	Peon-cum-watcher	27
20.	Cleaner	2
21.	Electrician	1
22.	Sweeper	1
	Total	162

Source : Pay Acquittance Roll of the AMCS, Tikabali, 1998-99.

The society has opened 84 procurement centres (permanent 7and seasonal) scattered all over the district to increase the collection work of the MFP and SAP. In order to store products, the AMCS, Tikabali has constructed 50 godowns at different procurement centres. For this purpose, the Government has also given financial assistance. Besides these, the AMCS has hired 74 godowns at different procurement centres. According to the quality of production, the number of hired godowns varies from year to year. The blockwise procurement centres of the society during 1998-99 is reflected in Table. 5.4. The blocks which are famous for procurement of MFPs are Raikaia, Phiringia, Baliguda, Daringibadi, Tumudibandha and Kotagarh. The Baliguda Forest Division includes all those blocks. Due to less density of forests in Boudh District, Kantamal, Harabhanga and Boudh blocks have least numbers of collection centres.

Block-wise Collection Centres and Fair Price Shops of the AMCS, Tikabali

*Minor Forest Produce (MFP)**

At the initial stage, the main item of procurement of the AMCS was turmeric. At that time it was known as "Turmeric Growers' Society". Later the business of the society was extended and it collected minor forest produce from the members and non-members. Till the year 1999-2000, the AMCS was the monopoly lease holder of the MFPs in the district of Boudh and Kondhmals. Different forest products such as siali plates, hill brooms, tamarind, mats, genduligum, markingnut, harida, bahara and anla are collected by the society under MFP items. Table 5.5 shows clearly the blockwise collection of MFP in the districts of Khandhamal and Boudh. It is depicted in the table that all the blocks in the scheduled areas of Kandhamal district have been collecting MFPs to a large extent. Although the AMCS, Tikabali deals in several items of MFP and SAP, the collection of siali plates is considered as a major item of procurement. During a year, for about 9 months, the siali plates are collected by the society. The members and non-members of the tribal

* The classification of forest produce into major and minor is basically made having regard to the revenue collection by the particular produce. Timber and Firewood are included in major forest produce. Other items of the forest are minor forest produce. The Forest Dept. has made such distinction because the revenue of the Government of Orissa is comparatively very low in connection with these items. But MFP is considered as a major source of income for the poor tribals. *Source:* Minor Forest produce—its role in the life of tribals—"A case study", Tribal Research and Training Institute, Pune, 1992, p. 14.6

Table—5.4 ***Block-wise procurement centres of the AMCS in 1998-99***

Sl. No.	*Name of the block*	*Name of the procurement centres*
1.	Tikabali	(i) Tikabali (ii) Paburia (iii) Risingia (iv) Gutingia (v) Bastingia (vi) Padangi
2.	G. Udayagiri	(i) G.Udayagiri (ii) Lingagarh (iii) Kalinga (iv) Kurmingia
3.	Raikia	(i) Manikeswar (ii) Shugadabadi (iii) Raikia (iv) Karada (v) Baraba (vi) Mandakia (vii) Indragada (viii) Gudrighasi (ix) Ranaba
4.	Chakapad	(i) Chakapad (ii) Shankarakhole (iii) Linepada (iv) Nidhiaberena (v) Kutrasingi (vi) Pairimala (vii) Chahali (viii) Nakidikia
5.	Phulbani	(i) Keridi (ii) Dadki (iii) Phulbani
6.	Khajuripada	(i) Khajuripada (ii) Sudrukumpa
7.	Phiringia	(i) Phiringia (ii) Balandapada (iii) Ratanga (iv) Nuapadar (v) Kelapada (vi) Kasinipadar (vii) Katapanga (viii) Gochhapada
8.	K. Nuagon	(i) K. Nuagon (ii) Gunjibadi (iii) Sarangada (iv) Chanchedi
9.	Daringibadi	(i) Daringibadi (ii) Simanbadi (iii) Badabanga (iv) Tilori (v) Jhinjiriguda (vi) Godapur (vii) Padasi (iv) Terabadi (x) Manipur (xi) Gumikia
10.	Baliguda	(i) Baliguda (ii) Bataguda (iii) Rutungia (iv) Budaguda (v) Barakhama (vi) Sudra
11.	Tumudibandha	(i) Tumudibandh (ii) Jhiripani (iii) Belaghar (iv) Guma (v) Kurtamgada (vi) Lankagada (vii) Bilamal (viii) Mandalpadar (ix) Pairamala (x) Dharinimaska (xi) Paramapanga
12.	Kotagarh	(i) Kotagarh (ii) Subarnagiri (iii) Sreerampur (iv) Sutaghati (v) Bandaka (vi) Laduri
13.	Harabhanga	(i) Charichhak (ii) Madhapur (iii) Adenigarh (iv) Badala (vi) Talagaon
14.	Kantamal	(i) Narayan Prasad
15.	Boudh	(i) Baghiapada
	Total	84 centres

Source : Annual Administrative Report of the AMCS, Tikabali, 1998-99 pp. 5-6.

Table—5.5 Block-wise collection of MFP in the districts of Kandhamal and Boudh by the AMCS

Sl. No.	*Name of the block*	*Name of the minor forest product procured*
1	Tikabali	Siali plates, Tamarind, Markingnut, Simulicotton, Mahua flowers, Sunari bark
2.	Chakapad	Siali plates, Marking nut, Genduligum
3.	G. Udayagiri	Siali plates, Tamarind
4.	Raikia	Siali plates, Tamarind, Mahua flower
5.	Phulbani	Mahua flower, Siali plates
6.	Khajuripada	Siali plates, Mahua flowers, Genguligum
7.	Baliguda	Siali plates, Tamaridn, Mats, Harida, Bahada, Honey wax, Sikaya, Sal resin, Siali fibre
8.	K. Nuagon	Siali plates, Mahua flower
9.	Daringibadi	Siali plates, Sal resin, Arrowroot, Mahua flower
10.	Phiringia	Siali plates, Tamarind, Genduligħum, Anla
11.	Tumudibandha	Siali leaves, Hill brooms, Mahua flowers, Marking nut, clearning nut.
12.	Kotagarh	Siali plates, Hill brooms, Lac, Cane, sal resin
13.	Harabhanga	Siali plates, Hill brooms, Marking nut, Cleaning nut, Siali fibre, Karanja seeds
14.	Kantamal	Mahua flower, Markingnut
15.	Boudh	Mahua flower

Source : Collection Registers of the procurement centres of the AMCS, Tikabali.

community get much benefit due to sale of siali plates to the Society. The reasonable fixed price received by the tribals by selling the siali plates to the society mostly supplements their income for earning livelihood in Kandhamal district.[65]

Siali Leaves (Bauhinia-vahlil)

Siali plant is a climber. Siali leaves are collected from this plant in different regions of Kandhamal district. If old leaves are collected from this plant, the new leaves grow. It is the special botanical character of this plant.[66] This plant is grown abundantly in the whole of the district of Kandhamal. Baliguda, Tumudibandh, Daringibadi, Raikia, G.Udaygiri, Phiringia and Tikabli blocks are well known for the preparation of good quality siali leaves. Generally the women of the tribal community in the district are engaged in plucking the siali leaves from the creepers. After seasoning the leaves with the help of sun-light, those are stitched by bamboo pins for the preparation of siali plates. These plates vary in size ranging from 12 inches to 18 inches in diameter. Each siali plate bundle contains 80 to 100 number of plates. The centre supervisors of the AMCS work at different collection centres and collect the siali plates from the tribal people at the approved rate fixed by the Government. The tribal families on an average get Rs. 100 to Rs. 120 every week by selling the siali plates to the society.[67] For the purpose of improving the quality and marketability of the plates, modern method of stitching is introduced in some areas. The siali plates of AMCS, Tikabali are sold in different states such as Orissa, Andhra Pradesh, Tamilnadu, Kerala, Maharastra and Rajasthan.[68]

Broom Grass (Thysanolaenamaxima)

Broom grass is mostly grown on the banks of forest streams in the mountains terraines.[69] Belghar, Kotagarh, Tumudibandh, Baliguda, Raikia, Kalinga, G.Udayagiri, Phulbani and Tikabali areas are famous for production of broom grass. The broom sticks are the flowers of this plant.[70] The collection of the broom sticks is a very difficult and dangerous task. The girls of the tribal community collect these flowers from the forest from January to April during the year. After collection, the flowers are dried in the sunlight on the next day. With the help of Siali fibres or plastic ropes, the broom sticks are bundled in size. For the purpose of better processing of broom sticks, the tribals are imparted training by the society to use modern techniques for improving the quality and marketability of the product. It is not only sold in different markets of Orissa but also is marketed outside Orissa such as Mumbai, Kolkata and Chennai. The ACMS, Tikabali had opened a sales branch at Mumbai for the growth of marketability of broom sticks. Now due to problems in management, the sales branch at Mumbai is closed and the broom sticks are sold in local markets of Orissa.

Tamarind (Tamarindus Indica)

The Tamarind trees are abundantly grown in Tikabali, G. Udayagari, Phiringia, Daringibadi, Tumudibandh, Phulbani, Khajuripada and Raikia Blocks in the district of Kandhamal. It is a self-grown plant which is found in waste lands, uplands and also roadsides throughout the tropical region.[71] Although tamarind is included in minor forest produce, it is not a forest tree.[72] During winter the dried fruits of the tree are plucked by the triabals and processed for consumption. Tamarind is an important condiment used as a sour ingredient in the Indian diet. It is collected from February to April during a year. The tamarind of Kandhmal is not only sold in different places of Orissa but also marketed outside the state namely Andhra Pradesh, Tamilandu, Maharastra etc. As the quality of product is very good, it is also exported to foreign countries like Iraq, Iran and Arabian countries.[73] For the purpose of export and preservation for a long period of time, tamarind is deseeded, defibred and processed. The AMCS, Tikabali procures an average of 7,000 quintals per annum which constitutes about 40 per cent market surplus of the districts.[74] In Kandhamal district, tamarind is also procured by some other agencies such as TDCC, FMCS and private traders.

Mats

In the river banks or water areas of the forests of Kandhamal and Boudh districts, a certain kind of wild grass is grown. Mats are produced by the reeds of such grass. During winter season, mat reeds are collected by the people of the tribal community in the district.[75] After seasoning the mat reeds in the sunlight, those are used for weaving mats of different designs. Mat reeds are abundantly grown in Baliguda and Tumudibandh areas of Kandhamal district. The mats are procured by the society in terms of pennals. A mat consists of some pennals. The breadth of one pennal is about ½" to 1. These products are generally produced in small scale and cottage industries and are mainly sold in neighbouring districts of Kandhamal.

Arrowroot

The botanical name of arrowroot is curcumaangustifolia. This commodity is included in MFP and is mainly found in Daringibadi, Kotagarh and Tumudibandh blocks. During rainy season, these roots are collected by the tribals in these blocks. A paste is produced by rubbing these roots on plain stones. After the filtration of the paste, the material is dried in the sun for about two weeks till it gets hard. The method of processing is a difficult task and tedious.[76] Arrowroot is sold in the market at a high price. It is used as a material for manufacturing biscuits in the biscuit industry. The product is also used as a diet for the sick persons.

Genduligum

In Kandhamal sub-division and Chakapad block of Balliguda sub-division, Genduli trees (starculiacuens) are found in large numbers. The tribals of the district make a hole on the tree and collect juice from it.[77] Then after processing properly, it is sold to the society. The gum is used as a raw material in plastic industries in our country. The product is also exported to some foreign countries and government gets large amount of foreign currencies. As the society has much bargaining power, Genduligum is sold to the private businessmen at a reasonable price. Selling of Genduligum is a profitable business for the tribals.

Markingnut

Markingnut(semacarpusanacardium) is a wild collection.[78] In the district of Kandhamal, the people of the tribal community pluck the fruits from the trees. They consume the fruits and sell the dried seeds to the AMCS. The seeds are used for various purposes. The liquid produced from these seeds is used for the preparation of a black colour. This colour is helpful for the protection of the body of the ship from water.[79] This black colour is also used in railways and handloom industries. The people in the tribal community use this colour for medicine and tattooing the body of females.[80]

In addition to those products, the society also procures some other minor forest produces like Sabai grass, Siali fibres, Sal resin, Mahua flower, Honey wax, Simuli cotton, Sikaya, Karanja sees, Harida, Bahada, Anla, Neem seeds etc., in Balliguda and Phulbani Sub-division of Kandhamal district and Harabhanga, Kantamal and Boudh of Boudh District. The tribals in the district get ample scope of self-employment opportunities due to collection and processing of minor forest produces. The Society also helps the tribals by providing necessary funds and training for proper collection and processing of MFPs in Kandhamal district.

Surplus Agricultural Produce (SAP)

The private traders deal with the SAPs. The businessmen of neighbouring districts come on migrating to Kandhamal district and settle there for carrying on business in the tribal belt of the district. They give loans to the tribals before harvesting season and make secret agreements for the establishment of trade relations with the innocent tribals.[81] Thus the private traders directly purchase the SAPs from the tribals and exploit them.

The AMCS, Tikabali, in the first year of its inception started the procurement and sale of turmeric in order to save the tribals from the clutches of the private traders and to provide them a remunerative price for their produce.[82] Now-a-days carrying on business in the SAPs is not an important activity of the society. In order to safeguard the economic interest of the tribals, the society deals in these products.[83] The collection of SAP in different blocks is shown in Table 5.6.

Table—5.6 Block-wise collection of SAPs by the AMCS in the districts of Kandhamal and Boudh

Sl. No.	*Name of the block*	*Items of SAPs procured*
1.	Tikabali	Turmeric, Maize, Mahua seeds
2.	Chakapad	Greengram, Horsegram, Ragi
3.	Phulbani	Mahua seeds, Maize
4.	Phiringia	Maize, Turmeric, Mahua seeds
5.	Raikia	Niger, Mahua seeds, Turmeric, Hillgram
6.	G. Udayagiri	Mahua seeds, Turmeric, Mustard, Niger
7.	Nuagaon	Mahua seeds, Maize, Niger
8.	Khajuripada	Maize, Mahua seeds, Turmeric
9.	Balliguda	Mahua seeds, Blackgram, Hillgram, Horsegram, Mustard, Niger
10.	Daringibadi	Mustard, Turmeric, Niger, Maize, Mahua seeds, Blackgram, Horsegram
11.	Tumudibandh	Jawar, Niger, Turmeric
12.	Kotagarh	Maize, Mustard, Ragi, Blackgram, Jawar
13.	Harbhanga	Blackgram, Greengram, Horsegram, Maize
14.	Kantamal	Mahua seeds, Millets, Maize, Ragi
15.	Boudh	Mustard, Maize, Ragi, Minor Millets

Source : Centre-wise collection Register of the AMCS, Tikabaili, 1991-92.

Table 5.6 reveals that in different blocks of the district of Kandhamal and Boudh, turmeric is one of the important items of procurement of the society.

At present the amount of collection of turmeric by the society is much less than the previous years. Mustard, millets, niger seeds, blackgram, hillgram, ragi, jowar etc. are some other important items of procurement of AMCS.

Mustard (Brassica Juncea)

The high and medium lands of Kandhamal district are suitable for the cultivation of the mustard. It is extensively cultivated in the district[84]. Mustard is not only used as a condiment but also used as an edible oil. Out of the total mustard cultivated area in the state, nearly 15 per cent area lies in the district.[85] Due to poor red laterite soil and red sandy soil, the yield of mustard per hectare is much less in comparison with other districts. The tribals in the district sell mustard immediately after harvest during Feburary to April. The AMCS procures mustard at reasonable price. As mustard oil cake contains 5.7 per cent nitrogen, it is mainly used as cattle feed. The climatic conditions in the tribal areas of the district is also congenial of the cultivation of this crop.[86] So the tribals are given different incentives for the production of mustard in order to increase their standard of living.

Millets (Eleusinecoracane)

Millet is used by the tribals as an important food item. It is known as coarse grains.[87] The production of the crop has much importance on the agricultural economy of the tribals. Millet is a quick growing and drought resisting nutritious foodgain.[88] It is cultivated in Tikabali, Raikia, Baliguda, Kotagarh and Phulbani in Kandhamal district and Boudh block of Boudh district. As the amount of production of ragi, bazra and smell millets in the district is relatively low, marketable surplus is quite less. Most of these crops are procured by TDCC and AMCS, Tikabali.

Niger (Guiztiaabyssinica)

Niger is an oilseed and is considered as a minor cash crop in Orissa. For the cultivation of this crop, Light and Red solid are suitable. It is also cultivated in rough, rocky and laterite soil on hill tops and slopes.[89] As a mixed crop, it is cultivated mostly with ragi, minor millets and pulses. As a Khariff crop it is harvested during November and December. After harvesting, the tribals sell the crop in the market. Generally the merchants of rural areas deal in this product. The crop is mostly cultivated in Baliguda and Tikabali blocks.[90] Niger is used for the production of oil and oil cakes. The AMCS, Tikabali procures the product at different collection centres. It is sold in Andhra Pradesh, West Bengal, Tamilnadu and Karnantaka.[91] For the plantation of coffee, the by-products of nigers are used as manures.

Turmeric (Curcuma Longa)

Turmeric is an important cash crop. It is mostly cultivated by the tribals in rainfed highlands at an altitude of 4000 feet from the sea level.[92] In Kandhamal district, the tribals cultivate this crop on the hill tops. They practise shifting (podu) cultivation for the production of turmeric. The red laterite soil is generally preferred for the cultivation of this crop. In Kandhamal district, Baliguda, G. Udayagiri, Raikai, Khajuripada and Tikabali blacks are famous for the cultivation of this crop. Out of the total production of turmeric in the state, nearly 50 per cent of the product is produced in Kandhamal district.[93]

The cultivation of this crop is labour-intensive. Its cultivation involves many difficult time-consuming process. After harvesting crop, it is cleaned-boiled, dried and polished for the purpose of improving the quality.[94] Turmeric is not only used in different festivals and auspicious functions but also is required in textile industries. It has also much medicinal value. In Khandamal district, turmeric is purchased by different organisations such as TDCC, RCMS and LAMPS.[95] The quality of the product is of high standard and is demanded in markets of foreign countries such as U.S.A., U.K., Singapore, Sri Lanka and South Africa.[96]

Marketing Operation

The AMCS was selling MFP and SAP to the private traders at its head office situated at Tikabali up to the year 1962. But after the establishment of a big sales centre at Berhampur, 128 kms. away from its head office, and an important commercial centre in Southern Orissa, the AMCS sells its products at this centre. The society has a large godwon at Berhampur to keep plenty of stock of MFP and SAP for quick transportation to different places situated inside and outside the state with the help of railways. The AMCS sells these products to the private traders at a higher price at the time of favourable marketing conditions. The State Tribal Development Co-operative Corporation also purchases these products from the society on agreed terms and conditions. For the prupose of marketing the products at reasonable price, the AMC always keeps a close contact with the traders inside and outside the state to exploit the favourable business opportunities.

Fair Price Shop

The AMCS also renders service to the tribals in Kandhamal district by opening fair price shops at different places such as Belghar, Lankgada, Jhirpani, Guma, Tikabali and Daringibadi. Different essential consumer goods, kerosene, stationeries, controlled cloth etc. are supplied to the members of the society at a reasonable price in these fair price shops.

REFERENCES

1. Rath Sibram, Evaluation of the Role of AMCS, Tikabali in Marketing Minor Forest Produces, Report on AMCS, 1992, p. 9.
2. Kansal A.P., "Success Story of the AMCS, Tikabali, Rainbow", Bhubaneswar: Orissa Co-operative Union 1983, p. 1.
3. Rath Sibram, *op cit*, pp. 4-5.
4. Kansal A.P. *op. cit*. p. 2.
5. "Audit Report of the 'Turmeric Growers Society, Tikabali for the year 1947-48", p. 1.
6. Kansal, A.P., *op. cit*., p. 2.
7. *Ibid*.
8. *Ibid*.
9. "Audit Reports", Tikabali *op. cit*., 1948, p. 2.
10. "Evaluation Report of the Role of AMCS", Rath S, pp.9-10.
11. *Ibid*, p. 2.
12. "Report of the Working of the Co-operative Society in Orissa", Government of Orissa, 1952, pp. 42-43.
13. Rath S, *op. cit*., p. 31.
14. *Ibid*, p. 10.
15. Rath S, *op. cit*., p. 15.
16. Rath, S, *op. cit*., pp. 14-15.
17. Kansal, A.P., "Success Story of AMCS Ltd., Tikabali", pp. 3-4.
18. Rath S., *op. cit*., p. 9.
19. "Annual Report on the Working of the Co-operative Societies in Orissa", 1950-51, Government of Orissa, 1958, Chapter-vii, p. 28.
20. *Ibid* pp. 28-29.
21. "Bye-Laws of the Agency Marketing Co-operative Society Ltd. Tikabali", 1952, p. 1.

22. Annual Report on the Working of the Co-operative Societies in Orissa, *op. cit*, 1953, p. 29.
23. "Final Audit Report of AMCS, Tikabali", 1957, p.1.
24. Rath S, *op. cit.*, p. 7, 25.
25. Final Audit Report of AMCS, Tikabali, 1957-58, p. 1.
26. *Ibid.*
27. *Ibid.*
28. "Annual Report on the Working of Co-operative Society in the State of Orissa", 1958, Cuttack, 1962, p. 66.
29. "Final Audit Report of the AMCS, Tikabali", 1958.
30. Kansal, A.P., op. cit, pp. 8-9.
31. Annual Report of the Working of Co-operative Society, Orissa, *op, cit.*, p. 66.
32. "Evaluating of the Role of the AMCS, Tikabali", Rath S, *op. cit.*, pp. 27-28.
33. Annual Report on the Working of Co-operative Society, Orissa, 1957-58, pp. 66-67.
34. Annual Report on the Working of the Co-operative Society, Orissa, 1961-62, pp. 55.
35. Rath S., *op. cit*, p.15.
36. *Ibid.*, p. 16.
37. *Ibid.*, p. 15.
38. *Ibid.*, p. 15
39. "Final Audit Report of AMCS, Tikabali, 1973.
40. Rath S., *op.cit.*, p. 16.
41. Annual Administrative Report of AMCS, Tikabali, 1982-83, p. 3.
42. *Ibid.*
43. *Ibid.*
44. "Statistics in Co-operatives", 1992-93, Government of Orissa, Bhubaneswar, p. 57.
45. "Bye-laws of the Agency Marketing Co-operative Society, Tikabali, 1952, p. 1.
46. "Final Audit Report of the AMCS, Tikabali for the Year 1947", p. 1.
47. "Annual Administration Report", 1998-99, AMCS, Tikabali, p. 2.
48. Bye-laws of AMCS, Tikabali, 1952," pp. 2-3.
49. The Bye-laws of the AMCS, Tikabali, *op. cit.*, p-3.
50. *Ibid.*

51. *Ibid*.
52. *Ibid*.
53. *Ibid*, p. 4.
54. "The Bye-laws of AMCS, Tikabali".
55. Annual Administrative Report, the AMCS, Tikabali.
56. "Orissa Co-operative Society Act", 1962, Orissa Law Times and Orissa Co-operative Society Rule of 1965, 1966, p. 2.
57. "The Bye-laws of AMCS", Tikabali, p. 8.
58. *Ibid*, pp. 8-9.
59. *Ibid*., pp. 10-11.
60. "The Bye-laws of AMCS", Tikabali, p. 11.
61. *Ibid*, p. 4.
62. *Ibid*, p. 5.
63. *Ibid*, pp. 6-7.
64. "Evaluation Report of the Marketing of MFP", Rath S. *op.cit*, p. 18.
65. "Survey Report of the ARCS Office, Phubani, Co-operative Circle, Phulbani, 1993.
66. Pattnaik, H.K., "Revised Working Plan for the Reserved Forest of the Ghumsur North Division", 1970-71 to 1998-90, Section-II, p. 408.
67. Rath S. "Evaluation of the Role of AMCS in Marketing Minor Forest Products", p. 23
68. *Ibid*., p. 19.
69. "The Wealth of India (Natural Resources)", CSIR, New Delhi, Vol-VII, 1959, p. 268.
70. Pattnaik, H.K, *op.cit*., p. 408.
71. Mishra, H.K, "Working Plan for the Reserved Forest of Baliguda Division", Working Plan Circle, Berhampur, 1981, pp. 269-271.
72. "Market Study Report", No. 5, TDCC, Orissa, Bhubaneswar, 1977, p. 1.
73. *Ibid*, p. 16.
74. Rath S., *op.cit*., p. 33.
75. Rath S., *op.cit*., p. 33
76. *Ibid*, p. 35.
77. Patnaik, H.K., *op. cit*. Section - II, p. 414
78. "Performance Report of the ACMS", 1986-87, p. 15.
79. Mishra, H.K. *op. cit*., p. 272.
80. Rath S., *op.cit*., p. 29.

81. "Success story of the AMCS, Tikabali", *op. cit.*, pp. 4-5.
82. *Ibid.*
83. "Annual Audit Report of the AMCS", 1989-90, pp. 1-3.
84. "Agriculture Information Diary", *op. cit.*
85. "Market Study Report", No. 8, *op. cit.* pp. 3-4.
86. "District Credit Plan", 1974-75, Boudh Kandhamals, pp. 25-27.
87. "The Wealth of India", CSIR, 1952, Vol. III, pp. 169-170.
88. Market Study Reports", No. 3, 1976, p. 5
89. "Market Study Reports", No. 3, 1976, p. 5
90. "Agricultural Information Diary", Office of the ADAO, Phulbani, 1992-93.
91. "Market Study Report", *op. cit.* p.4.
92. Market Study Report", No. 2, TDCC, 1976, pp. 1-2.
93. *Ibid.*
94. Palo, R.N., "Tribal Development Fostered Through AMCS, Tikabali", p. 240.
95. "Market Study Report", No.2, *op.cit.*, pp. 8-10.
96. *Ibid.*

6

Marketing of Minor Forest Produce and Surplus Agricultural Produce : An Analysis

Introduction

Marketing of Minor Forest Produce (MFP) and Surplus Agricultural Produce (SAP) is an important factor which need due consideration for economic growth of tribals and others of Kandhamal district.

This chapter deals with the marketing of MFP and SAP from 1991-92 to 1999-2000 in Kandhamal district under the leadership of Agency Marketing Co-operative Society (AMCS), Tikabali and under the new policy of the Government of Orissa (Appendix-II) For the purpose of study, 1000 sample respondents of Kandhamal district are taken into consideration. This chapter tries to examine from various angles, the positive steps taken by AMCS for marketing of MFP and SAP and also the steps taken by the Panchayats to appoint the agents under new government policy to meet the requirements of the poor tribals in Kandhamal district of Orissa.

Marketing of MFP and SAP according to the Land Holding Pattern

Out of 1,000 sample respondents, 500 respondents are taken from MFP and the rest 500 respondents are taken from SAP for analysis, which is illustrated in Table.6.1 and in Diagram No.6.1.

Table—6.1 Marketing of MFP and SAP according to the land holding pattern

Sl. No.	*Land holding*	*MFP*	*SAP*	*Total*
1.	Upto 1 acre	169	21	190
2.	1 acre-2 acres	123	34	157
3.	2 acres - 3 acres	92	59	151
4.	3 acres-4 acres	56	97	153
5.	4 acres-5 acres	37	126	163
6.	5 acres and above	23	163	186
	Total	500	500	1000

Source : Compiled from the questionnaires.

Diagram—6.1
Marketing of MFP and SAP According to Land Holding Pattern

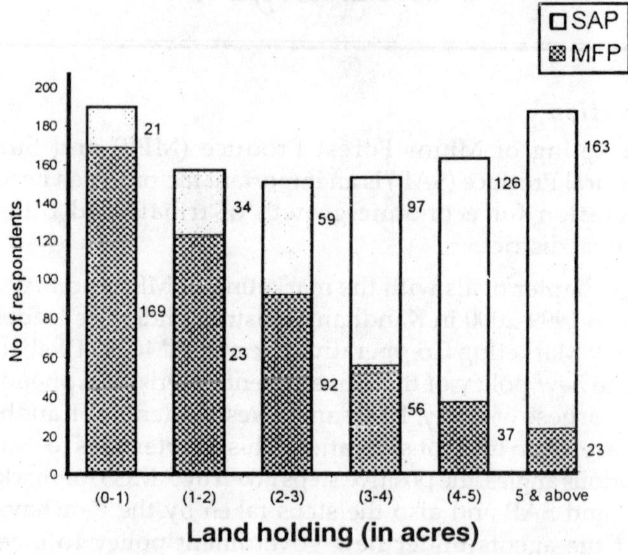

The land holding pattern of the people of Kandhamal is classified into six categories. It is clear from table 6.1 that the people of Kandhamal who hold less/no land i.e. agricultural labourers and marginal farmers are engaged in procurement and marketing of MFP to AMCS, Tikabali. But the people who have more land i.e. the small, medium and big farmers are mostly engaged in marketing of SAP's to the society. Table 6.1 shows that 169 tribals and others who own up to one acre of land collect MFP and sell to the society. But when land holding of the respondent is more i.e. 5 acres and above, 23 persons or 4.6 per cent sample respondents come forward to sell the MFP at AMCS, Tikabali. The study shows that 163 i.e. 32.6 per cent respondents coming under this category come forward to sell agricultural produce to the society. But when land holding pattern decreases, the supply of SAP by the respondents decrease and vice versa. This is because the persons who do not have land or own small piece of land mostly collect MFP from the forest area, and sell these products at AMCS, Tikabali. But the persons who possess land, instead of collecting MFP, produce agricultural products and sell them at AMCS collection centres.

Marketing on the Basis of Illiteracy/Literacy

The sample individuals of Kandhamal have been divided into two categories—illiterates and literates. The persons approach the AMCS, Tikabali with their produce according to their educational qualification is illustrated in the table 6.2. and diagram no.-6.2.

Table—6.2 Respondents approaching the procurement centres of AMCS, Tikabali according to qualification

Sl. No.	*Qualification*	*No. of persons*	*Percentages*
1.	Illiterate	462	46.2
2.	Upto Class-III	242	24.2
3.	Class II to V	166	16.6
4.	Class V to VII	78	7.8
5.	Class VII to X	30	3.0
6.	Class X to XII	16	1.6
7.	Class XII to Graduation	06	0.6
8.	Beyond graduation	—	—
	Total	1000	100%

Source : Compiled from questionnaires.

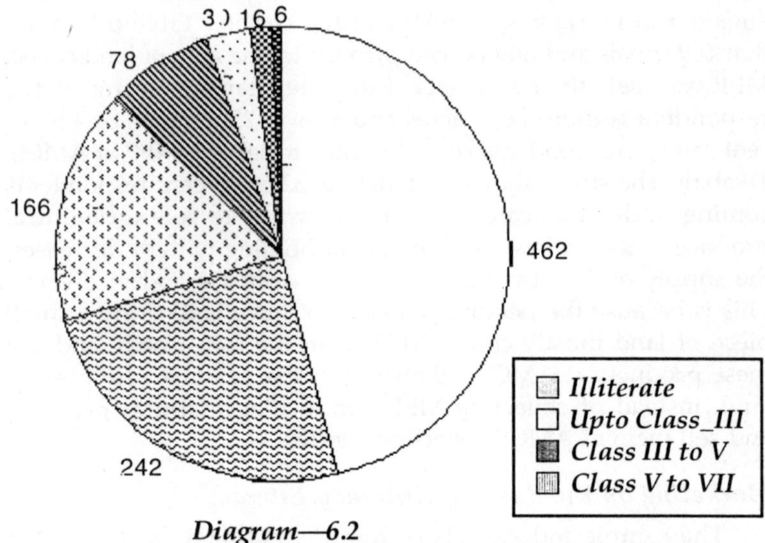

Diagram—6.2

Respondents approaching the procurement centres of AMCS, Tikabali according to qualification.

Table-6.2 reveals that out of 1000 sample individuals, 462 (46.2%) are illiterates and rest 538 (53.8%) are literates. The literates are further divided into seven categories, starting from up to class III to graduation level. No sample individual has crossed his educational qualification beyond graduation. From the table it is clear that, when educational qualification increases, the persons hesitate to approach the marketing centre for marketing of their products and vice-versa. The persons whose qualification is below standard III, approach the marketing centres 242 in number, but when their qualifications come to +2 level or more, only six persons approach the marketing centres with their produce for marketing. So it is presumed that the qualified persons are very much prestige conscious about their qualification and hesitate to approach the AMCS, Tikabali with their produce.

Marketing of Produce according to Caste

The sample individuals of study district are divided into four categories such as General, Scheduled Caste, Scheduled Tribe and Other Backward Caste. Their share in marketing of produce both MFP and SAP at AMCS, Tikabali is explained in Table. 6.3 and Diagram No. 6.3.

Table—6.3 Approach made by the sample individuals to AMCS procurement centres according to their caste

Sl. No.	*According to caste*	*No. of persons*	*Percentage to total*
1.	Scheduled Tribe	462	46.2
2.	Schedule Caste	342	34.2
3.	Other Backward Caste	118	11.8
4.	General	78	7.8
	Total	1000	100%

Source : Compiled from questionnaires.

Diagram—6.3
Approach made by the sample individuals to AMCS procurement centre according to their caste

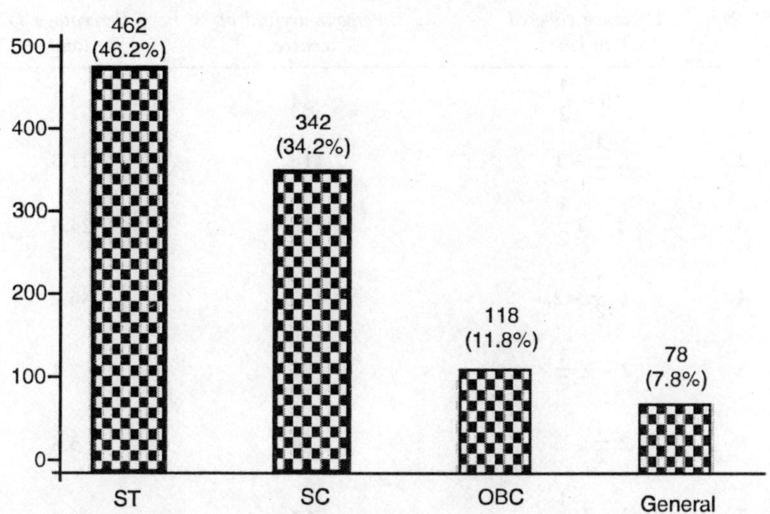

Out of 1000 sample persons of Kandhamal district, 462 are ST, 342 are S.C., 118 are other backward caste and rest 78 General category. The ST and SC both contribute 80.4 per cent of total sample individuals and other two categories (OBC + General caste) contribute only 19.6 per cent of the sample individuals. As the other backward caste people and general caste persons are engaged in other activities, they do not give much importance for collection of minor forest produce; so they are less in number.

Distance Covered by MFP and SAP Respondents at AMCS Tikabali and Other Collection Centres.

The AMCS, Tikabali collects minor forest produce and surplus Agricultural produce from the persons on different days at different centres located in different blocks/panchayats and also at AMCS, Tikabali. To approach the collection centres, the sample respondents have to cover some distance for marketing their produce. So the distance covered by them divided into eight categories, starting from 0- ½ km to 3½ kms. and above. The distance (as per km) covered by the sample individuals of Kandhamal district to sell their produce at different marketing centres are explained in the Table. 6.4.

Table—6.4 Distance covered by sample individuals for disposal of MFP and SAP at collection centres opened by AMCS, Tikabali

Sl. No.	*Distance covered in km*	*Persons arrived at centre*	*Percentage to total*
1	$0 - \frac{1}{2}$	34	3.4
2	$\frac{1}{2} - 1$	118	11.8
3	$1 - 1\frac{1}{2}$	246	24.6
4	$1\frac{1}{2} - 2$	362	36.2
5	$2 - 2\frac{1}{2}$	74	7.4
6	$2\frac{1}{2} - 3$	58	5.8
7	$3 - 3\frac{1}{2}$	64	6.4
8	$3\frac{1}{2}$ – and above	44	4.4
	Total	1000	100%

Source : Compiled from the questionnaires.

Table 6.4 reveals that out of the 1000 samples, 608 (60.8%) individuals cover a distance of 1 km. to 2 kms. to approach AMCS for selling their produce. There are only 34 individuals who cover a maximum distance of ½ kms while 108 individuals cover a distance ranging from 3 kms. and above for the purpose. Thus it is clear from the table that the most of the collection centres are situated within a radius of 2 kms.

Approaching the Procurement Centres According to Age Group

The tribals and others approach the AMCS, Tikabali and its recognised procurement centres to sell their produce according to the age group are explained in table. 6.5.

Table 6.5 shows that out of 1000 sample individuals, 848 are females and rest are males. So it is clear that the females mostly visit the procurement centres to sell the produce. The tribals and others in the age group of 10-20, 20-30 and 30-40 mostly visit the procurement centres established by AMCS, Tikabali in the district of Kandhamal. These age groups account for 380, 212 and 136 individuals. Out of 1000 sample persons, the above age groups constitute 728 (72.8 per cent) and rest 272 (27.2 per cent) persons are of the age group of 40 years and above. This is because mostly young aged women come to the centres for marketing of their produce than other age groups of females.

Table—6.5 Age-wise approaching the AMCS and collection centres by the sample respondents

Sl. No.	*Age (years)*	*Males*	*Females*	*Total*	*Percentage to total*
1.	Less than 10	24	72	96	9.6
2.	10-20	54	326	380	38.0
3.	20-30	28	184	212	21.2
4.	30-40	22	114	136	13.6
5.	40-50	16	82	98	9.8
6.	50-60	08	44	52	5.2
7	60 and above	--	26	26	2.6

Source : Compiled from questionnaires.

Approaching of the Sample Tribals and Others at Collection Centres in Different Blocks of Kandhamal District

The sample tribals and others approach at the collection centres opened by AMCS, Tikabali in different blocks of the district are explained in table 6.6.

Table—6.6 Blockwise approaching of sample triabls and others at collection centres

Sl. No.	*Name of the Blocks*	*Persons approaching the centres in blocks*	*Percentage to total*
1.	Tikabali	281	28.1
2.	G.Udayagiri	63	6.3
3.	Raikia	93	9.3
4.	Chakapad	58	5.8
5.	Phulbani	39	3.9
6.	Khajuripada	22	2.2
7.	Phiringia	24	2.4
8.	Nuagaon	26	2.6
9.	Daringibadi	112	11.2
10.	Baliguda	42	4.2
11.	Tumudibandh	174	17.4
12.	Kotagarh	66	6.6
	Total	1000	100%

Source : Compiled from the questionnaires.

Marketing of Minor Forest Produce and Surplus Agricultural Produce

Tribals and others of sample district generally arrive at the AMCS, Tikabali, and other marketing centres with minor forest produce and surplus agricultural produce. Analysis has been made to find out how many sample individuals come to the centres with SAP and MFP is explained in table 6.7 and diagram no. 6.4.

From the above table 6.6, out of 1000 sample respondents, 392(39.2%) of Tikabali block approach the AMCS centres to sell their products because AMCS is located in their block. In Raikia block, there are 9 collection centres. Daringibadi block has 10 collection centres and Tumundibandh block has 11 collection centres. So the approaches made by the persons are highest in three blocks.

Diagram—6.4
Arrival of Sample Individuals at AMCS Centres to Cell MFP and SAP

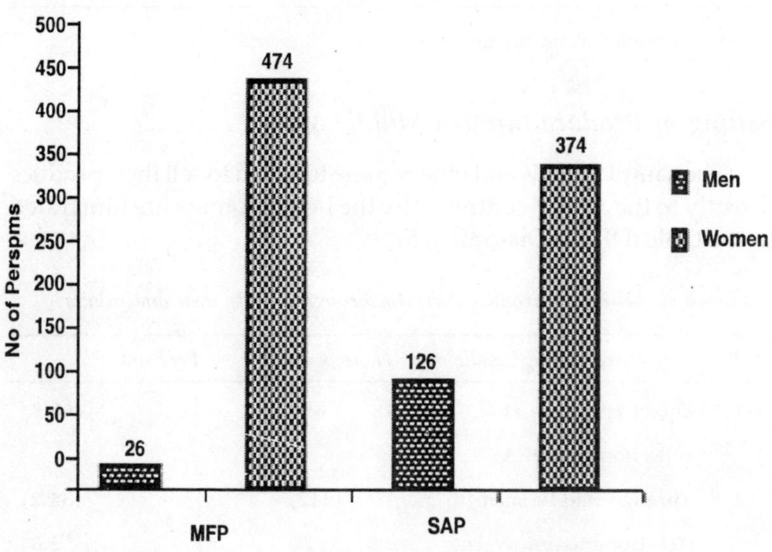

From table. 6.7 it is clear that out of 1000 samples persons only 152 men (15.2 per cent) approach the centres for marketing of their produce. Out of 152 men, 126 men approach with SAP and rest 26 with MFP. Similarly out of 848 women, 474 women approach with MFP and rest 374 women approach with SAP. So women approach less with SAP and more with MFP.

Table—6.7 Arrival of sample individuals at AMCS centres to sell MFP and SAP

Sl. No.	*Items*	*Men*	*Women*	*Total*
1.	Minor Forest Produce (MFP)	26	474	500
2.	Surplus Agricultural Produce (SAP)	126	374	5000
	Total	152	848	1000

Source : Compiled from the questionnaires.

Selling of Produce through Middle Men

The sample tribals and others come forward to sell their produce directly to the AMCS centres or by the help of others are illustrated in the table 6.8 and Diagram 6.5.

Table—6.8 Selling of produce directly/through middle men and others

Sl. No.	*Direct selling/middle men*	*No of persons*	*Percentage*
1.	Direct approach at collection centre (A)	658	65.8
2.	Through middle men (B)	(342)	(34.2)
	(i) Commission Agent	26	2.6
	(ii) Village Head (Mukheea)	102	10.2
	(iii) Ward Members	56	5.6
	(iv) Co-operative staff	124	12.4
	(v) Others	34	3.4
	Total A + B	1000	100%

Source : Compiled from the questionnaires

Diagram—6.5
Selling of produce directly/through middle men and others

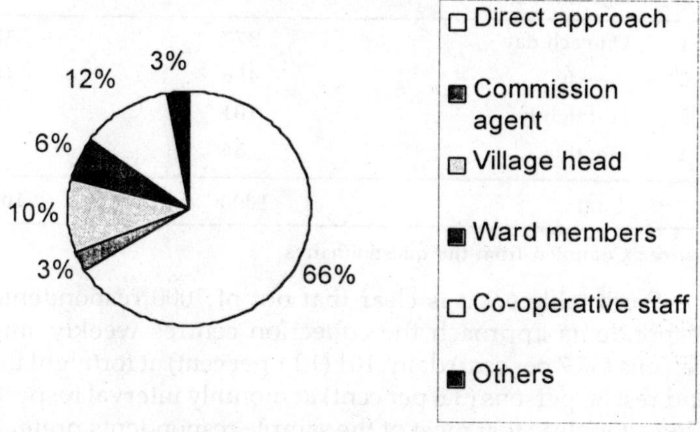

The tribals and others approach the marketing centres directly or being influenced by middle men and others. The table 6.8 reveals that out of 1000 sample persons, 658 (65.8 per cent) approach the AMCS Tikabali/organised centres directly without taking the help of others. But only 342 (34.2 per cent) approach the centres being influenced by the middle men. Commission agents, villages heads, ward members, co-operative staff and others (friends, relatives etc.) come into the fold of middlemen. To Co-operative staff i.e. the staff of AMCS and village head (Mukheea) both influence 226 persons to approach the marketing centres (out of 342 persons). From the table it is clear that the sample tribals and others are not mostly influenced by the middle men or the middle men do not come forward to induce them to sell their produce at co-operative centres, because they will do not get any benefit out of this.

Approaching the Marketing Centres at Different Time Interval

The sample respondents of Kandhamal district approach the AMCS collection centres daily, weekly, fortnightly and monthly gap to sell their produce are illustrated in table 6.9 and diagram 6.6

Table—6.9 Sample respondent's approach the AMCS collection centres to sell their produce at different time interval

Sl. No.	Approaching the centre at different time	No. of persons	Percentage to total
1.	On each day	377	37.7
2.	Weekly	486	48.6
3.	Fortnightly	101	10.1
4.	Monthly	36	3.6
	Total	1000	100

Source : Compiled from the questionnaires

From table 6.9 it is clear that out of 1000 respondents, 486 respondents approach the collection centres weekly, and 377 persons (37.7 per cent) daily, 101 (10.1 per cent) at fortnight interval and rest 36 persons (3.6 per cent) at monthly interval respectively. Thus, it is clear that most of the sample respondents prefer to sell their produce weekly on the days of weekly markets.

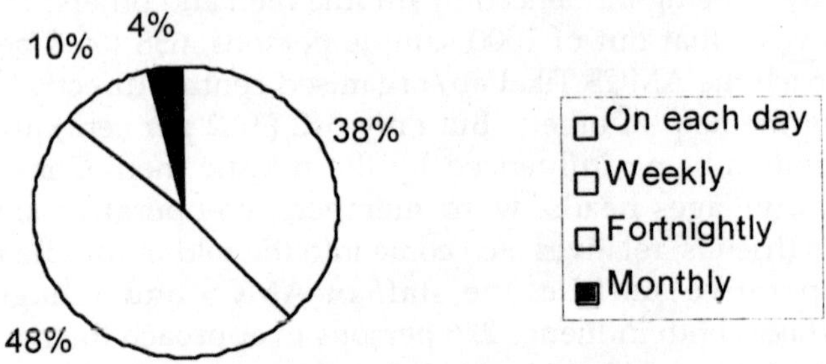

Diagram—6.6
Sample respondents' approach AMCS collection centres to sell their produce at different time interval

Mode of Transport Availed by the Sample Individuals to Approach the Marketing Centres

The tribals and others of the sample district approach the AMCS Tikabali and its procurement centres by some mode of transport. The mode availed by them are illustrated in table 6.10 and in diagram no. 6.7.

Total—6.10 Mode of transport availed by the tribals/others to attend the collection centres of AMCS, Tikabali

Sl. No.	*Mode of transport*	*No. of tribals/ others*	*Percentage to total*
1.	Walking	673	67.3
2.	Bullock Cart	72	7.2
3.	Bicycle	129	12.9
4.	Trolley	07	0.7
5.	Rickshaw	29	2.9
6.	Mini-Bus & other motor driven	72	7.2
7.	Other Mode	18	1.8
	Total	1000	100

Source : Compiled from the questionnaires

Diagram 6.7
Mode of transport availed by the tribals/others to attend the collection centres of AMCS, Tikabali

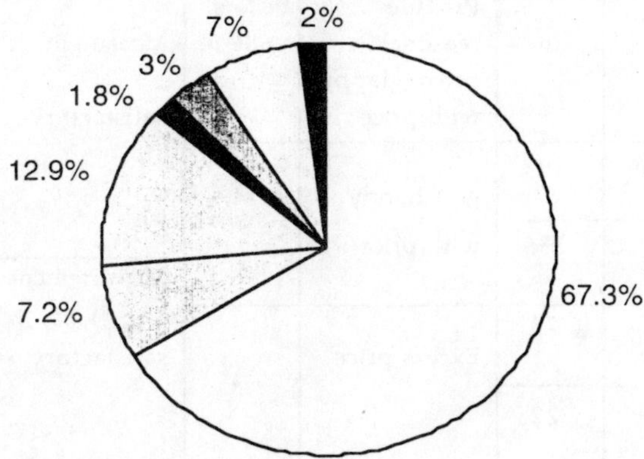

According to table 6.10, it is found that the sample individuals approach the marketing centres mostly by walking. They carry their produce on their head and go to the centre to sell the produce. Out of 1000 sample persons, 673 (67.3 per cent) use walking as their main mode of transport. Bicycle occupies second mode of transport of sample individuals. As many as 129 persons use by-cycle as mode of their transport . Mini Bus and other motor driven vehicles occupy third position in the mode of transport. Saventy-two persons use this as their mode of transport. Due to inadequate transport facilities and poverty of the sample individuals are poor in character, they usually prefer walking.

Payment Style of AMCS, Tikabali to the Sellers of MFP and SAP

When products which are delivered at AMCS, Tikabali and its procurement centres, the personnel of the society keep them after proper measurement and pay the price as fixed for each produce. They first give slips to the sellers about their quantity of produce and the payment is made according to the money available at that time. After receiving all the produces from the sellers, they at last start payment. The style of payment and the reaction of sellers are illustrated in table 6.11.

Table—6.11 Payment style of AMCS, Tikabali to the sample sellers of MFP and SAP of Kandhamal district

<table>
<tr><th>Payment style</th><th>No. of sellers</th><th colspan="2">Does AMCS provide reasonable price?</th><th colspan="2">Measurement made by AMCS</th></tr>
<tr><td>Payment made on the same day</td><td>467</td><td>Provide reasonable price/Happy with price</td><td>Sellers 886</td><td rowspan="2">Measurement is satisfactory</td><td rowspan="2">Sellers 918</td></tr>
<tr><td>Within two days</td><td>102</td><td rowspan="2">Not happy with price</td><td rowspan="2">114</td></tr>
<tr><td>Within 7 days</td><td>336</td><td rowspan="3">Measurement is not satisfactory</td><td rowspan="3">82</td></tr>
<tr><td>Within 15 days</td><td>73</td><td rowspan="2">Excess price</td><td rowspan="2">--</td></tr>
<tr><td>Within one month</td><td>22</td></tr>
<tr><td>Total</td><td>1000</td><td></td><td>1000</td><td></td><td>1000</td></tr>
</table>

Source: Compiled from the questionnaires

Table 6.11 reveals that out of 1000 sample respondents, 467 sellers of MFP and SAP get their price of the produce on the same day. But 336 persons (33.6 per cent) are able to get their price within 7 days. 102 sample individuals get their price within two days. The personnel of AMCS, personnel pay the cost of the produce at reasonable price fixed by the Government. So out of 100 respondents sample, 886 persons are happy with the price and rest 114 individuals are not happy with the price paid by the AMCS. Similarly, out of 1000 individuals, 918 sample sellers are happy with the measurement done by the personnel of AMCS and 82 are not happy with the measurement. So overall performance of AMCS, Tikabali is satisfactory.

Amount Spent by the Sellers at Marketing Centres to Get Early Payment

To get early payment after the delivery of the products at procurement centres of AMCS Tikabali, whether the sellers are giving any commission to the personnel of AMCS and others are examined in table 6.12.

Out of 1000 respondents, 937 (93.7 per cent) do not spend any amount to get their payment in reasonable time, but 63 sample respondents (6.3 per cent) spend some amount at different levels as mentioned in table 6.12 to receive sale proceeds early.

Table—6.12 Payment of expenses by the sellers of MFP and SAP at marketing centres to get early payment

Amount paid by the sellers to get early payment	*No. of persons*	*Any misbehaviour to sellers made by AMCS personnel at the time of payment*	
A. 1. AMCS personnel	12	(A) yes	(B) No
2. Village Heads	04		
3. Middle Men	27		
4. Friends & relatives	13	22	978
5. Others	07		
B. Not paid to any persons	937		
Total A + B =	1000	Total = A + B = 1000	

Source : Compiled from the questionnaires

Source of Income of Sample Respondents

The sample tribals and others mostly depend on minor forest produce and on agricultural produce. The source of income of sample respondents are illustrated in table. 6.13 and in diagram-6.8.

Table—6.13 Income of sample respondents under different heads.

Sl. No.	*Family income on different items*	*Persons*	*Percentage to total*
1.	Agriculture	302	30.2
2.	Industry	15	1.5
3.	Wages/Salary	223	22.3
4.	Selling forest produce	387	38.7
5.	Any other sources	83	8.3
	Total	1000	100

Source : Compiled from the questionnaires.

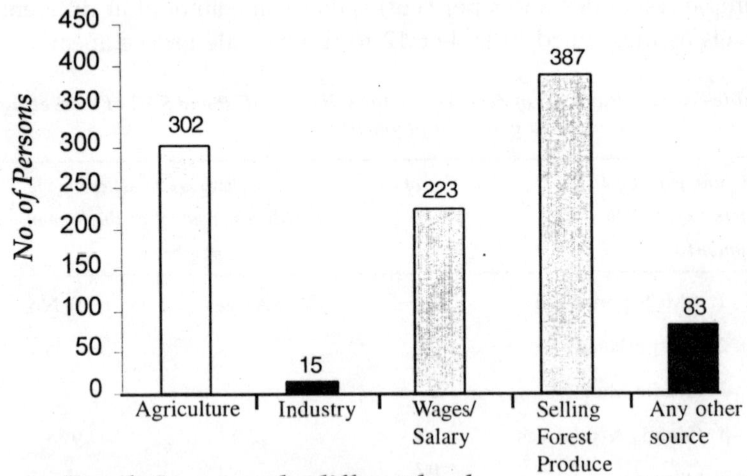

Family Income under different heads

Diagram—6.8
Income of sample respondents under different heads

Though most of the sample respondents sell MFP and SAP, they also depend on other sources of income which are illustrated in the table 6.13. From this Table it is clear that 689 sample individuals (68.9 per cent) depend on agriculture and forest produce and rest 311 (31.1 per cent) persons depend on other sources.

Borrowing from Different Institutions

The sample beneficiaries borrow loan from the banking institutions and non-banking institutions for procurement/ production of MFP and SAP as illustrated in table 6.14 and in diagram no. 6.9.

Table—6.14 *Borrowing by the sample individuals from the institution and non-institutional agencies.*

Sl. No.	*Different banks*	*Persons borrowed*	*Persons not taken any loan*
1.	Commercial banks	118	
2.	RRBs	122	
3.	AMCS	102	
4.	Co-operative banks	87	59
5.	Non-institutional Agencies	512	
	Total	941	+59 = 1000

Source : Compiled for the questionnaires.

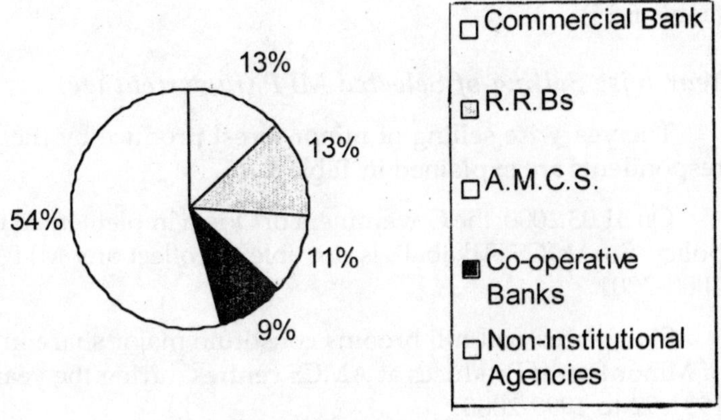

Diagram—6.9
Borrowing by sample individuals from the institutional and non-institutional agencies

Out of 1000 sample respondents, 941 (94.1 per cent) of them have taken loan from different agencies. Out of these 941 respondents, 512 have taken loan from non-institutional agencies and rest 429 have taken loan from institutional agencies. Only 59 persons have not taken any loan from any agencies. Thus it is clear that most of the sample respondents depend on non-institutional source of finance to carry out their operations.

Year-wise Selling of SAP (in percentage)

A period of ten years from 1991-92 to 2000-2001 has been taken for the purpose of the study. The AMCS collect the produce from the tribals and other sellers of the district Kandhamal and sell the same at different marketing centres of the state. This importance is measured in percentage. This is illustrated in table 6.15.

Turmeric, ginger and mustard are most important surplus agricultural produces of the people of Kandhamal. But, from year to year, the importance of ginger has been reduced due to less demand and lack of cold storage facility. Ginger cannot be stored for longer periods. Blackgram and Ragi have taken their place in case of ginger. In the year 1998-99 turmeric, mustard, blackgram and rasi constitute 93 per cent of total agricultural produce. (Table 6.15).

Year-wise Selling of Selected MFP (in percentage)

The yearwise selling of minor forest produce by the sample respondents are explained in Table 6.16.

On 31.03.2000, the Government of Orissa implemented the new policy. So AMCS, Tikabali, is not able to collect any MFP during 2000-2001.

Siali plates and hill brooms constitute major share in selling of Minor Forest Produces at AMCS centres during the years from 1991-92 to 1999-2000.

Marketing of Selected MFP and SAP

Out of the various minor forest produce and surplus Agricultural Produce, generally very few items are marketed by the

Table—6.15 **Procurement of Selected surplus agricultural produce from the year 1991-92 to 2000-2001 (in percentage)**

Year	Different SAP's (in percentage)								
	Turmeric	*Ginger*	*Mustared*	*Blackgram*	*Tila*	*Katangi*	*Rasi*	*Others*	*Total*
1991-92	29%	36%	23%	--	4%	--	6%	2%	100%
1992-93	28%	27%	24%	3%	6%	1%	81%	3%	100%
1993-94	30%	21%	26%	5%	7%	--	8%	3%	100%
1994-95	33%	14%	27%	10%	5%	--	9%	2%	100%
1995-96	33%	09%	29%	11%	6%	--	10%	2%	100%
1996-97	34%	04%	29%	13%	6%	--	12%	2%	100%
1997-98	34%	--	30%	15%	5%	--	15%	1%	100%
1998-99	33%	--	30%	15%	5%	--	15%	2%	100%
1999-2000	32%	--	31%	14%	6%	--	14%	3%	100%
2000-2001*									

* During the year 2000-2001, due to the new policy of Government of Orissa, AMCS was not able to procure SAP.

Source : Compiled from the questionnaires.

Table—6.16 ***Yearwise sale of selected produce by the sample respondents (in percentage)***

Year	*Selected MFP (in percentage)*									
	Siali plates	*Hill brooms*	*Mohua flower*	*Arrow root*	*Genduli gum*	*Marking nut*	*Honey*	*Cleaning nut*	*Other produce*	*Total percentage*
1991-92	46	22	10	04	--	--	07	05	06	100
1992-93	48	21	09	05	--	--	06	05	06	100
1993-94	41	29	05	03	01	--	06	08	07	100
1994-95	39	30	05	03	03	02	08	07	03	100
1995-96	38	35	06	02	01	01	09	06	02	100
1996-97	39	35	06	04	--	02	07	04	03	100
1997-98	39	33	07	06	01	0.1	07	04	02	100
1998-99	39	20	09	07	04	--	06	10	05	100
1999-2000	35	32	11	06	04	--	07	10	05	100
2000-2001*										

* Due to New Policy, no respondent approaches the AMCS Tikabali Centre.

Source : Compiled from questionnaires.

people of Kandhamal. The selected items along with number of persons selling the produce is illustrated in table 6.17.

Table—6.17 Marketing of selected MFP and SAP at different marketing centres of AMCS, Tikabali

Sl. No.	*Important items of MFP*	*No. of persons selling the produce*	*Proportion to total (%)*	*Important items of SAP*	*No. of persons selling the produce*	*Proportion to total (%)*
1.	Siali plate	227	45.4	Turmeric	203	40.6
2.	Hill broom	124	24.8	Ginger	14	2.8
3.	Mahua flower	61	12.2	Mustard	102	20.4
4.	Arrow root	43	8.6	Tila	42	8.4
5.	Genduligum	07	1.4	Katangi	07	1.4
6.	Making nut	06	1.2	Ragi	51	10.2
7.	Money	21	4.2	Blackgram	43	8.6
8.	Cleaning nut	05	1.0	Green gram	23	4.6
9.	Others	06	1.2	Others	15	3.0
	Total	500	100		500	100

Source : Compiled from the questionnaires.

From table 6.17 it is found that from among the Minor Forest Produce, siali plates, hill brooms and mahua flowers contribute lion share i.e. 82.4 per cent and rest contribute only 17.6 per cent. Similarly from among the Surplus Agricultural Produce, turmeric, mustard and rasi contribute 71.2 per cent and rest contribute 28.8 per cent.

Training facilities provided by AMCS, Tikabali to the Tribals and Others to Get Finished Produce

The AMCS, Tikabali provides training facilities to the persons to procure finished products/good products from MFP and SAP. For this purpose, various training centres are established. These training centres impart necessary training to tribals and others to prepare better quality products like siali plates, hill brooms and to bring raw honey to a saleable condition. Similarly, the society provides training regarding the processing of turmeric and ragi for production of turmeric power and til oil respectively.

Table—6.18 Training facilities provided by AMCS personnel to the sample beneficiaries to Get Finished Produce

Training facility provided by AMCS Tikabali	*M*	*W*	*Total*	*Percentage to total*
A. Persons dealing in MFP	98	233	331	33.1
Persons dealing in SAP	109	246	355	35.5
Total	207	479	686	68.6
B. Training is not provided to sample persons	35	279	314	31.4
Total (A+B)	242	758	1000	100%

M = Men, W = Women

Source : Compiled for the questionnaires.

Table. 6.18 reveals that out of 1000 sample respondents, only 686 persons or 68.6 per cent are given training facilities, but rest 314 persons (31.4 per cent) are not provided with any type of training facilities by AMCS, Tikabali. Training facilities provided by AMCS, Tikabali to the tribals and others (as per castewise) is illustrated in Table 6.19.

Table—6.19. Training facilities provided by AMCS, Tikabali to the sample respondents as per caste-wise

Sl. No	*According to caste*	*No. of persons selected as sample*			*Training given*			*Training not given*		
		W	*M*	*Total*	*W*	*M*	*Total*	*W*	*M*	*Total*
1.	S.T.	417	45	462	308	43	351	109	02	111
2.	S.C.	325	17	342	193	14	207	132	03	135
3.	OBC	103	15	118	68	14	82	35	01	36
4.	General	03	75	78	--	46	46	03	29	32
	Total	848	152	1000	569	117	686	279	35	314

W = Women, M = Men, ST = Scheduled Tribe, SC = Scheduled Caste, OBC = Other Backward Caste

Source : Compiled from the questionnaires.

From table 6.19 it is clear that out of 152 sample men only 35 men are not at all provided with training facilities. But of this 35 men who were not provided with training facilities, from among them 29 are from general caste, 77 men are selected from ST, SC and OBC category, out of this 77 men 71 are given training facilities.

Reaction of the Tribals and Others of Sample District Respondents on New Government Policy

The Government of Orissa adopted a new policy during the year 2000-2001 regarding collection of non-timber forest produce (Appendix—II) to facilitate tribal people of the state. This hampers the marketing process and monopoly of AMCS, Tikabali. The reaction of sample individuals regarding the new policy is illustrated in the Table 6.20.

Table—6.20 Reaction of sample respondents on new policy of Government

Item	*Views on new policy*			*Views on AMCS, Tikabali*		
	On prince	*On measure-ment*	*Influence by middle-men to sell the produce*	*On price*	*On measure-ment*	*Influence by middlemen to sell the produce*
Satisfactory	414	312	803	886	918	342
Not Satisfactory	502	607	No Influence	107	78	No Influence
Not Replied	84	81	197	07	04	658
Total	1000	1000	1000	1000	1000	1000

Source : Compiled from the questionnaires.

Table 6.20 reveals that out of 1000 sample individuals, 502 (50.2 per cent) are not satisfied with the minimum support price fixed by new policy of the Government whereas 107 persons are not satisfied with the price fixed by AMCS, Tikabali. Similarly on measurement 607 (60.7 per cent) are not satisfied/not happy on the measurement made by the Agents appointed by the Panchayats, whereas 78 persons are not happy on the measurement done by AMCS, Tikabali. As many as 803 sample individuals are influenced by the middle men to sell their produce at the centres opened by the village trader, but only 342 sample tribals and others were influenced by middlemen and others to sell their produce at AMCS centres.

Reaction of Sample Respondents on New Policy on Different Issues

The impart of new policy, the center are located at Panchayat level by the private trader establishment of collection centre at door step it helped the seller in saving time transport expenses etc. The reaction of sellers as different issues on new policy of the Government as SAP and MFP are illustrated in table 6.21.

From table 6.21 it is clear that the sample individuals have no such good impression on the local traders appointed as per new policy. The sample tribals and others have positive reaction on less transport expenses, time saving and less distance which indicate good sign, but on otherhand the reaction of sample persons not indicate good sign. Regarding payment of commission to the Agents and behaviour to sellers, more than 60 per cent of sample individuals are not happy. Influence made by the agents appointed by the local traders (under new policy) to influence the tribals and others to sale their produce.

Under the new policy of 2000 the local trader appointed by the Panchayats are authorised to purchase the produce from the local persons. These local traders take the help of same individuals and others to produce the minor forest produce and surplus agricultural produce. This is explained in Table 6.22.

Table 6.22 reveals that out of 1000 sample respondents 803 (80.3 per cent) are influenced by different persons of the locality to sell their produce to the local traders, and rest 197 (19.7 per cent) persons are not influenced by the persons nominated by the local traders. But of 803 respondents, 504 are influenced by the commission agents.

Borrowing Loan from Local Traders

After the new policy the local trader come forward to provide loans to the local tribals at the time of need and influence them to sell their produce at local centre instead of selling at AMCS centres. This is illustrated in table 6.23.

Table—6.21 *Reaction of new policy of the government as different issues by the sample respondents.*

Reaction of seller	*Less transport expenses*	*Time saving*	*Delivery at less distance*	*Collected at door step*	*Early clearance of produce at centre*	*Proper dealing with the seller*	*Payment of price of produce at reasonable time*	*Any Commission paid to the Agents*	*Any Misbehaviour to sellers*
Positive	803	678	634	127	326	238	267	648	603
Negative	197	322	366	873	674	762	733	352	397
(in person)									
Total	1000	1000	1000	1000	1000	1000	1000	1000	1000

Source : Compiled from questionnaires

Table—6.22 Influence made by the local traders to the sample respondents after new policy 2000

Sl. No.	*Persons influenced by different categories (A)*	*No. of persons*	*Percentage to total (803)*
1.	Friends	92	11.6
2.	Relatives	54	6.7
3.	Village Head (Mukheea)	78	9.8
4.	Commission Agents	504	62.7
5.	Ward Members	52	6.5
6.	Others	13	2.7
	Total	803	80.3/1000 = 80.3
7.	Persons not influenced by any person (B)	197	197/1000 = 19.7
	Total A + B =	1000	100

Source : Compiled from questionnaires.

Out of total of 1000 sample respondents 884 persons (88.4 per cent) borrowed money from local traders and rest 116 (11.6 per cent) persons did not borrow money from the local traders. Out out of this 116 persons, 71 were from general caste.

Table—6.23 Borrowing from the local traders as per caste

Sl. No.	Caste	No. of respondents	No. of persons borrowed	No. of persons not borrowed
1.	ST	462	432	30
2.	SC	342	330	12
3.	OBC	118	115	03
4.	General	78	07	71
	Total	1000	884	116

Source : Compiled from questionnaires

Quantum of Loan Sanctioned by the Local Traders

The local traders provided some loan to the sample respondents. The amount of loan sanctioned by them are illustrated in table 6.24.

The loan provided to the respondents are divided into 5 categories. Only four persons are provided loan within the range of Rs. 1000-2000. The traders are exploiting the sample respondent by giving little amount of loan. They have provided loan to 622 persons within the range of 0-100 rupees.

Table—6.24 Amount of loan sanctioned by the local traders to the sample tribals and others

Sl. No.	*Amount of loan (in Rs.)*	*No. of persons borrowed (A)*	*Proportion to total %*
1.	0 – 100	622	70.3
2.	100 – 500	205	23.2
3.	500 – 1000	53	6.0
4.	1000 – 2000	04	0.5
5.	2000 & above	--	--
	Total	884	884/1000 = 88.4
	No. of persons not borrowed (B)	116	116/1000 = 11.6
	Total A + B =	1000	100

Source : Compiled from questionnaires

Interest Charged by the Traders for the Loan Amount Sanctioned by Local Trader

The local traders charge abnormal rate of interest on the loan provided by them to the local tribals and others. The rate of interest varies from person to person. The percentage of interest charged by the local traders are illustrated in table 6.25 and in diagram-6.10.

The rate of interest fixed by the trades is from 0-5%, 5-10%, 10-15%. 15%- and above respectively. As many as 329 loanees have paid interest within the range of 10-15% and 306 respondents have paid interest within the range from 15 and above per cent.

Table—6.25 The rate of interest charged by the local traders to the local tribals and others

Sl. No.	*Rate of interest*	*No. of persons*	*Percentage of total*
1.	Upto 5%	53	5.9
2.	5% – 10%	196	22.1
3.	10% – 15%	329	37.3
4.	15% and above	306	34.7
	Total	884	100

Source : Compiled from questionnaires

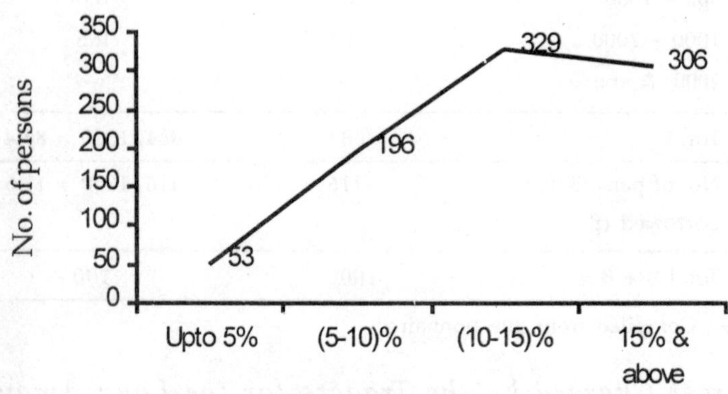

Diagram—6.10
Rate of interest charged by the local traders to the local tribals and others

7

Findings and Suggestions

Introduction

This being the concluding chapter of the study, it highlights the summary of some major/important findings. Further, in this chapter, hypotheses formulated in the introductory chapters are tested with the help of analysis and a few important suggestions are put forth for consideration of Government, local bodies and others. This chapter also includes the practical utility of the study and ends with a list of key issues for further research.

Summary of Major Findings

The chapter-wise important findings of the study are presented below:

Socio-economic Profile of District Kandhamal

On 1st April, 1936, Orissa became a separate province and Kandhamal was taken as a sub-division of Ganjam district of Orissa. On 1st January 1948, a separate district named Boudh and Kandhamal was formed. At present Kandhamal district comprises two sub-divisions, viz., Phulbani and Baliguda, with 4 Tahasils, 12 Blocks and 144 Gram Panchayats. The district lies between 19.36ºS and 20.53ºN latitude and 83.33º W and 84.48º E longitude. The total geographical area of the district is 7650 sq. kms. which is 4.9 per cent of the geographical area of the state. The soil of the district is moderately fertile and the average rainfall of the district is 159.76 cm. It is rich in forest resources which occupies 58.27 per cent of the total geographical area of the district. The total population of the district was 6,47,912. Out of this 3,22,674 were males and 3,25,238 were females (2001 census). In this district 37.23 per cent of the total population are literates. The district has 2336 inhabited and 179 uninhabited villages.

Agriculture is the important occupation of the people of Kandhamal district. Paddy and maize are the principal crops of the district. There is no large and medium industry in this district, but only 4 S.S.I have been established in the district till 2001-2002. The district has no national highway and no railways. The district has only 34 kms of state highways since 1997. The district has one sub-divisional hospital, 13 ayurvedic, 16 homoeopathic hospitals having 406 beds in total. Only 46.33 per cent villages are electrified. The tribals of the district live in very small houses made of jungle wood and take *mohuli*, the local liquor. They generally speak 'Qui' language as their mother tongue. They worship Gods like 'Shiva', 'Ganesh' and a number of local goddesses. The average per capita income of the people of Kandhamal district is Rs. 660 per annum which is very less in comparison to other districts of Orissa. About 88 per cent of their income is spent by them on food and liquor. The living style of the people of Kandhamal is very simple and their standard of living is very poor.

Growth of Co-operative Movement in India and in Orissa

Co-operatives played an important role for the growth and development of rural poor of the country. There were 1,59,939 co-operative societies in the country at the end of First Plan period. But during Second Five Year Plan, the same has increased to 3,32,000. In third Plan period, the co-operatives have covered 5,02,816 villages out of 5,63,629 total villages of the country. During the Fourth Five Year Plan period, various steps were taken for development of marketing societies. During Eighth Plan period, more importance was given on the growth of co-operatives in the tribal areas of the country. The Tribal Development Co-operative Corporation (TDCC) was organised for collecting and marketing of minor forest produce. In Ninth Plan period, Krishi Vigyan Kendras were established at Panchayat level for improvement of agriculture.

In Orissa, 21 co-operative societies were in operation in the year 1905. Berhampur Urban Co-operative Bank was established in the year 1906, which was the first co-operative institution in South Orissa. After Orissa became a separate state on 1st April 1936, the co-operative societies were increased rapidly. The Co-operative Land Mortgage Bank was established in the year 1938-39 at

Berhampur to advance long-term loans to the agricultural sector. During 1950-51, there were 5145 societies in Orissa, but the same has increased to 8,623 at the end of the period 1955-56. At the end of the second Plan period there were 11,206 societies in Orissa. During Third Plan period, more importance was given on Marketing Co-operative Societies and 12 RMCS were organised in Orissa. Aska Co-operative Sugar Factory (a medium industry), was established during this plan period. At the end of Fourth Plan period, there were 7001 co-operative societies working in the state. During Fifth Plan period, 57 RMCS, 30 forest marketing co-operative societies along with AMCS, Tikabali were operating in the state. During Sixth Plan period, 7108 societies were functioning in Orissa. During Seventh Plan period, 221 LAMPS were organised in tribal areas of the state. During Eighth Five Year Plan, Rs. 4368 lakhs was invested for socio-economic development of tribals. In 9th Five Year Plan 3,55,764 Kissan Credit Cards were issued to the farmers to provide timely and adequate credit facilities.

Approach and Strategies for the Development of Co-operative Marketing

Marketing is considered as a vital factor for the economic growth of a country. Indian marketing system thus begins at farmers field and is seasonal in character. To overcome the various problems faced by the Indian agriculturists regarding marketing of products, the co-operative marketing system was introduced. Different Committees have also recommended the need of co-operative marketing in India. At the end of 1943-44, the states like Madras, Bombay, Uttar Pradesh, Bihar, Punjab took various steps for co-operative marketing. By the end of June 1950, there were 6,907 primary marketing societies in India having 13 lakh members. The number of marketing societies increased to 9,778 at the end of June 1956. On 30th June, 1961, 24 state marketing societies, 171 central societies and 3,108 primary marketing societies were functioning in India. By the end of 1984-85, 4,130 marketing societies were functioning in India. During Eighth Plan period, NAFED was able to export 3,60,220 tonnes of onion to keep the price of onion stable in our country. By the end of 1996-97, 229 cold storages having 6.35 lakh tonnes capacity were functioning in the country.

The value of agricultural produce marketed by co-operatives is expected to increase to Rs. 7,500 crores during the year 2001-2002.

History and Growth of AMCS, Tikabali

Till the year 1950, the minor forest produce were purchased by the private traders of Kandhamal district. So the tribals were exploited by local traders. To save the tribals from the clutches of the local traders, Agency Marketing Co-operative Society (AMCS) was established on 19th November, 1947 with the sincere efforts of Sri Pravakar Patnaik. Due to lack of government interference, the tribals were exploited by the local businessmen. The Asst. Registrar of co-operative society, Berhampur established 9 godowns at Tikabali to store minor forest produce of the district. During the year 1952-53, the AMCS Tikabali extended its business activities to Madras, Nagpur, Calcutta and Tata Nagar. Bombay marketing centre of AMCS was opened on 1958 and created a goodwill in the country. In the year 1969-70, the society purchased turmeric worth Rs. 14.50 lakhs and paid higher price to the tribals than the private traders. Due to war with Pakistan, the wagons were not available. So the society was not able to sell the turmeric outside the state for which in the year 1971-72, it incurred loss to the tune of Rs. 6 lakhs. But during the year 1982-83, the financial position of the AMCS improved. The members who were 200 in the year 1950-51, increased to 64,371 during the year 1998-99. The AMCS has 84 Procurement Centres located at different places of the district. The society constructed 50 godowns at different places and hired 74 godowns from private bodies to store minor forest produce. The AMCS mainly purchases siali leaves, broom grass, mats, arrowroot, turmeric, genduli gum etc at reasonable price to save them from the exploitation of the local private traders. The products of the society were also exported to foreign countries like USA, UK, Singapore, Sri Lanka and South Africa. The AMCS also supplied essential commodities to the tribals at reasonable price to save them from the clutches of local traders.

Marketing of Minor Forest Produce and Surplus Agricultural Produce—an Analysis

Marketing of Minor Forest Produce and Surplus Agricultural Produce need due consideration for economic development of tribals and others who are living in sample district Kandhamal. For the purpose of the analysis, 1,000 samples are taken (500 for MFP and 500 for SAP), Out of the samples, 462 (46.2 per cent) are illiterates and rest 538 (53.8 per cent) are literates. From among the sample respondents, 462 (46.2 per cent) belong to ST, 342 (34.2 per cent) from SC, 118 (11.8 per cent) from OBC and rest 78 (7.8 per cent) are from general caste. To approach the collection centres, the sample respondents have to cover a distance, within the range of 0.5 km to 3.5 kms. Highest number of respondents i.e. 362 (36.2 per cent) approach the centres within the range of 1.5 kms to 2 kms. Out of the total respondents, 848 (84.8 per cent) are female respondents and rest 152 are male respondents. The sample individuals are classified into seven categories according to their age group. 380 (38.0 per cent) respondents are from the age group of 10-20 years which is highest among all the categories who are approaching the marketing centres. AMCS, Tikabali has 77 procurement centres in 12 blocks of the district Kandhamal. The respondents of Tikabali block approaching the marketing centres are highest among all (281 respondents). From among the total respondents, 658 respondents (65.8 per cent) directly approach the centres to sell their produce, but 342 (34.2 per cent) take the help of some middle men to sell their produce at AMCS marketing centres. Out of total sample, 486 (48.6 per cent) approach the centres weekly, 377 (37.7 per cent) on each day, 101 (10.1 per cent) on fortnight interval and rest 36 (3.6 per cent) respondents monthly. The sample respondents mostly approach the marketing centres with the produce on their heads by walking. 673 (67.3 per cent) respondents approach the centre by walking and rest 327 (32.7 per cent avail other modes of transport like bicycle, trolley, mini bus etc. 886 (88.6 per cent are happy on the price paid by the AMCS Tikabali, but rest 114 (11.4 per cent) are not happy with the price paid to them by AMCS.

The sample respondents mostly sell turmeric, ginger, mustard, blackgram, green gram, tila, ragi, etc as SAF and siali plates, hill brooms, mahua flower, arrow root, genduligum, honey, cleaning nut etc. as MFP. AMCS, Tikabali also provide training facilities to the tribals and others to sell their produce in an improved condition. 686 (68.6 per cent) are provided with training facilities and rest 314 (31.4 per cent) respondents are not provided with training facilities. The Government of Orissa, during the year 2000-2001, introduced (Appendix—II) a new policy for marketing of non-timber forest produce to the local traders appointed by village panchayats. 502

respondents are not happy on the price paid by the local traders; 607 are not happy on the measurement system adopted by the local trades; 762 are not happy with the dealing of the local traders. In order to influence the respondents, the local traders provided some loans at high rate of interest. 884 respondents have taken loans but rest 116 have not taken any loans from the local traders. From among the 884 respondents who have taken loan, 622 (70.3 per cent) are provided loan only up to Rs. 100; 205 (23.2 per cent) are provided loan within the range of Rs. 100-500, 53 (6.0 per cent) are provided with loans within the range of Rs. 500-1000 and rest 4 (0.05) per cent) are provided with loan facilities within the range of Rs. 1000-2000. Regarding the rate of interest, 53 persons are provided with loans at the rate of interest up to 5%, 196 respondents are given loan within the range of 5-10% interest, 329 respondents are provided with loan within the interest rate of 10-15% and 306 respondents are provided with loan at the monthly rate of 15% and above.

Testing of Hypotheses

In the light of the above findings, the hypotheses formulated in the fist chapter are tested here.

1. *The personnel of AMCS, Tikabali influence the sample respondents to sell their produce at different recognised centres of AMCS.*

As per the analysis, out of 1,000 sample respondents taken for the purpose of the study from the sample district Kandhamal of Orissa, 658 respondents (65.8 per cent) approached the collection centres of AMCS, Tikabali without any influence. But 342 sample respondents (34.2 per cent) are influenced by middlemen, like Commission Agents, Village Mukheeas (Head), ward members of the villages, and co-operative staff (AMCS staff) and others to sell their produce at centres of AMCS (Table 6.8). So according to the analysis, it is clear that more than 50 per cent of sample respondents are not influenced by any persons. So hypothesis taken here is proved to be correct and positive. Hence the hypothesis is accepted.

2. *Mostly females and illiterate respondents come forward to sell their produce at different procurement centres*

From the analysis it is found that out of 1,000 respondents, 462 (46.2 per cent) respondents are illiterates and rest 538 (53.8 per cent) are literates. From among the literate respondents, 242 (24.2 per cent) read up to class III, 166 (16.6 per cent) read up to class V,

78 (7.8 per cent) read up to class VII, 30 (3.0 per cent) read up to 10th class, 16 (1.6 per cent) read up to +2 level and 6 respondents (0.6 per cent) read up to Graduation level (Table 6.2).

Similarly, out of 1,000 respondents selected for the purpose of the study, 848 or 84.8 per cent are female respondents and rest 152 or 15.2 per cent are male respondents (Table 6.5). Hence hypothesis taken here is partially incorrect and partially correct. As 46.2 per cent of respondents are illiterate a female respondents, the hypothesis indicates negative symptom for one portion and positive symptom for another portion. So it is half rejected and half accepted.

3. ***The sample respondents mostly approach the marketing centres every day to sell their produce***

According to the analysis (Table 6.9), out of the thousand sample persons taken for the purpose of the study, 377 respondents (37.7 per cent) approach the marketing centres to sell their produce every day. But rest 633 respondents approach the centres weekly, fortnightly or monthly. Out of 623 respondents, 486 approach the centres weekly, 101 fortnightly and 36 respondents monthly. From this analysis it is clear that 37.7 per cent sample tribals and others approach the marketing centres to sell their produce every day. So hypothesis taken here for the purpose of the study is not 100 per cent correct; it is correct up to 37.7 per cent and is rejected for 63.3 per cent.

4. ***Mostly elderly women of the sample district Kandhamal are approaching the marketing centres with their produce to sell at the centres***

From the analysis, it is found that out of 1000 respondents, 848 (84.4 per cent) are ladies and rest 152 (15.2 per cent) are gents. The sample respondents are classified into 7 categories according to the age group (Table 6.5). For the purpose of the analysis, the age groups are classified as less than 10 years, 10-20 years, 20-30 years, 30-40 years, 40-50 years, 50-60 years and 60 years and above.

Out of 848 lady respondents, 72 are from below 10 years of age, 326 are from the age group of 10-20 years, 184 respondents are from the age group of 20-30 years, and 114 respondents are from the age group of 30-40 years; so rest 152 lady respondents are from age group of 40-50, 50-60, and more than 60 years of age. So it is clear from the analysis that up to the age group of 40, ladies are 696. So hypothesis taken is not correct and proved negative; hence it is not accepted.

5. The staff of AMCS, Tikabali provide necessary training facilities to the sample tribal ladies and other ladies to procure finished products from the minor forest produce and agricultural produce

As per the analysis (Table 6.18) for the purpose of the study, it is found that out of the sample of one thousand respondents, only 686 persons (68.6 per cent) are provided with training facilities by the staff of the AMCS Tikabali; but rest 314 individuals (3.14 per cent) are not provided with any training facilities by the AMCS staff. The staff provided training facilities to the respondents dealing in minor forest produce and also dealing in surplus agricultural produce. Our of 686 respondents 331 (48.2 per cent) are taken from the individuals dealing in minor forest produce and rest 355 (51.8 per cent) are taken from Surplus Agriculture Produce. Out of 686 respondents who are provided with training facilities, 479 (69.8 per cent) are females and rest 207 (30.2 per cent) are males. So from the analysis it is found that the staff of AMCS provide training facilities to both female and male respondents. Out of 758 lady respondents, 479 respondents (63.3 per cent) are given training facilities. Hence the hypothesis taken here is proved positive and is accepted.

6. The sample respondents save their time, transport expenses etc. as the local traders come to their door-steps after implementation of New Government Policy, 2000

In course of the analysis it is found that out of 1,000 respondents taken for the purpose of the study, 803 respondents (80.3 per cent) showed positive attitude regarding transport expenses. The above respondents (803) have their views that due to new policy, each village has traders, and the respondents approach the trader without any transport expenses to sell their produce. Due to the village traders, the respondents were able to save their time. Out of 1,000 respondents, 678 respondents (67.8 per cent) give their positive views on saving of time. But regarding collection of non-timber forest produce at the door-step of the sample respondents, 873 (87.3 per cent) persons expressed their views in negative manners. Similarly, regarding early clearance of produce at the centre, only 326 (32.6 per cent) showed their positive views and rest 674 (67.4 per cent) respondents indicate their views in a negative manner. Regarding the proper dealing with respondents, 762 respondents (76.2 per cent) were not happy with the dealing of local traders. Further 603 respondents (60.3 per cent) were misbehaved by the local traders and 733 (73.3 per cent) are not happy with the payment of price of the produce in reasonable time. So the hypothesis taken here is half positive and half negative. So it is neither accepted nor rejected.

7. The traders appointed by Panchayats influence the tribals and others to sell their produce at their local collection centres instead of selling at AMCS, Tikabali

In the course of the analysis it is found that out of 1000 respondents, 803 (80.3 per cent) respondents are influenced by different persons nominated by the local traders, so that they will not sell their produce at AMCS marketing centres. Out of 803 respondents, 504 (62.5 per cent) tribals and others are influenced by commission agents. Only 197 persons i.e. 19.7 per cent are not influenced by the local traders. As more than 80 per cent respondents are influenced by different persons selected by the local traders, the hypothesis proved to be positive and correct; so, it is accepted.

Suggestions

The Government of India and Orissa need to take some definite corrective measures to improve the scenario of marketing of tribal produce. It is true that there is no early solution to check this old malady. But adequate steps should be taken to tackle the situation efficiently and effectively depending on the circumstances of the case. The following few suggestions are put forth to improve the situation:

1. The rural lending institutions should come forward to provide credit facilities to the rural poor of the district Kandhamal regarding procurement of minor forest produce and surplus agricultural produce to save them from the non-institutional agencies;
2. Proper education and training is to be provided to the sellers of the produce, so that they will not be cheated by the local businessmen;
3. The tribals should be provided with adequate training facilities, so that they can prepare finished produce from the raw products and also they may be educated for storing of produce for a long time;
4. More qualified and efficient staff should be provided to the AMCS, Tikabali so that they can approach the sellers at

different levels and educate the tribals to sell their produce at AMCS centres instead of at local traders' centres;

5. The AMCS, Tikabali, should provide some credit facilities to the sellers of the minor forest produce and surplus agricultural produce at reasonable rate of interest so that the tribals will come to AMCS centres to sell their produce and repay the loan;
6. As the rural areas of the district have no proper communication facilities, the AMCS staff should approach the sellers of the produce at their doorstep so that it will save time and energy of the sellers and large amount of collection can be done by adopting this method;
7. The AMCS Tikabali should be free from the influence of the political persons. The honest officers should be appointed by the Government, and a target is to be fixed for each of them;
8. Instead of creating a competition attitude between AMCS Tikabali and local traders, the collection of products should be divided among the AMCS and local traders to avoid competition;
9. The Government should provide adequate fund to the AMCS Tikabali for construction of cold-storage, warehouses to keep the produce for a larger time;
10. The AMCS, Tikabali should bring some extension programmes for the tribals of Kandhamal district, like education at night hours, free health services, proper training for procurement of goods, storing of goods, drinking water facilities so that good relationship can be established between the staff of AMCS and tribals. If it is implemented, they would come forward to sell their produce at AMCS centres instead of at local traders.

Practical Utility of the Study

The study has highlighted on the marketing of Minor Forest Produce and Surplus Agricultural Produce at AMCS, Tikabali and after the change of government policy at the collection centres of different local traders selected at panchayat level. The study may prove useful for planners as well as central and state governments while formulating policies on tribals of the country.

This work is expected to provide suitable information to different departments such as Co-operative, Forest, Agriculture, Commerce and Transport to initiate suitable measures to improve the scenario.

It may also provide an insight to the tribal departments of Government of India and Orissa to take definite/positive steps for the development of tribal people by providing suitable measures for marketing of their produce at reasonable price and quality.

Above all, national, state as well as district level social organisations should come forward to work in Kandhamal district of Orissa to improve the socio-economic standard of the tribals and necessary steps should be taken to save them from the clutches of local traders, middlemen etc.

Scope for Further Research

This study needs an in-depth and extensive work in the field of marketing of forest produces. Some of the areas that need further study are explained in detail:

1. A study may also be undertaken by inducting a large number of samples for better generalisation and to make the analysis more detail and comprehensive;
2. The study is confined only to one district i.e. Kandhamal of Orissa. Therefore, the scope of the study can be extended to the entire state. On the other hand, for micro analysis, separate studies could be undertaken for each of the districts or sub-divisions of the region;
3. The present study is confined only to the marketing of Minor Forest Produce and Surplus Agricultural Produce, mostly of tribal people of a district. The problems faced by the tribals in collection of produce and cultivation are not taken into consideration in this study. So a detailed study regarding the economic-conditions of the people of Kandhamal is to be undertaken;
4. This study is confined only to the marketing side of the tribals and others of a tribal district. But other factors i.e. before marketing of the produce, the problems faced by the tribals are not taken in this study;
5. The problems faced by the staff of Tikabali and local traders appointed by the panchayats (as per new policy) are also not taken into consideration in this study.

APPENDIX—I

Marketing of Tribal Products —A Case Study of Agency Marketing Co-operative Society, Tikabali

Questionnaire

PART-I : GENERAL INFORMATION

1. *Name and Address :*

   (A) Name :

   (B) Village/Town :

   (C) Block :

   (D) District :

   (E) Age :

   (F) Sex :

   (G) Married/Unmarried :

   (H) Caste—SC/ST/General :

   (I) Religion :

2. *Occupation :*

   (A) Main : (B) Subsidiary :

3. *Educational Qualification :*

   (A) Illiterate :

   (B) Literate : Education up to :

4. *Family Members :*

	Male	Female	Total
(A) Adults			
(B) Children			
			Total

5. *Land Holding :*

(A) Marginal Farmer

(B) Small Farmer

(C) Big Farmer

6. *Pattern of Cultivation :* Rice

Commercial Crops

I. Own Land

(A) Irrigated Area

(B) Non-Irrigated Area

II. Share Cropping

(A) Irrigated Area

(B) Non-Irrigated Area

III. Shifting Cultivation

Total

7. *Family members employed :*

	Male	Female	Children	Total
No.				
Monthly Income		(Rs)		

8. *Family Income (Annual) :*

(A) Agriculture Rs.

(B) Industry Rs.

(C) Wages/Salary Rs.

(D) Selling Forest Products Rs.

(E) Any other source Rs.

Total Rs.

PART—II : BORROWINGS FROM SOCIETY FOR SALE OF TRIBAL PRODUCTS AT SOCIETY

9. *Borrowings during last 10 years :*

Year	*Short term*		*Long Term*	
	Loan	Repaid	Loan	Repaid
1991-92				
1992-93				
1993-94				
1994-95				
1995-96				

1996-97

1997-98

1998-99

1999-2000

2000-2001

10. ***Expenses for borrowings (Last Loan)***

Commission paid to	Before Loan (Rs.)	After Loan (Rs.)	Total
(A) Society Officials			
(B) Private Persons			
(i) Panchayat Member			
(ii) Local Politician			
(iii) Village Broker			
(iv) Relative/Friend			
(v) Travelling Expenses			
(vi) Other Expenses			
(vii) Mandays Lost/Wages Lost Rs.			
(For Borrowing Loan)			

11. ***Time-Lag for getting Loan :***

(A) Date of Application :

(B) Date of receiving First Instalment :

(C) Date of Final Instalment :

12. ***Security for the Loan :***

(A) Have you provided any security for the Loan : Yes/No

(B) If provided the type of security :

(i) House Rs.

(ii) Land Acres Rs.

(iii) Gold Rs.

(iv) Any other thing Rs.

PART—III : REPAYMENT

13. ***Mode of Repayment of Loan :***

Institution	Collected at Residence (Rs)	Deposited at Office (Rs)	Deposited after Notice	Total (Rs) (Rs)
(A) Commercial Bank				
(B) Co-op. Bank				
(C) RRB				
(D) AMCS				
(E) Private				

14. ***Have you fully utilised the loan ?*** Yes/No

If not Why? Reasons:

(A) Utilised for payment of other institutional loan for which the due date has been expired.

(B) Utilised for payment of private loans which was regarded urgent for which loan taken for the
  (i) Cultivation and
  (ii) For the household requirements

(C) Any other reason.

15. ***If loan is not repaid in due time what action the institutions have taken?***

(A) Requested personally for repayment

(B) Issued notices regularly.

(C) Taken legal action.

(D) Organised loan recovery melas

(E) Any other method.

PART—IV: MARKETING OF TRIBAL PRODUCTS BY THE TRIBAL PEOPLE

(A) Sales to the Society

(i) Siali Plates	Yes/No
(ii) Hill Brooms	Yes/No
(iii) Tamarind	Yes/No
(iv) Turmeric	Yes/No
(v) Mat Grass	Yes/No
(vi) Genduli Gum	Yes/No

(vii) Ginger Yes/No

(viii) Medicinal Herbs & Roots Yes/No

(B) Sales in Local Market (items of sales to be mentioned)

(i) Daily Market

(a)

(b)

(c)

(ii) Weekly Market

(a)

(b)

(c)

(C) Sales to Private Traders (List of items)

(i) Siali Plates Yes/No

(ii) Hill Brooms Yes/No

(iii) Tamarind Yes/No

(iv) Turmeric Yes/No

(v) Mat Grass Yes/No

(vi) Genduli Gum Yes/No

(vii) Ginger Yes/No

(viii) Medicinal Herbs & Roots Yes/No

PART—V : OPINION OF THE TRIBAL PEOPLE ABOUT THE SOCIETY

(i) Is the AMCS paying reasonable price?

(ii) If No—Why?

(a) Due to poor quality

(b) Due to less quantity

(c) Due to any other reasons

(iii) Are they getting the sale proceeds?

(a) Immediately on delivery of the products

(b) After some days of delivery—Week/Fortnight Month

(iv) Do the personnel of the Society approach them before Yes/No procurement

(v) (a) Whether the price fixed by the society is reasonable? Yes/No

(b) If not reasonable, at what price they purchase?

(vi) Whether the wholesalers or other private traders give reasonable price? Yes/No

If not at what price they pay?

(vii) Do the officials of the society take bribe from them to purchase their products? Yes/No

(viii) Do they sell direct to the society or through the middleman?

(ix) If they sell through middleman, whether they charge anything for their services?

(x) Do they sell forest produces to the traders through middleman?

(xi) Does the Society distribute bonus at the end of the year?

PART—VI : OPINION OF THE TRIBAL PEOPLE REGARDING NEW POLICY OF THE GOVERNMENT

(i) Are they satisfied by selling their products through panchayat level agents? Yes/No

(ii) Are these agents paying reasonable price? Yes/No

(iii) Do the panchayat level agents force or misbehave while purchasing goods from them? Yes/No

(iv) Do they make payment immediately on delivery of the products? Yes/No

(v) Do they prefer new policy or the old one? Yes/No

(vi) Any other suggestion

Signature of the Investigator Signature of the Informant

Signature of the Superviser

APPENDIX—II

Government of Orissa Forest and Environment Department

Resolution No.5503/E & E

Dated. Bhubaneswar the 31st March, 2000.

Sub : Policy on procurement and trade of non-timber forest produce.

1. Non-Timber Forest Produce (NTFP) has traditionally been perceived as an important source of forest revenue. According to policies relating to NTFP over the years have generally tended to aim at maximization of revenue. However, NTFP is an important source of livelihood of tribals and the rural poor. These gatherers of NTFP, majority of whom are women, have limited access to the market, and their primary concern is getting a fair price for the NTFP gathered by them and being above to dispose of the produce gathered. The prevailing system does not adequately provide these facilities to the primary gatherers. At the same time, it is also equally important that collection of NTFP must be on non-destructive basis so that sustainability of forests is long term sustainability of the NTFP based livelihood can be reasonably ensured.

2. The State Government have had under their consideration proposals for formulation of an appropriate policy on Non-Timber Forest Product, keeping in view the consideration outlined in the preceding paragraph, while formulating the policy the provision of the panchayats (Extension to scheduled areas) Act 1996 have also to be kept in view. The term 'minor forest produce' has not been defined. Under

the policy of Joint Forest Management, the local communities are being closely involved as partners of Forest Department in the management of degraded forests; and the members of the Bana Saramkshyana Samiti are entitled to share of the usufructs, including the entire NTFP gathered from such a forest area. Considering all aspects of the matter, Government have been pleased to approve of the following policy guidelines for streamlining the system of collection and disposal of various Non-timber Forest Produce items :

Minor Forest Produce

3.(a) The items of Non-Timber Forest Produce listed in Annexure-A will be treated as Minor Forest Produce (MFP), and the term MFP will only mean and include items listed in Annexure-'A'. The list of items of NTFP to be treated as MFP may however be modified by government from time to time, Gram Panchayat, Gram Sabha in the scheduled areas will have the ownership over MFP produced within its territorial jurisdiction, i.e in respect of the MFP produced is collected from the Government lands and forest lands within the limits of the revenue comprising the gram panchayat. Under law, ownership MFP in non-scheduled areas is not vested in Gram Panchayats. Gram Panchayats both in scheduled and non-scheduled areas, will however, have the authority to regulate purchase, procurement (as distinct from collection by primary gatherers) and trading in MFP in accordance with the policy outlined in the succeeding paragraph.

3.(b) No Gram Panchayat, whether situated within or outside the scheduled area will have ownership over MFP produce in Reserve Forests, in forest areas under wildlife Sanctuaries and National Parks which are outside the limits of revenue villages. The Gram Panchayats will not therefore have the right to grant lease or licence to any individual or agency for collection of Minor Forest Produce from any Reserve Forest or Sanctuary or National Park. However, members of Vana Samrakshyana Samities, and tribals, artisans, etc. as part of their customary rights will be free to collect Minor Forest Produce from forest areas excluding sanctuaries and

National parks. When such MFP collected from forest areas is brought to a village, i.e. into the territory within a Gram Panchayat, it will come under the Gram Panchayat's powers to regulate procurement and trading. Where Bana Samrakshyana Samiti has been formed, the Samiti and its members will have priority over the Gram Panchayat in the matter of collection and disposal of Minor Forest Produce of the respective forest area.

3.(c) Any person desirous of purchasing MFP for primary gatherers or trading in MFP so purchased shall apply for registration to the concerned Gram Panchayats and the Gram Panchayat may register such dealers or traders for a season from the first day of October to the last day of September of the following year. Dealers and Traders will have to seek fresh registration for the next season. Gram Panchayats shall make all efforts to promote free competition in procurement of MFP by engaging as may dealers for each item of Minor Forest Produce as reasonably practicable. The Gram Panchayat shall also levy an annual registration fee from such dealers or traders at such rate as may be determined by the Gram Panchayats and shall issue a certificate of registration by the Gram Panchayats will have to furnish a monthly return to the concerned Range Officer indicating the item of MFP procured, quantity procured and the GP from which procurement was made during the month. No person will be allowed to operate as a dealer/Trader in MFP in any area without being registered as such by the concerned.

3. (d) The collection of MFP by the primary gatherers will be subject to reasonable control to be exercised by the DFO in accordance with the provisions of law and should silvicultural principals laid down in the Forest Working Plan which shall be given publicity in advance in the adjoining GPs.

3. (e) The Government agencies like Orissa Forest Development Corporation, Tribal Development Co-operative Corporation etc. may also register themselves with one or more Gram Panchayats for procurement and trading in one or more items of Minor Forest Produce.

3.(f) A Gram Panchayat may cancel the registration of any dealer/trader or may refuse to grant registration for the subsequent season if after summary enquiry in course of which the affected party shall be given an opportunity to show cause it is satisfied that the declare/trader has procured by MFP from the primary gatherers at a rate lower than the minimum procurement price fixed for that item MFP under para 5 of this resolution for the relevant year.

3.(g) No lease shall be granted by Government in respect of any Minor Forest Produce nor shall it levy any royalty on these items after commencement of this Resolution. No Forest Development Transit permit will be required thereafter for transport/ movement on any Minor Forest Produce within the State.

Other items of NTFP

4.(a) The trade in kendu leaf will continue to be directly controlled by the State Government as there are well laid down statutory provisions for control of trade in this item. Sal seed which is one NTFP item notified forest produce under Orissa Forest Produce (Control of Trade) Act, 1981 will also be dealt with in accordance with the provisions of law by Government keeping the overall interest of the rate, the industries and the gatherers in view.

4.(b) Certain items, namely sal leaves, gums and resins of different trees. Khaira and catechu, the barks of different trees and climber and roots of various species which have medicinal or other uses will not be leased out, as the collection of these items on commercial scale has adverse impact on the sustainability of the particular species and the forest. In particular localities, however, based on sound assessment of silvicultural availability and enforcement of appropriate collection procedure, any of these lease-barred items may be allowed to be collected either directly by field organisation of Forest Department or a Government undertaking.

4.(c) The remaining items of NTFP as per the list at Annexure-B, which may be modified by Government from the time to time, will be allowed to be procured and traded by the dealers who have been registered for the purpose under this Resolution by the concerned Divisional Forest Officers. Individuals, Societies, Co-operative, Government Undertakings and Co-operations may be registered as a dealer for the above purpose. Such registration shall ordinarily be granted by the Divisional Forest Officers for a season (form the first day of October to the last day of September of the following Calendar year) to applicants seeking such registration, unless there are valid reasons for refusing registration. The DFOs will endeavour to promote competition among the traders and dealers by registering as many dealers as reasonably practicable for a specified area. For each item, as many dealers as may come forward can be engaged for each Forest Division/Range, TFDC, TDCC, Co-operative Societies like LAMPS etc. will also be eligible to register themselves with the DFOs and should be encouraged to engage themselves in trading in these items. The Vana Samrakshyana Samiti, Mahila Samiti, recognised groups of primary gatherers may also get themselves registered for this purpose. The fees to be paid for registration shall be prescribed by Government.

4. (d) The registered dealers will be required to finish the names of their authorised agents/nominees and the names of their collection and storage centres to the concerned Divisional Forest Officers, and will also record the daily transactions in prescribed formats. The dealers will have to enter into an agreement with the concerned DFOs under which the dealers will be responsible for achieving a minimum target of procurement to be fixed by the Divisional Officer of a particular item during a collection season. If the collection method of any particular item in any particular area is to be harmful or injurious to the forest, the DFO may impose temporary ban on such collection.

4. (e) The registered dealers will have to pay royalty to the local forest Range Officer at the rate fixed for the quantity of produce collected. The rate of royalty shall ordinarily not be less than 10 per cent of the procurement price for the particular item, but this rate may be varied by Government from time to time,. Suo moto or on proposals submitted by the Divisional Forest Officers.

4. (f) The registered declares will be required to take transit

permits from competent Forest Officers for movement/ transport of the produce out of the collection centres after setting the royalty dues, etc.

4. (g) The Divisional Forest Officer may cancel the registration or refuse registration of any dealer/trader in after summary enquiry in course of which the affected party shall be given an opportunity to show cause it is found that the dealer has procured any forest produce from the primary gatherers at a price less than the minimum procurement price fixed for the relevant year under para-5 of the Resolution or has failed to achieve the minimum target of procurement, or has failed to file the prescribed returns or has failed to settle the royalty dues in time.

5. For all NTFP items including NFP, the Committee appointed by Government in SC & ST Development Department will fix the minimum procurement price for each collection season or part thereof. These procurement prices shall be announced every year ordinarily during the month of September and will be given wide publicity as decided by Government.

By Orders of the Governor,
H.S. Chahar,
Commissioner-Cum-Secretary to Govt.

Anexure A: List of Non-Timber Forest Produce Items

SI. No.	*Common trade name of the item of forest produce*	*SI. No.*	*Common trade name of the item of forest produce*
1.	Tamarind Tamarind seed	13.	Cleaning Nut (Nirmala)
2.	Mahua Flower	14.	Honey
3.	Hill Brooms	15.	Siali Leaves
4.	Thorn Broom (Jhadu or Ghoda Lanji)	16.	Sabai Grass
		17.	Mango Kernel
5.	Phula Jhadu	18.	Thatch Grass
6.	Broom Grass	19.	Simul Cotton
7.	Nux Vomica (Kochila Seeds)	20.	Arrow root (Palua)
8.	Harida (Myrobolps)	21.	Dhatuki Flower
9.	Bahada (Myrobolps)	22.	Putrani
10.	Amla (Myrobolps)	23.	Sikakai
11.	Soap Nut (Ritha Phala)	24.	Junger Jada or Gaba
12.	Marketing Nut (Bhalia)	25.	Palasa Seed

26. Siali Seed
27. Indra Jaba (Ko ai Seed)
28. Gila (Seed and Coat)
29. Benachera
30. Bana Haladia
31. Bana Kolatha
32. Gaba
33. Basil
34. Makhana Seeds
35. Tala Makhana Seed
36. Baidanka Seeds
37. Baghanakhi Seeds
38. Kamals Gundi Fruit
39. Landa Baguli
40. Bela
41. Chiratta (Bhui Neem)
42. Khajuripata
43. Rohini Fruit
44. Bhursunga Leaves
45. Rasna Root
46. Phenaphena Fruit
47. Sidha Fruit
48. Sathabari
49. Katha Lai
50. Atundi Lai
51. Kheula Lai
52. Suam Lai
53. Eksira Fruit
54. Katha Chhatu (Mushroom)
55. Mat Beed
56. Ananta Mula
57. Antia Pata
58. Nageswar flower
59. Mankad Kendu
60. Atundi Fruit

ANNEXURE—B

List of other NTFP which may be modified by Government

1. Mohula Seed
2. Kusum Seed
3. Karnja Seed
4. Neem Seed
5. Char Seed
6. Chakunda Seed
7. Babul Seed
8. Any other item (s) as may be notified by Government.

Items Covered Under Para 4(b)

1. Sal leaves

2. Sal resn (Jhuna)
3. Gums (Dharua Gum, Babul gum, Genduli gam, Bahada gum, Palas gum, Selai gum etc.)
4. Khaira and Catechu
5. Barks of trees/climbers (Sunari, Lodha, Medha, Phenphena, Arjuna barks etc.)
6. Roots of Patala Garuda (R.S. roots)
7. Sandal wood
8. Tassars cocoon
9. Canes

OFFICE OF THE REGISTRAR OF CO-OPERATIVE SOCIETIES, ORISSA, BHUBANESWAR.

Memo No. 6845/ Date 10.05.2000

XLV-F-55/97-Mkt.-III(5)

Copy forwarded to the All Deputy Registrars of Co-operative Societies, in the State for information and necessary action. They are requested to circulate the Government policy among the concerned institution coming under their administrative control.

Sd/

Joint Registrar, C.S. (Marketing)

Memo No. 6846/Date. 10.05.2000

Copy forwarded to the Secretary, Tikabali, Agency Marketing Co-operative Society Ltd., Tikabali/Managing Director, MARKFED, Bhubaneswar/Secretary, Mujagada F.M.C.S. Mujagada, Ganjam, Pin. 761132/Managing Director, Kunduli LAMPS, Similiguda, Dist. Koraput.

Sd/

Joint Registrar, C.S. (Marketing)

APPENDIX—III

District-wise growth rate in Orissa

Rank in the state	*District*	*Growth rate 1991-2001*	*Rank among the districts of India*
	Orissa	***15.94***	
1.	Khordha	24.79	208
2.	Bhadrak	20.47	326
3.	Nabarangapur	20.26	333
4.	Baleshwar	19.24	351
5.	Kandhamal	18.60	366
6.	Anugul	18.55	368
7.	Kalahandi	17.99	388
8.	Mayurbhanj	17.89	389
9.	Baudh	17.45	400
10.	Jajpur	17.08	412
11.	Debagarh	17.02	416
12.	Kendujhar	16.79	421
13.	Sundargarh	16.26	429
14.	Ganjam	16.01	433
15.	Rayagada	15.27	449
16.	Jharsugude	15.13	451
17.	Puri	14.80	457

(Contd...)

Rank in the state	*District*	*Growth rate 1991-2001*	*Rank among the district of India*
18.	Koraput	14.41	466
19.	Sambalpur	14.17	472
20.	Gajapati	14.02	477
21.	Cuttack	14.00	479
22.	Malkangiri	13.71	489
23.	Sonapur	13.39	494
24.	Kendrapara	13.25	497
25.	Jagatsinghpur	13.15	502
26.	Nuapada	13.00	507
27.	Dhenkanal	12.46	510
28.	Bargarh	11.47	524
29.	Nayagarh	10.39	534
30.	Balangir	8.52	554

Source : Census of India, 2001 (Series 22, Paper—II), p-48

APPENDIX—IV

District-wise density of population : 2001

Rank in the state 2001	*District*	*Growth rate 1991-1992*	*Rank among the districts of India*
	Orissa	**236**	
1.	Khordha	666	128
2.	Jagatsinghpur	633	140
3.	Cuttack	595	157
4.	Jajpur	560	175
5.	Bhadrak	532	191
6.	Baleswar	532	192
7.	Kendrapara	492	203
8.	Puri	431	238
9.	Ganjam	382	267
10.	Jharsuguda	245	373
11.	Dhenkanal	239	383
12.	Sonapur	231	390
13.	Bargarh	231	391
14.	Nayagarh	222	399

(Contd...)

Rank in the state 2001	*District*	*Growth rate 1991-1992*	*Rank among the districts of India*
15.	Mayurbhanj	213	407
16.	Balangir	203	423
17.	Nabarangapur	192	438
18.	Sundargarh	188	444
19.	Kendujhar	188	445
20.	Anugul	179	454
21.	Kalahandi	168	466
22.	Sambalpur	140	499
23.	Nuapada	138	504
24.	Korapur	134	508
25.	Boudh	120	522
26.	Gajapati	120	523
27.	Rayagada	116	526
28.	Debagarh	93	537
29.	Malkangiri	83	541
30.	Kandhamal	81	543

Source : Census of India, 2001 (Series 22, Paper—II), p-61

APPENDIX—V

Block-wise land utilisation pattern of the district Kandhamal for the year 1992-93

Sl. No.	Name of the block	Forest area	Miscellaneous tree crops and groves not included in net area sown	Permanent pasture and other grazing lands	Culturable waste
1.	Tumudibandha	11,026	46	869	1,963
2.	Kotagarh	18,939	18	805	665
3.	Daringibadi	23,275	35	1,295	969
4.	Raikia	12,301	48	685	144
5.	G. Udayagiri	367	83	137	307
6.	Chakapad	7,179	149	866	1,201
7.	Tikabali	7,446	108	480	1,514
8.	Nuagaon	18,874	162	1,070	910
9.	Baliguda	19,491	161	656	725
10.	Phiringia	9,488	99	1,139	2,594
11.	Phulbani	7,208	81	588	1,426
12.	Kajuripade	6,903	73	574	1,446
	District–Total	1,42,497	1,063	9,164	13,864

Source : District Statistical Handbook 1993 Kandhamal, p-14.

APPENDIX—VI

Raiffeisen and Schulze Co-operative Models

Raiffeisen Model of Co-operatives

1. Membership was limited to the rural masses, especially farmers and cultivators.
2. Limited Liability of the members.
3. Small area of operation.
4. Small loans were given to the members which were recovered over a long period.
5. Loans were given on the basis of personal security of the members and only for productive purposes. Emphasis was on the personal character of the borrowers.
6. Nominal Share Capital
7. Profit earning was not the motive and even under the co-operative law only a small portion of profits was distributed to the members as dividend.
8. Losses and profits were transferred to the reserve fund and endowment fund. The endowment fund was indivisible.
9. The society management was honorary.
10. Emphasis was given on moral as well as material well-being.

Schulze–Ditilizch

1. Membership was limited to artisans, industrial workers and middle class people living in cities and towns.

2. Limited liability of the members.
3. Large area of operation.
4. The amount of loans advanced was bigger and the period of repayment was short.
5. Loans were given on the security of tangible assets. Although loans were advanced for productive purposes, no supervision over the utilisation of the loans was made.
6. A Strong Share Capital.
7. Profit earning was the chief motive and the rate of dividend was quite high.
8. Not much emphasis was given to the reserve fund. Reserve fund was used for making up the losses. But it was required to be made good as soon as possible.
9. The management was paid.
10. The chief concern was with the material well-being of the members.

Source : Co-operative Democracy *vis-a-vis* Members Education, Daman Prakash, Co-operative Times, New Delhi pp. 43-44.

APPENDIX—VII

Plan-wise expenditure on co-operation in Orissa from first plan to seventh plan period

Sl. No.	Plans/Periods	Total expenditure	On co-operation	Percentage variation
1.	First Five Year Plan (1951-56)	18.42	0.17	0.92
2.	Second Five Year Plan (1956-61)	86.59	0.97	1.12
3.	Third Five Year Plan (1961-66)	224.60	2.37	1.05
4.	Annual Plans (1966-69)	124.95	1.72	1.37
5.	Fourth Five Year Plan (1969-74)	249.34	6.75	2.70
6.	Firth Plan (1947-78)	453.68	9.89	2.18
7.	Annual Pan (1978-80)	190.28	4.79	2.52
8.	Annual Plan (1979-80)	195.01	5.49	2.81
9.	Sixth Plan (1980-85)	1500.00	30.00	2.00
	(1980-81)	248.21	6.52	2.62
	(1981-82)	182.17	5.81	3.20
	(1982-83)	300.84	9.20	3.05
	(1983-84)	345.00	3.13	1.00
	(1984-85)	341.24	5.93	1.74
10.	Seventh Five Year Plan			
	(1985-90)	2700.00	50.00	1.85
	(1985-86)	444.59	5.96	1.34
	(1986-87)	574.26	10.31	1.80
	(1987-88)	696.25	19.24	2.87
	(1988-89)	727.14	18.57	2.55
	(1989-90)	851.00	18.85	2.21
	(1990-91)	1000.00	10.87	1.10

Source : Co-operative Movement in Orissa, 1980-90, Registrar of Co-operative Society, Orissa, Bhubaneswar, p-13.

APPENDIX—VIII

Year-wise enrolment of membership of the AMCS, Tikabali, from 1947-48 to 1997-98

Sl. No.	*Years*	*'A' Class Adivasis*	*'B' Class Non-adivasis*	*'C' Class Traders*	*'D' Class Government*
1.	1947-48	200	--	--	1
2.	1951-52	48	--	--	--
3.	1952-53	311	--	--	--
4.	1953-54	217	5	--	--
5.	1954-55	407	27	5	--
6.	1955-56	88	--	3	--
7.	1956-57	309	--	--	--
8.	1957-58	527	101	--	--
9.	1958-59	432	--	--	--
10.	1959-60	227	--	--	--
11.	1960-61	309	9	--	--
12.	1961-62	450	9	--	--
13.	1962-63	508	4	--	--
14.	1963-64	409	--	3	--
15.	1964-65	729	22	2	--
16.	1965-66	657	--	--	--
17.	1966-67	101	7	--	--
18.	1967-68	412	8	3	--
19.	1968-69	503	--	--	--
20.	1969-70	208	--	--	--
21.	1970-71	627	8	--	--

(Contd.....)

Sl. No.	*Years*	*'A' Class Adivasis*	*'B' Class Non-adivasis*	*'C' Class Traders*	*'D' Class Government*
22.	1971-72	417	--	--	--
23.	1972-73	159	--	--	--
24.	1973-74	488	208	--	--
25.	1974-75	284	--	29	--
26.	1975-76	406	--	--	--
27.	1976-77	629	235	119	--
28.	1977-78	408	127	--	--
29.	1978-79	619	107	10	--
30.	1979-80	984	110	--	--
31.	1980-81	1127	202	623	--
32.	1981-82	784	315	168	--
33.	1982-83	2127	1318	794	--
34.	1983-84	1087	208	--	--
35.	1984-85	501	281	--	--
36.	1985-86	398	428	--	--
37.	1986-87	408	328	--	--
38.	1987-88	357	284	--	--
39.	1988-89	81	287	--	--
40.	1988-90	26	16	--	--
41.	1990-91	31	6	--	--
42.	1991-92	332	216	--	--
43.	1992-93	47	40	--	--
44.	1993-94	25,330	3008	--	--
45.	1994-95	410	--	31	--
46.	1995-96	869	--	--	--
47.	1996-97	3,733	--	--	--
48.	1997-98	6,050	--	32	--
	Total	55,771	7,924	85	1

Source : Final Audit Reports of the AMCS. Tikabali for the year 1947-48 to 1997-98 and membership share register of the AMCS, Tikabali 1947-48 to 1997-98.

APPENDIX—IX

Procurement Price-List of different MFPs and SAPs of the AMCS, Tikabali for different periods

Sl. No.	*Item*	*1951-52*	*1956-57*	*1961-62*	*1965-66*	*1970-71*	*1975-78*	*1980-81*	*1985-86*	*1990-91*	*1993-94*	*1994-95*
						MFP						
1.	Siali Plate (Per Chaki)	0.12	0.12	0.15	0.20	0.36	0.50	0.63	1.40	2.50	3.50	4.00
2.	Tamarind (Per Kg.)	0.8	0.30	0.20	0.25	0.33	0.50	1.19	1.00	1.35	2.00	2.50
3.	Broom Strick (Per Bundle)	20p	20p	25.00	0.20	0.37	0.25	0.25	0.35	0.95	4.50	5.00
4.	Mat Reeds (Per Pannels)	2.00	1.50	0.05	0.05	0.08	0.12	0.20	0.25	0.25	0.60	0.60
5.	Marking Nut (Per Kg)	NA	--	--	--	0.06	0.10	0.25	0.25	0.50	0.50	0.75
6.	Harida (Per Kg)	NA	--	--	--	0.13	0.15	0.30	0.50	0.50	0.50	1.00
7.	Bahada (Per Kg)	NA	--	--	--	0.08	0.07	0.14	0.10	0.10	0.75	0.50
8.	Amla (Per Kg)	NA	--	--	--	0.08	0.07	0.50	0.50	0.50	0.25	1.50
9.	Gerduli gum (Per Kg)	--	--	--	--	4.31	3.50	5.00	12.00	15.00	0.00	20.00

(Contd.....)

Sl. No.	Item	1951-52	1956-57	1961-62	1965-66	1970-71	1975-78	1980-81	1985-86	1990-91	1993-94	1994-95
10.	Arrowroot (Per Kg)	--	--	2.00	--	4.00	4.00	6.00	15.00	--	25.00	30.00
11.	Sunari bank (Per Kg)	--	--	--	--	0.27	0.15	0.20	--	--	--	--
12.	Cleaning Nut (Per Kg)	--	--	--	--	--	--	--	0.50	--	2.00	2.00
13.	Karanja Seeds (Per Kg)	--	--	--	--	0.40	0.40	0.66	1.00	--	--	--
14.	Cane (Nos)	--	--	--	--	--	--	0.15	0.50	0.60	1.25	1.25
15.	Mahua Flower (Per Kg)	--	--	--	0.25	0.50	0.50	1.00	--	--	--	--
16.	Salresin	--	--	--	--	3.50	3.50	0.50	--	--	--	--
17.	Honey	--	--	1.05	--	5.00	5.00	--	1.00	--	30.00	30.00
						SAP						
1.	Turmemic (Par Kg)	0.40	0.76	1.05	0.75	2.75	--	2.30	4.00	7.00	NA	NA
2.	Niger (Per Kg)	0.36	0.36	0.50	1.00	1.54	--	3.25	3.75	6.00	7.80	8.00

(Contd.....)

Sl. No.	Item	1951-52	1956-57	1961-62	1965-66	1970-71	1975-78	1980-81	1985-86	1990-91	1993-94	1994-95
3.	Mustard (Per Kg)	--	0.36	0.50	1.20	2.00	--	4.56	3.90	5.60	NA	NA
4.	Blackgram (Per Kg)	--	--	--	--	1.11	--	2.86	3.82	6.40	6.60	7.00
5.	Greengram (Per Kg)	--	--	--	--	1.26	--	3.75	--	5.20	NA	NA
6.	Hillgram (Per Kg)	--	--	--	--	0.90	--	2.45	2.55	4.00	NA	NA
7.	Mahua Seeds (Per Kg)	--	--	--	0.25	0.35	--	0.45	--	--	NA	NA
8.	Kuttingi (Per Kg)	--	--	--	0.60	1.20	--	2.00	2.21	2.35	3.00	3.50
9.	Lingly (Per Kg)	--	--	--	0.65	1.74	--	4.37	--	6.20	--	--
10.	Ragi (Per Kg)	--	--	--	0.35	0.50	--	0.78	--	--	--	--
11.	Maize (Per Kg)	--	--	--	0.40	0.50	--	0.86	--	--	--	--
12.	Horsegram (Per Kg)		--	--	--	--	--	1.04	--	--	--	--

Source : Audit Report for the years 1951-52 to 1994-95, AMCS, Tikabali

APPENDIX—X

Botanical names of the Minor Forest Produce (MFP) available in Kandhamal district

Sl. No.	*M.F.P*	*Botanical Name*
1.	Anla	*Emblica offianalis*
2.	Arrowroot	*Curcum angustilfolia*
3.	Assan	*Grewia tesiifolia*
4.	Bahada	*Terminalia bellirica*
5.	Cane	*Calamus tenuis*
6.	Gendligum	*Sterculia cuens*
7.	Harida	*Jerminalia chebula*
8.	Brooms	*Thysanlaena maxima gross*
9.	Jhuma	*Sal Resin Power*
10.	Karanja Seeds	*Pangamia pinnta*
11.	Mahua flower	*Modhuca longifolia*
12.	Marking Nut	*Semecarpus anacardium*
13.	Neem seeds	*Azadirachta Indica*
14.	Sabai grass	*Ischaemum anguistifolicum*
15.	Sal resin	*Shorea robusta*
16.	Sikaya	*Sapindus robusta*
17.	Simuli Cotton	*Bombax ciba*
18.	Sanari Bark	*Caassia fistula*
19.	Tamarind	*Tamarindus indica*

Source : Dr. Mishra, M and Mishra, A. "Udvida Parichaya" (in Oriya), Berhampur, 1985 and 'The Wealth of India' (Natural Resources), CSIR, New Delhi 1952, 1959 Vol. III. IV, V, VI, VII.

APPENDIX—XI

Botanical names of Surplus Agriculture Produces (SAP), grown and procured by the AMCS, Tikabali

Sl. No.	*Name of SAPs*	*Botanical Terms*
1.	Blackgram	*Phasedusmumgo*
2.	Castorseeds	*Ricinuschommunis*
3.	Green Gram	*Phaseolus aureus*
4.	Hillgram	*Cajunuscajon*
5.	Horsegram	*Dolishesbiflorus*
6.	Jawar	*Sorghumvulgare*
7.	Jingliseed	*Sesamumouentale*
8.	Mahua flower	*Madhucalongifolia*
9.	Mustard	*Brassicajuncea*
10.	Maize	*Zeamays*
11.	Niger	*Guiztiaabyssinica*
12.	Ragi	*Eleusinecoralana*
13.	Turmeric	*Curcumalenga*

Source : Dr. Mishra, M.K. and Mishra, N, 'Udvida Parichaya', (in Oriya) 1985, Taratarini Pustakalaya, Berhampur.

APPENDIX—XII

Incumbency chart of the secretaries of the agency Marketing Co-operative Society, Tikabali

Sl.No.	Name	Disignation	From	To
1.	Sri Prabhakar Pattnaik	SARCS	19.11.1947	19.2.1950
2.	Sri Harihara Pada	SARCS	20.2.1950	12.2.1953
3.	Sri P. Ramamurty Patra	SARCS	13.2.1953	15.4.1955
4.	Sri Kamalkanta Chatterji	SARCS	16.4.1955	8.8.1958
5.	Sri Gangadhar Misra	SARCS	9.8.1958	4.11.1965
6.	Sri B.B. Singsamant	SARCS	5.11.1965	4.1.1970
7.	Sri A. K. Panda	SARCS	5.1.1970	10.9.1972
8.	Sri Arakhita Sethi	SARCS	11.9.1972	8.9.1973
9.	Sri Sibaram Rath	ARCS	9.9.1973	6.7.1976
10.	Sri Chatrubhuja Sundaray	SARCS	7.7.1976	9.2.1977
11.	Sri Puma Ch. Pattnaik	ARCS	10.2.1977	30.4.1979
12.	Sri Laxmi Narayan Sahu	ARCS	1.5.1979	30.6.1981
13.	Sri Balamakund Mohanty	ARCS	30.6.1981	18.5.1982
14.	Sri Bipin Ch. Pattnaik	Inspector	19.5.1982	10.6.1982
15.	Sri Santanu Kumar Mohanty	ARCS	11.6.1902	31.5.1985
16.	Sri Dhuleswer Panda	ARCS	1.6.1985	9.5.1988
17.	Sri Sentana Kumar Mohanty	ARCS	10.5.1988	17.10.1989
18.	Sri Maheswar Khiller	ARCS	18.10.1989	31.12.1990
19.	Sri Amulya Kumar Majhi	ARCS	1.1.1991	27.6.1991
20.	Sri B.B.Bhuyan	DRCS	2.9.1992	28.9.1992
21.	Sri B.K. Mohanty	DRCS	29.9.1992	21.12.1992
22.	Sri Jura Padhy	ARCS	22.12.92	31.7.1998
23.	Sri Prabhat Nayak	Inspector	1.8.1998	15.8.1998
24.	Sri Rangadhar Duria	DRCS	16.8.1998	31.7.1998
25.	Sri John Mojes	Inspector	1.8.1999	18.10.2001
26.	Sri Alok Dash	Supervisor	19.10.2001	—

Source : Succession List of Secretaries of the AMCS, Tikabali, Phulbani

APPENDIX—XIII

Incumbency chart of the Presidents of the Agency Marketing Co-operative Society, Tikabali

Sl. No.	Name	Designation	From	To	Remarks
1.	Sri. Pyarimohan Mohapatra	Deputy Tahasildar	19.11.1947	19.2.1950	--
2.	Sri. Dinabandhu Pradhan	--	20.2.1950	11.11.1954	--
3.	Sri. Pada Mallick	--	12.11.1954	20.12.1970	--
4.	Sri. Debeswar Kanhar	--	31.12.1970	16.07.1975	--
5.	Sri. Nagarjun Pradhan	--	17.7.1975	30.1.1978	--
6.	Sri. Bhaskar Pradhan	--	31.1.1978	31.12.1979	--
7.	Sri. Nagarjun Pradhan	--	12.8.1980	11.8.1984	--
8.	Sri. Siba Prasad Nayak	DRCS, B.K.D. PC6	12.8.1984	5.11.1984	Authorised Officer
9.	Sri. Nagarjun Pradhan	--	6.11.1984	11.11.1988	--
10.	Sir. Subas Ch. Mallick	DRCS, PC6	12.11.88	27.8.1989	Authorised Officer
11.	Sri. B.B. Bhuyan	DRCS, PC6	28.8.1989	25.6.1992	Authorised Officer
12.	Sri. Ranjit Pradhan	--	13.5.1990	25.6.1992	Chairman of advisory council.
13.	Sri. Ranjit Pradhan	--	26.6.1992	31.10.2000	--

Source : Succession List of AMCS, Tikabali.

APPENDIX—XIV

Statement of working capital, share capital & government subsidies of the AMCS, from 1951-52-1993-94

(Rs. in lakhs)

Sl. No.	*Years*	*Working capital*	*Share capital*	*Government subsidies*
1.	1951-52	0.79	0.36	0.06
2.	1952-53	1.08	0.04	0.07
3.	1953-54	0.87	0.04	0.02
4.	1954-55	1.23	0.06	0.09
5.	1955-56	1.18	0.07	—
6.	1956-57	3.02	0.08	—
7.	1957-58	NA	NA	0.36
8.	1958-59	2.35	0.09	0.18
9.	1959-60	NA	0.09	0.07
10.	1960-61	1.76	0.10	0.33
11.	1961-62	3.62	0.20	0.02
12.	1962-63	3.87	0.21	—
13.	1963-64	4.16	0.92	0.01
14.	1964-65	4.60	0.94	—
15.	1965-66	5.59	0.95	—
16.	1966-67	6.25	1.00	—

Contd.....

Sl. No.	Years	Working capital	Share capital	Government subsidies
17.	1967 -68	7.16.	0.97	—
18.	1968-69	13.63	1.27	—
19.	1969-70	19.65	1.53	—
20.	1970-71	26.27	1.78	—
21.	1971-72	24.62	1.79	—
22.	1972-73	23.24	6.76	0.03
23.	1973-74	33.31	2.09	0.24
24.	1974-75	34.81	12.09	0.95
25.	1975- 76	9.39	12.65	0.43
26.	1976- 77	17.78	12.65	0.38
27.	1977-78	22.36	13.15	0.41
28.	1978- 79	36.20	13.16	0.80
29.	1979-80	46.08	13.16	0.15
30.	1980-81	51.39	13.16	—
31.	1981-82	62.86	13.16	1.47
32.	1982-83	65.05	13.16	0.06
33.	1983-84	109.33	13.65	1.38
34.	1984-85	125.75	13.74	0.07
35.	1985-86	153.35	12.74	—
36.	1986-87	141.23	17.98	0.52
37.	1987-88	168.00	18.46	0.19
38.	1988-89	176.04	18.46	1.7
39.	1989-90	216.52	21.86	—
40.	1990-91	222.23	21.86	3.4
41.	1991-92	229.32	22.47	—
42.	1992-93	210.08	22.47	—
43.	1993-94	256.00	22.75	3.23

Source : Column 3,4 compiled from Final Audit Reports of the AMCS, Tikabali from 1951 - 52 to 1993-94, and Column 5 compiled from Subsidy Ledger or AMCS.

(Contd.....)

APPENDIX—XV

Year-wise abstract of procurement and sale of Minor Forest Produce (MFP), Surplus Agricultural Produces (SAP) and Consumer goods by A.M.C.S., Tikabali (Orissa)

(Rs. in lakhs)

Year	Minor forest produces		Surplus agricultural produces		Consumer goods		Total	
	Purchase	Sale	Purchase	Sale	Purchase	Sale	Purchase	Sale
1951-52	0.49	0.77	0.12	0.26	0.89	0.65	1.50	1.68
1952-53	0.34	0.61	0.13	0.26	0.31	0.34	0.78	1.21
1953-54	0.23	0.59	0.16	0.35	0.42	0.45	0.81	1.39
1954-55	0.22	1.01	0.41	0.44	0.44	0.49	1.07	1.94
1955-56	1.04	1.96	0.84	0.74	0.48	0.10	2.36	2.80
1956-57	1.04	2.06	0.71	0.50	1.43	1.00	3.18	3.56
1957 -58	1.16	1.13	0.30	0.54	0.37	1.00	1.38	2.97
1958-59	2.38	2.59	1.37	0.51	0.60	0.60	4.35	6.70
1959-60	1.73	3.86	1.61	1.56	1.50	1.50	4.84	6.92
1960-61	3.16	4.14	0.65	0.50	0.25	0.26	4.06	4.90
1961-62	3.46	4.85	1.05	1.34	1.12	2.75	5.63	8.94
1962-63	2.10	5.50	1.16	0.81	5.24	5.09	8.50	11.40
1963-64	2.20	5.48	1.44	0.33	7.45	7.52	11.09	14.33
1964-65	2.75	6.28	2.30	2.20	10.24	10.86	15.29	19.34
1965-66	4.00	7.34	1.74	2.56	8.39	8.46	14.43	18.36
1966-67	4.30	9.52	4.69	7.47	11.32	11.54	20.31	28.53

(Contd.....)

	Purchase	*Sale*	*Purchase*	*Sale*	*Purchase*	*Sale*	*Purchase*	*Sale*
1967 -68	4.66	8.66	3.05	4.04	13.11	13.95	20.82	27.01
1968-69	4.53	8.95	4.61	4.51	7.74	7.53	16.88	20.99
1969-70	5.52	10.31	14.47	4.47	7.21	7.45	36.20	22.23
1970-71	8.40	11.85	4.91	4.69	3.25	3.93	16.56	19.47
1971-72	5.36	12.74	1.04	7.09	3.52	4.44	9.92	24.81
1972-73	7.04	13.82	0.84	2.71	7.28	7.33	15.16	23.86
1973-74	3.77	13.42	2.34	3.24	3.05	3.02	9.16	19.68
1974-75	11.68	19.09	4.25	4.79	8.41	8.91	24.34	32.79
1975-76	10.54	19.50	2.97	2.72	5.47	5.60	18.98	17.82
1976-77	17.80	27.47	1.40	2.07	3.80	3.82	23.00	33.36
1977-78	17.90	36.69	2.02	1.32	5.20	5.01	25.12	43.02
1978-79	20.77	43.75	2.68	2.73	3.57	3.65	27.02	50.13
1979-80	23.27	48.87	1.40	1.94	1.09	2.18	25.76	52.99
1980-81	24.95	47.44	6.84	3.41	1.72	1.86	33.53	52.71
1981-82	49.91	80.03	8.60	8.68	4.92	5.08	63.43	93.79
1982-83	54.91	11.23	6.17	9.27	6.99	7.27	68.07	115.77
1983-84	57.51	112.43	6.09	4.68	9.25	8.89	72.85	126.00
1984-85	75.82	129.22	7.99	5.11	8.19	7.80	92.00	142.13
1985-86	50.37	110.30	8.79	14.91	7.63	8.43	66.97	133.64
1986-87	92.95	136.15	13.55	15.74	13.21	12.79	119.71	164.68
1987-88	68.44	148.76	17.30	13.08	9.37	10.89	95.11	172.73
1988-89	76.34	119.77	13.31	6.11	6.07	11.56	95.72	137.44
1989-90	131.45	202.52	15.07	30.71	8.34	9.39	154.86	242.62
1990-91	207.40	220.23	1.65	10.90	12.02	11.78	221.07	242.95
1991-92	161.17	206.32	5.33	1.12	5.18	7.20	171.68	214.54
1992-93	182.30	279.28	3.30	5.44	5.26	6.22	190.86	291.94
1993-94	217.02	358.00	2.31	0.02	4.23	3.62	221.32	361.64
1994-95	183.08	299.85	2.57	7.82	2.20	2.66	187.85	310.33
1995-96	172.47	379.38	16.47	14.08	3.95	3.27	192.89	396.73
1996-97	289.03	340.63	6.70	6.49	4.17	2.05	299.90	349.17
1997-98	326.99	429.54	3.77	12.04	3.61	3.82	334.37	445.40
1998-99	309.32	363.93	0.16	0.17	2.46	2.04	311.94	366.14

Source : Final Audit Reports of Agency Marketing Co-operative Society, Tikabali for the years from 1951-52 to 1998-99 and statistics on Co-operative.

APPENDIX—XVI

Profit and loss account of different years of the Agency Marketing Co-operative Society, Tikabali

(Value in Rs.)

Year	*Amount of net profit (Rs.)*	*Amount of net loss (Rs.)*	
1951-52	7,363.30	—	--
1952-53	9,927.15	—	--
1953-54	9,955.70	—	--
1954-55	14,948.12	—	--
1955-56	—	3,628.70	—
1956-57	—	15,003.40	—
1957-58	—	1,11,908.33	—
1958-59	90,767.13	—	—
1959-60	31,218.34	—	—
1960-61	Nil	Nil	—
1961-62	29,056.18	—	—
1962-63	30,374.12	—	—
1963-64	39,111.47	—	—
1964-65	81,188.53	—	—
1965-66	89,244.76	—	—
1966-67	96,647.21	—	—
1967-68	4,15,145.53	—	—

(Contd.....)

Year	*Amount of net profit (Rs.)*	*Amount of net loss (Rs.)*	
1968-69	—	3,90,131.80	—
1969-70	1,03,493.40	—	—
1970-71	—	2,97,952.81	—
1971-72	—	11,49,282.20	—
1972-73	—	36,103.78	—
1973-74	—	2,21,571.92	—
1974-75	1,53,820.42	—	—
1975-76	2,48,469.43	—	—
1976-77	2,49,111.85	—	—
1977-78	6,92,736.50	—	—
1978-79	8,02,089.77	—	—
1979-80	10,39,904.52	—	—
1980-81	1,52,784.59	—	—
1981-82	2,23,379.98	—	—
1982-83	5,31,516.15	—	—
1983-84	5,94,722.10	—	—
1984-85	5,73,319.50	—	—
1985-86	6,14,669.49	—	—
1986-87	5,56,761.24	—	—
1987-88	5,65,119.62	—	—
1988-89	4,00,370.89	—	—
1989-90	2,56,63,978.85	—	—
1990-91	4,53,817.33	—	—
1991-92	—	18,62,091.26	—
1992-93	—	46,28,815.71	—
1993-94	—	44,17,763.86	—
1994-95	32,41,267.11	—	—

Source : Profit & Loss Account for the Year Ending on 30th. June 1951-52 to 1994-95, Final Audit Reports of AMCS, Tikabali.

APPENDIX—XVII

Botanical names of Surplus Agriculture Produces (SAP), procured by AMCS, Tikabali

Sl. No.	*Name of SAPs*	*Botanical Terms*
1.	Black-gram	Phasedusmumgo
2.	Castor seeds	Ricinuscommunis
3.	Green-gram	Phaseolus aureus
4.	Hill-gram	Cajunuscajon
5.	Horse-gram	Dolishesbiflorus
6.	Jawar	Sorghumvulgare
7.	Jungli Seed	Sesamnmoventale
8.	Mahua flower	Madhucalongifolia
9.	Mustard	Brassicajuncea
10.	Maize	Zeamays
11.	Niger	Guiztiabry ssinica
12.	Ragi	Eleusinecoralana
13.	Turmeric	Curcumalenga

Source : Dr. Mishra, M.K. & Mishra, N, 'Udvida Parichaya' (in Oriya), Taratarini Pustakalaya, Berhampur, 1985.

APPENDIX—XVIII

Prcurement of minor forest produces by A.M.C.S, Tikabali

Year	Sialiplates		Hill Brooms		Tamarind		Mats		Genduligum		Magkingnut	
	Quantity (chakis)	Value	Quantity (Nos.)	Value	Quantity (quintals)	Value	Qnantity (penk)	Value	Quantity	Value	Quantity	Value
1970-71	4,73,888	1,67,635	4,96,127	182569	1082.1600	3571194	415,2158	912948	138.17.500	59,548	105.000	32.00
1971-72	9,83,647	2,95,094	5,21,250	197432	412900.000	227789	135367	1082036	140.25.000	61,210	3.22.500	9.67
1972-73	13,38,786	3,82,972	5,44,988	114625	2415.62150	123280	141248	11849	88.47.500	34,162	464.16.500	2,392
1973-74	4,78,310	4,44,828	5,47,131	426829	2447.94000	292597	227516	1671385	85.52.500	33,462	218.50.500	1,091
1974-75	18,08,128	6,50,764	4,08,985	103429	5972. 77000	211115	192959	2332054	224.23.000	89,687	180.50.000	985
1975-76	13,07,905	6,53,952	3,50,000	87502	568400.000	284200	234456	2339548	220.10.000	84,251	230.00.000	1,120
1976-77	NA	NA	NA	NA	NA	NA	271115	27052	NA	NA	NA	NA
1977-78	26,86,7 49	13,43,374	5,00,712	128606	3159.38	166483	140211	13990	67.35.000	27,662	2682.92.500	38,870
1978-79	28,10,009	14,05,004	6,40,158	160808	5650.66	286904	132269	1322690	89.84.000	57,616	223183.500	34,423
1979-80	35,55,050	19,64,147	3,71,712	93395	1500.19.500	89610	61511	8151.10	114.05.500	56,500	1314.11.000	19,711
1980-81	32,03,795	20,32,158	3,14,911	79692	214706000	175069	152285	31358	12.67.700	7,774	3873.32.000	96,074
1981-82	8,91,702	6,24,191	4,05,129	133692	494000000	494000	111281	23202	37.70.000	15,080	583.00.000	14,575
1982-83	32,08,887	28,47,941	8,08,177	293271	1985358500	1985358	63462	12692.40	0.05.800	20.00	7526.37.000	1,88,056
1983-84	44,97,404	43,691,99	5,24,469	172601	107851500	1077466	48513	10115.20	0.35.000	274.00	2870.52.500	71,835.00

(Contd....)

Year	Sialiplates		Hill Brooms		Tamarind		Mats		Gendulgum		Markingnut	
	Quantity (chakis)	Value	Quantity (Nos.)	Value	Quantity (quintals)	Value	Quantity (penk)	Value	Quantity	Value	Quantity	Value
1984-85	55,91,238	64,68,363	2,82,321	99973.75	822226000	82222600	18628	3725.60	1.58.000	1774.00	2541.39.000	63,534.00
1985-86	31,79,832	44,51,683	416871	144404	273821000	27382100	30366	7289.40	7.78.500	9,335.00	2817.12.000	70,426.00
1986-87	53,74,207	77,14,824	76764	268679	1178025000	1173229	29043	7260.75	4.73.000	5,546.00	2366.14.000	92,270.00
1987 -88	40,11,522	59,98,623	700423	245148	394803000	368576	121372	31198.70	1.12.000	1,630.00	5517.81.500	2,20.712
1988-89	53,63,370	1,101,767	446703	156346	117086200	1774669	15552	4205.00	2.63.000	3,945.00	4374.18.000	2,18,063
1989-90	36,89,454	64,45,946	533263	186642	5586775000	757495	59188	14797.00	4.42.000	6,616	5325.51.000	2,66,270
1990-91	75,51,028	19,028,555	759200	265720	644289000	1288578	50608	17746	1.26.000	1,890.00	717.20.000	35.860
1991-92	44,62,287	13,386,861	861377	301482	115988000	2319777	47006	17923.30	0.30.000	457.00	336.45.000	18,822
1992-93	52,87,532	15,862,596	532508	186378	10438965000	2087793	32336	15608.80	0.50.000	755.00	1438.96.000	50,125
1993-94	59,62,732	20,084,386	120428	188109	633257000	1266514	4606	2764.00	0.06.000	90.00	2781.40.000	12,66,574

Source : Audit Reports for the years 1970-71 to 1993-94, AMCS, Tikabali.

APPENDIX—XIX

Procurement of Surplus Agricultural Products (SAP) by Agency Marketing Cooperative Society (AMCS), Tikabali (from 1970-71 to 1997-98)

Year	*Turmeric* Quantity (Otl)	*Turmeric* Value (Rs.)	*Niger seeds* Quantity (Otl)	*Niger seeds* Value (Rs.)	*Mustardseed* Quantity (Otl)	*Mustardseed* Value (Rs.)	*Black gram* Quantity (Otl)	*Black gram* Value (Rs.)	*Hill gram* Quantity (Otl)	*Hill gram* Value (Rs.)	*Jinjly seed* Quantity (Otl)	*Jinjly seed* Value (Rs.)
1970-71	3390.17	9,32,298	900.00	1,038	563.01.300	1,12,400	7.26	805.00	11.47	1,034	73.98	12,872
1971-72	419.12	41,954	536.00	64,000	426.40	64,577	68.22	9.768	71.24	4719	3.2.900	449
1972-73	332.34.250	67,666	1.61	227.00	1.53	267.00	20.00	4,800	12.00	1,297	5.31	1,348
1973-74	221.00	54,291	414.3	98.250	141.77	44,190	105.75	12.900	7,57.500	982	4.10	1.016
1974-75	250.00	61,415	260.00	55,181	166.21	65,120	121.00	14,725	32.00	5121	8.11	2,536
1975-76	165.05	56,877	265.21	59,280	180.00	60,600	106.00	12,826	36.00	5,512	28.00	8,876
1976-77	175.00	60,325	141.21	32,120	135.00	40,120	78.00	9,497	20.24	3,797	40.00	12.712
1977-78	181.16	65,424	153.83	36,521	136.57	48.000	6.29	1,493	4.16	758	25.00	11,123
1978-79	201.34	79,710	233.00	45,530	68.50	26,240	100.54	26,858	15.14	2,848	19.44	4,972
1979-80	61.14	17,098	148.82.500	40,807	293.65	1,34,171	50.00	13,190	18.00	3,411	5.73	2,047
1980-81	10.99.500	2,533	451.50	1,47,171	345.00	1,38,000	425.27	1,22,000	230.34	54,490	41.00	17,940
1981-82	51.45	12,862	317.43	1,27,000	183. 71	70,000	68.00	20,371	22.00	220.00	1000	3.662
1982-83	–	–	1362.00	4,79,000	148.00	76,000	34.57	10,101	133.13	31,000	16.73	8,000

(Contd.....)

Year	*Turmeric* Quantity (Otl)	*Turmeric* Value (Rs.)	*Niger seeds* Quantity (Otl)	*Niger seeds* Value (Rs.)	*Mustardseed* Quantity (Otl)	*Mustardseed* Value (Rs.)	*Blackgram* Quantity (Otl)	*Blackgram* Value (Rs.)	*Hillgram* Quantity (Otl)	*Hillgram* Value (Rs.)	*Jinjly seed* Quantity (Otl)	*Jinjly seed* Value (Rs.)
1983-84	15.00	17,670	1121.13	4,26,000	145.00	65,000	18036	60,450	0.56	500.00	16.46	9,020
1984-85	9.00	10,602	1362.00	5,73,000	327.00	1,27,000	257.07	1,24,000	8.70	10,000	18.00	6,480
1985-86	–	–	1296.55	4,86,000	360.00	1,49,000	360.04	1,38,000	293.80	67,800	25.000	9,000
1986-87	151.61	1,09,895	1166.26	6,26,000	436.14	2,70,000	52.58	2,21,000	112.67	45,000	31.00	11.160
1987-88	333.60.500	2,47,454	1557.88	9,48,000	444.60	3,22,000	13.38	58,000	152.20	68,000	157.02	11,120
1988-89	0.02.000	14	1934.00	11,33,000	112.70	60,000	106.78	4,72,920	30.00	12,00	166.00	1,03
1989-90	026	182	2008.00	12,21,000	6.33	3600.00	280.47	1,87,000	–	–	9206.000	78,000
1990-91	–	–	34.67	32,000	–	–	–	–	196.56	1,33.000	–	–
1991-92	–	–	491.16	5,33,000	–	–	–	–	–	–	–	–
1992-93	–	–	374.18	3,31,000	–	–	–	–	–	–	–	–
1993-94	–	–	274.04	2,14,478	–	–	2.00	1,320	–	–	–	–
1994-95	7361.5	69,708.50	14,704	1,58,158	2.00	22,00	–	–	15.00	7,500	–	–
1995-96	11,069	1,03,856	51,504	5,83,471	3.60	4,815	69,909	9,25,429	51,504	5,83,471	6,532	29,394
1996-97	44.725	6,70,122	–	–	–	–	–	–	–	–	–	–
1997 -98	25,037	3,73,993	–	–	1.5	2,300	1.00	1,450	–	–	–	–

Source : Collected and Compiled from Annual Administration Report on the working of Co-operative Societies, RCS, Orissa for the years (1951-52 to 1960-61), Centre-wise collection register of SAP Secretary, AMCS, Tikabali for the year (1962-63 to 1997-98).

Bibliography

Books

Apte, S.G., *Anthology of Co-operative Thought*, National Co-operative Union of India, New Delhi, 1975.

Agarwala, V.P., *Forests in India*, Oxford and IBH Publishing Company, New Delhi, 1990.

Archana, G., *Integral Rural Development*, R.B. Publishing Co-operative, New Delhi, 1985.

Banerjee, J., *Co-operative Movement in India*, Navana Printing Work (P) Ltd., Calcutta, 1961.

Bedi, R.D., *Theory, History and Practice of Co-operation*, Loyal Books Depot, Meerut, 1986.

Bhorali, D., *Co-operative Banking and Economic Development*, Indian Book Centre (P) Ltd. Delhi, 1986.

Bhowmick, P.K., *Approach to Tribal Welfare*, Inter India Publication, New Delhi, 1982.

Borkar, V.V., and Ambewadikar, R.M., *Co-operative Movement and the Weaker Sections*, Ajanta Publication, New Delhi, 1989.

C. Mahesh, *Co-operative Problem in India*, Premier Publishing Company, New Delhi, 1991.

Choudhury, B., *Tribal Development in India*, Inter India Publication, New Delhi, 1982.

Datt. Ruddar, and Sundharam, K.P.M., *Indian Economy*, S.Chand & Company Ltd., New Delhi, 2001.

Dhal, P.C., *A Text Book of Co-operative Management*, Konark Publishers, New Delhi, 1989.

Dhingra, I.C., *The Indian Economy Resources, Planning, Development and Problems*, Sultan Chand and Company, 1972.

Dubashi, P.R., *Essays on Rural Development*, Kaveri Books, New Delhi, 1996.

Dutt, S.K., *Co-operative Society and Rural Development* (A politico economy study), Mittal Publication, New Delhi, 1991.

Elhance, D.N., *Role of Co-operative Credit in Agricultural Development*, Orient Longman Ltd., New Delhi, 1985.

Garg, V.K., *Rural Economics*, Premier Book Company, New Delhi, 1991.

Geral, M. Meier, *Problems of Co-operation for Development*, Oxford University Press, London, 1974.

Goel, B.B., *Management of Marketing Co-operatives*, Deep & Deep Publications, New Delhi, 1991.

Hajela, T.N., *Principles, Problems and Practice of Co-operation*, Shivalal Agarwala and Company, Delhi, 1975.

Hough, Elernor, M., *The Co-operative Movement in India*, Oxford University Press, Calcutta 1966.

Jena, B.B., *Orissa, People, Culture and Policy*, Kalyani Publisher, New Delhi, 1980.

Jena, K.C., *Socio-economic Conditions of Orissa*, Sundeep Prakashan, New Delhi, 1978.

Jha, D., *A Perspective on Co-operative Marketing*, Vikas Publishing House, (P) Ltd., New Delhi, 1997.

Karmat, G.S., *Managing Co-operative Marketing*, Himalaya Publishing House, Bombay, 1985.

L., Vinod Kumar., *Rural Development in India*, Ashish Publishing House, New Delhi, 1992.

Land, G.M., *Co-operative Banking in India*, The Co-operative's Book Depot Bombay, 1956.

Mahalingam, S., *Role of Co-operative Organisations in Developing Tribal Economy*, Mittal Publication, New Delhi, 1990.

Mathur, B.S., *Co-operation in India*, Sahitya Bhawan, Agra, 1973.

Misra, R.N., *Rural Banking in India*, Anmol Publication, New Delhi, 1995.

Misra, R.N., *Rural Development and Population*, Anmol Publication, New Delhi, 2001.

Panda, R.K., *Agricultural Indebtedness and Institutional Finance*, Ashish Publishing House, New Delhi, 1980.

Patnaik, U.C., *Introduction to Co-operative Management*, Kalyani Publisher, New Delhi, 1983.

Patnaik, U.C., and Roy, A.K., *Co-operation and Co-operative Management*, Lakyani Publishers, New Delhi.

Philip, K., *Marketing Management Analysis, Planning, Implementation and Control*, Prentice Hall of India, Pvt. Ltd., New Delhi, 1998.

Pratap, D.P., *Approach to Tribal Development*, Inter India Publication, New Delhi, 1981.

Rath, B.K., *Cultural History of Orissa*, Sundeep Prakashan, New Delhi, 1983.

Sahoo, B., *Backward Classes and Economic Development*, Satnetra Publication, Bhubaneswar, 1989.

Sen, K.K., *Indian Economics, Sultan Chand and Company*, New Delhi, 1992.

Sharma, D.P., and Desai, V.V., *Rural Economy of India*, Vikas Publishing House (P) Ltd., New Delhi, 1980.

Sinha, B.K., *Co-operative in India*, National Co-operative Union of India, New Delhi, 1977.

Suresh, K.A., and J. Mulley, *Co-operatives and Rural Development in India*, Asish Publishing House, 1990.

Tripathy, S.N., *Co-operatives : Its Growth and New Dimensions*, Discovery Publishing House, New Delhi, 2000.

Vidyarthi, L.P., and Rai, B.K., *The Tribal Culture of India*, Concept Publishing House, New Delhi, 1985.

Weerman, P.E., *Reading in Co-operative Management*, New India Press, New Delhi, 1977.

Reports

Report of the Committee on Co-operation, Government of India, New Delhi 1964.

Reports of the Study Team on Co-operatives in Tribal Development Projects, Ministry of Agriculture, Government of India, New Delhi, 1971.

Reports of the Committee on Forest and Tribals in India, Ministry of Home Affairs, Govt. of India, New Delhi, 1982.

First Five Year Plan, Planning Commission, Government of India, New Delhi.

Second Five Year Plan, Planning Commission, Government of India, New Delhi.

Orissa District Gazetteer, Boudh-Khondmals, Department of Revenue, Government of Orissa, 1983.

District Statistical Handbook of Phulbani District, District Statistical Officer, Phulbani, 1989-90, 1991-92, 1993-94, 1995-96.

District Credit Plan, Phulbani, State Bank of India 1983.

Third Five Year Plan, Planning Commission, Govt. of India, New Delhi.

Fourth Five Year Plan, Planning Commission, Govt. of India, New Delhi.

Fifth Five Year Plan, Planning Commission, Govt. of India, New Delhi.

Approach to Tribal Development in Sixth Plan, Planning Commission, Govt. of India, New Delhi.

Report of the Committee on the Welfare of Scheduled Caste and Scheduled Tribe, 1981-82.

Report of the Annual Administration of the Scheduled Areas, T & R.W. Department, Govt of Orissa, Bhubaneswar 1969.

Sixth Five Year Plan, Planning Commission, Govt. of India, New Delhi.

Seventh Five Year Plan, Planning Commission, Govt. of India, New Delhi.

Eighth Five Year Plan, Planning Commission, Govt. of India, New Delhi.

Annual Report on the Working of the Co-operative Society in Orissa, Govt. of Orissa, Bhubaneswar, 1952.

Economic Survey, Government of Orissa,

Directorate of Economics and Statistics.

Planning and Co-ordination Department, Bhubaneswar, 1995-1996, 1997-98, 1998-99, 1999-2000, 2000-2001.

District Statistical Handbook, Phulbani, District Statistical Office, Phulbani, 1989-90, 1990-91.

Report of Agricultural Census of Orissa, Board of Revenue, Orissa, Cuttack, 1992-93, 1995-96, 2000-2001.

Annual Report, Orissa Khadi and Village Industries Board, Bhubaneswar 1999-2000, 2000-2001.

Annual Credit Plan, Phulbani District, Lead Bank Department, State Bank of India, Bhubaneswar, 1991-92.

Ninth Five Year Plan, Planning Commission, Government of India, New Delhi.

Annual Administration Report, AMCS, Tikabali, 1995-96, 1996-97, 1997-98, 1998-99.

Dist. Statistical Handbook, Kandhamal, Directorate of Economics and Statistics, Orissa, Bhubaneswar, 1997, 1998, 1999.

Journals

Behura, N.K., *Tribes and the Forest—An Overview*, Vol. 32, No. 1., March, 1992.

Bhalla, G.S., and Bhalla, H.S., *Economic Programme for Rural Poor*, The Indian Journal of Commerce Vol, XIII, No. 162, March, 1990.

Bhuyan, B., and Mohanty, B., *A Critical Analysis of Indebtedness in Rural Sector of Orissa*, Orissa Economic Journal, Vol, XIV, 1981.

Gupta, S.K., *Co-ope 'ative Credit and Rural Development*, Rural India, Vol. 51, No.9, September 1988.

Kansal, A.P., *Success Story of the AMCS, Tikabali*, Rainbow, Orissa Co-operative Union, Bhubaneswar, 1983.

Kaul, *I., Indian Agriculture and Its Vast Potential*, Yojana, Vol., 34, Novemeber-15, 1990.

Misra, B., *Rural Development with Special Reference to Orissa*, Orissa Co-operative Congress, State Co-operative Union, Bhubaneswar, 1984.

Misra, B.N., *Agriculture Development Income Distribution and Social Change in India*, Orissa Economic Journal, January-June, 1981.

Misra, R.N., *Role of Credit Development in Agriculture*, Ganjam Economic Review, Vo1.5, 1994.

Misra, R.N., *Rural Credit Structure Performance of Co-operative Central Bank Ltd.*, Orissa Journal of Commerce, Vol. 21, 1997.

Misra, R.N., and Patnaik, U.C., *Management of Change in Rural Recovery Practices*, Financing Agriculture, Bombay, Vol. 23, No.2., April-June.

Prakash, Daman, *Co-operative Democracy vis-a-vis members education*, Co-operative Time, New-Delhi, 1988.

Reddy, D. Raghunath., *Rural Credit Structure in India with a special Reference to Co-operatives*, Agricultural Banker, Vol. 13, January-March, 1990.

Yeshwanth, I., *Co-operative Consumption Credit*, Agricultural Banker, April-June, 1981.

The Orissa Journal of Commerce, Orissa Commerce Association, Berhampur, Vol. 32, No.2, 2000.

The Journal of Commerce and Economics, Berhampur-1, Vol-lV-V, 1997.

The Orissa Journal of Commerce, Orissa Commerce Association, Vo. 31., No. 1, 1997.

Other Publications

Misra, R.N., *Role of Co-operative Bank in Financing Long Term Agricultural Credit*, Dissertation submitted for M. Phil, Berhampur University, 1983.

Misra, R.N., *Financing Agriculture by Rural Banking Institutions and Mounting Overdues* : A Study with special reference to Southern Orissa, Thesis submitted for Award of Ph.D, Berhampur University, 1992.

Mishra, Rabindra Nath, Co-operative Marketing in the Perspective of Economic Development of Orissa, Thesis submitted for award of Ph.D., Berhampur University, 1982.

Palo, R.N., *Tribal Development Fostered through Agency Marketing Cooperative Society*, Tikabali, Thesis submitted for award of Ph.D., Berhampur University, 1994.

Tribal and Rural Welfare Manual, Government of Orissa T. & R. W. Department, Bhubaneswar, 1966.

Tribal and Rural Welfare Manual, Government of Orissa T. & R.W. Department, Bhubaneswar, 1992.

Sub-Plan for Tribal Regions, T & R.W. Department, Government of Orissa, Bhubaneswar 1974-1979.

Annual Sub-Plan, T & R.W. Department, Bhubaneswar, 1983-84.

Bye-Laws of the Agency Marketing Co-operative Society Ltd., Tikabali, 1952.

Market Study Report, TDCC, Orissa, Bhubaneswar, No.5, 1977.

Census of India, Directory of Census Operations, Orissa, Bhubaneswar, 2001 (Paper I & II of series 22)

National Bank for Agriculture and Rural Development—Abstract, Rural and Development Supported Studies, Mumbai, 1997.

Co-operative Movement in Orissa, a Profile—Registrar, Co-operative Societies, Orissa, Bhubaneswar, 1997-98, 1998-99, 1999-2000.

Index

T

U

Y